WILD FISHING IN WILD PLACES

ADRIAN LATIMER

Foreword

By Orri Vigfusson
International Chairman, North Atlantic Salmon Fund

I am delighted to be able to provide a preface for Adrian Latimer's fine book. As angling becomes increasingly focused on technology it is refreshing to come across a work that devotes itself almost entirely to the sheer pleasure of our well-loved art. It is also fun to read about fishing in so many different locations, from Cape Wrath in Northern Scotland to adventures in deepest Montana in America and the wilds of Iceland.

Adrian Latimer clearly adores his fishing and has the unique ability of being able to share this enthusiasm with his readers. You feel that you were there when he landed his famous salmon on the River Don, you stumbled by his side along the cliff-like banks of the River Kirkaig, and enjoyed memorable Irish hospitality with him whilst hunting the huge trout of Lough Corrib. This is an angling book for all seasons and reading it has given me great pleasure

Orri Vigfusson
Reykjavik, July 2001

Preface

'It would be delightful to write about pleasures, if by doing so one could impart them to others'

Lord Grey of Falloden 'Fly Fishing' 1899

As the new Millennium starts, I cannot help wondering how many unpolluted, unexploited natural rivers and lakes will still exist and support stocks of wild fish at the end of this century. Will a mere hundred years see the destruction of watercourses and fish that have thrived since the Ice Age?

Fortunately today, if you are willing to travel, and not always that far, such havens still survive, precious oases of calm and balance amidst an ever rising ocean of information superhighways, mobile phones, laptops and endless stress. It is to these sanctuaries that I travel, both with fly rod and pen. If I can in any way help extend their preservation then it has been a valuable journey. In the meantime, I hope to convey some of the beauty, the emotion and the fun of fishing for wild fish in wild places - the electric flash of a kingfisher, the mighty sweep of osprey or eagle, the ageless majesty of mountain or fjord, and the sparkling purity of crystal waters. Finally, least we forget, the reel-spinning excitement, anguish and elation of an arched rod.

My thanks go to my family, friends and all those guides, gillies and boatmen who have added so greatly to my delight over the years, and from whom I have gained so much. If I can repay one small part of this enjoyment and kindness somewhere in this little book, then it was well worth the writing.

Adrian Latimer
Paris, 1999.

Chapter Headings

CHAPTER 1

Early Beginnings

'I am sometimes asked what strange alchemy it was that turned me – an apparently rationale fellow – into a lifelong fisherman...For a time I lapse into reverie, while an inner ear listens in again to a music I first heard as a young boy, beside a mountain stream and, ever since, have carried with me.'
David Street 'When all the World was Young' 1991

To non-fishers, fishing seems a strange way to live out a passion. Hours of shivering in the cold on your own to catch either nothing, or, even stranger, something that then gets promptly thrown back. Oh yes, and paying vast amounts for the privilege. Substituting bleak wilderness and savage weather for the more obvious delights of sun, sand and exotic nightlife. So just how does some seemingly normal individual ascend to this higher plane of enlightenment, and become a true brother of the angle? Just where and how does the rot set in?

In my case, no-one in my immediate family even fished, and living just west of London was hardly a would be fly fisher's paradise. Added to which, as a kid, I steadfastly refused to eat fish. Until I grew up that was, and wised up to the delicate flavour of a well poached salmon. Or was it just an excuse to uncork a fine bottle? I was continually confronted with a nagging refrain, a sort of leitmotif of my teens: "Oh but you fish so much and you don't even like eating fish", as if I was some kind of freak. No, it certainly wasn't family habit or a desire to eat finny prey that brought me to the waterside.

In fact, to be honest, I cannot remember why I bought my first tackle, but I do recall the day clearly, even twenty five years later. I had, for weeks and months, saved up my pocket money. It amounted to the princely sum of four pounds, a serious amount for a twelve-year-old in the early 1970's. My parents had continually advised me against wasting all my savings on something about which I knew precisely nothing. But determined, or plain stubborn I was. And so, one sunny summer day, I found myself in a fishing shop in Slough – what a place to start, things could only improve! I was amazed at the array of colourful floats, rods, nets and unimaginable paraphernalia: an Aladdin's cave of unknown delights. I bought a seven foot green fibreglass spinning rod, a fixed spool reel, five pound nylon, a couple of floats and a little guide book on how to fish. I went home over excited and triumphant with my thrilling new toys. Little did I know what I had let myself in for.

Of course, my parents were right. Two years later, the bright green stick was still in its wrapping, now at the back of a cupboard. I suppose someone older at school must have fished, and I must have thought that this really was 'it'. The trouble was, having actually bought the gear, I had no idea what to do or where. And so it gathered dust until an uncle of mine decided to get married in Devon. This may seem a strange trigger to a lifetime's passion in fishing, but I had a great uncle that lived in Devon and fished. In fact he even owned some fishing right at the bottom of the garden. My parents insisted that I take the fishing gear with me. Of course, like all childish fads, I was now not the slightest bit interested in my priceless, hard won purchase. Grudgingly, I agreed. A few hours later I was casting a small weight across the lawn. Once that was sufficiently mastered, I was able to graduate to a small red and black Mepps spinner on the river. I kept that favourite little spinner for sixteen years, before I was broken by a spring salmon on the same river due to old nylon. It was a dreadful moment. You can hardly have a sentimental attachment to a metal lure, but my great uncle had, by then, died. This was the last real link to him, and to my childhood beginnings with rod and line. It was also a salmon wasted due to my own stupidity, which made the double loss so much worse. I could even see the fish, charging around in the low water in front of me, just a few unattainable feet away. I was so close to an unexpected triumph, a springer caught in very unfavourable conditions. I could feel the pulse of excitement and future pride, the pleasure of later going home, producing the prize, and preparing dinner. Then it all went slack, and in just a second or two I realised the horrible truth. My stomach turned to lead and sank through my feet, a sort of spiritual evisceration. God, what a lousy feeling! And all because I used old nylon – it still upsets me years later, and I have lost a lot of fish since.

I digress. I doubt any fish were hooked, a parr perhaps, but I was, right through the scissors, and there was no catch and release in those days. I went back next Easter and eventually caught what must have been a six or eight inch brown trout. Thinking about it, I did release the fish, though I convinced myself it was a genuine half pounder. In between times I coarse fished, everywhere I could, as we lived close to the Thames and various gravel pits, my poor parents acting as a perennial taxi service. I moved up from gudgeon and bleak, at an ounce apiece, to pike and carp at a few pounds. The green rod finally disappeared one day down by the river. I was ledgering some foul bait on the bottom, the rod held in a homemade rod rest made out of a kitchen roll I think. All of a sudden it simply leapt out of the 'rest' and into the river – with me after it, and that was that. I guess some leviathan must have grabbed the bait and just headed off downstream, a large barbel perhaps. I was desolate, until one day I received a call at school to say some poor man had been playing a fish on the Thames when it suddenly came off, and instead, he had pulled out a cheap green rod with my name on. Kindly soul, he had looked up the phone book and rung round all the Latimers.

Every summer I would head down to Devon for a treasured week, having by this time bought a five in one combination rod. It had various sections that could be assembled by a sort of mix and match into anything from fly to seafishing rod. I would arrive having tied a box full of scruffy versions of the latest killer fly, and gulped down a hundred magazine articles and books. The main attraction of the Dartmoor stream, the Teign, was its night fishing for sea trout. By the age of sixteen, I was allowed to roam the river alone at night, and I was an avid disciple of Hugh Falkus. My first sea trout came in 1978, a genuine half pounder this time, and I can remember the commotion. The average four-ounce roach or bream can be simply reeled in, with a wriggle or two. A sea trout, fresh from the sea and having already leapt two weirs more than ten times its height poor, valiant little creature, was altogether different. It ran upstream and past me. There I was in pitch-blackness, unable to see the line or the fish, facing downstream whilst this spirited little beast cavorted about in the air behind me! Two nights later a brownie of similar size, but somewhat less acrobatic energy, joined the fridge. I had finally entered the game fishing records.

It was hardly epic stuff. As I grew older and had less time at home, I coarse fished less, swapping maggots, cheese and sweetcorn for Black Buzzers, Vivas and Sweeney Todds on the local stocked reservoirs, and Alexandras and Medecines on the Teign. By great chance, I made a friend at school whose parents owned and generously invited me up to Scotland to fish the River Eachaig in Argyll. Thus I first bumped into my ultimate dream – Mr Salmo Salar, the Atlantic Salmon in person. One of the nicest things about fishing is how often dreams come true. As a kid I read about the Tweed, Dee and Tay with awe and envy, convinced I would never be so fortunate as to fish them. Now I have, though the awe has rather faded as stocks have so sadly declined. Even so, it still gives me a kick to wade out into the middle of the River Dee, and think that there I am, really, in the Dee, and to recall that boyhood dream and hope. There are not many other pursuits that can do this, reviving dormant childhood memories, thrills and feelings.

So it was in 1981 that I saw for the first time the beautiful, steeply wooded banks of the River Eachaig, and marvelled at the rocks, rushing waters, red squirrels and contents of the fish book. It really was a dream world. In those days the river was still netted by the keeper to boost the estate's income, and I remember holding and pleading to return a fourteen pound sea trout, the finest fish I had (and have) ever seen. Every now and then a great bar of silver energy would crash through the surface to set the heartbeat soaring. The Teign is a peaty, moorland stream that meanders slowly down through grazing pastures. It is not great fly water, being too slow, especially now with the ever-lower water levels caused by increased abstraction. Nor is it exactly remote these days, having the main dual carriageway to the southwest belching carbon monoxide and endless noise alongside. In contrast, the Eachaig was a swashbuckling spate stream, hurrying along to the sea in a froth of impatient, dashing pools, perfect fly water. Well, perfect if you knew how to cast a fly and control a line, two minor essentials that I lacked in abundance.

Still, the river did try to offer a warm Highland welcome. On arriving, I was dispatched to the Rock Pool. Within half an hour of starting I was somehow manipulating an untidy line around past the rock, with one of my specially purchased Blue Charms. I was happy to tie trout and sea trout flies, but presumed that salmon required some magical skill, so I went to the fly shop and paid out what seemed like a vast expense for a bit of floss and bucktail. Mike, my friend and host, happened to be strolling by and as the fly landed in roughly the right place he kindly offered encouragement, quipping that a salmon would take hold any minute. A second later one did. I screamed out loud, then, horribly embarrassed, realised it was only the bottom and sheepishly announced so. Mike had steamed up, yelling at me to keep the rod up and get out of the water – he could see the bottom that I was supposedly hooked to – a six pound salmon! He was an expert – having actually caught at least three of these magical, unattainable beasts. Can you remember the excitement, the amazement, the fear and brink of utter joy; all that emotion hanging on that so greatly desired, never expected, first royal fish? I staggered out of the water, hanging on for dear life. At the other end of my trout rod the angry beast shook his head and thumped the rod tip down, quite unlike any fish I had encountered before. But not for long – and for the first time of, oh so many occasions, I felt the bitter slack of ruptured hope. Thereafter, life returned to normal, one six ounce sea trout being the week's tally, plus one lifelong memory and regret. There are certain fish, all salmon in my case, that I have lost over the years that I feel sharply even now. Will this continue until I am in my dotage I wonder? Whereas the thrill of a caught fish soon fades. Even the best salmon I have landed I can remember more from photos than from real sentiment. But those losses, they still burn, that sinking feeling is still there. It is an oddly inverted ratio of painful nightmare to pleasurable memory.

It must have been another five years, with the odd trip north, before I struck gold, or silver, again. It was dusk on the Teign, with the usual low and warmish midsummer water. I was, as always, routinely fishing the shallow run into the pool as night fell. The river cuts a long, deep, slack stretch which is quite good holding water, but steep banks, deep water and overhanging trees mitigate against fly fishing it, especially in darkness. It then broadens out and gurgles over pebbles, just six inches deep. Except for a yard wide run on the far bank where the water is a couple of feet deep. In the daytime you can see every stone on the bottom of this little run, with not a fish in sight. The run then hits the bank under an old tree and doglegs right into a deepening, wonderful holding pool. It is a most unprepossessing little stream within a stream. But at night the sea trout come up from the slack depths into the fast run, for oxygen or fun, I don't know.

When a fish took, I thought little of it. It was the usual place, right up at the neck, for a typical July Teign fish of a pound and a quarter or so. No big deal, even in those days I was quite used to that. But not when it set off, past the tree and leapt clear out of the water, a good thirty yards below me. I was ankle deep, but way out of my depth, never having faced an adversary of such power and sustained strength. Sea trout fight with vicious speed and gymnastics, but in short bursts and not for long. This was sustained, electrifying power. Once again, I guess I just hung on, and played the fish as best I could, or to be honest, I probably let the fish play me. Eventually the fish, somehow, was beached - try netting a six-pound fish in a trout net in darkness in just six inches of water. Shaking, I reached for the torch to see just what this huge sea trout was, and almost dropped it. In front of me lay my first salmon. Never has a hip flask been so handy!

Since then I have fished for all sorts of species, all over the world, in rivers, seas and lakes. Some are edible, others not, some beautiful, some ugly, some sleek, streamlined and fast, others flat, fat and slow. In weather benign, sultry, scorching or snow, with bait, spinner, fly or any weird and wonderful concoction, anything to attract, seduce and lure. There have been rare days when everything has worked to perfection, when I have cast like an angel and stalked like a star. Or days when I have asked myself just why I put myself through such pain, when I feel useless and incompetent, when I wonder if I will ever catch a decent fish again. Plus many, many more days of just mundane pleasure, neither great nor bad, a catch here or there, of no interest to anyone else, nothing to write about. Still, it is these days that are the very essence of fishing – pure, simple fun.

I don't feel the need to ask myself why I fish as it seems a question of no importance. I do it because it is a harmless, absorbing pastime that I always enjoy, a pursuit of pleasure as much as of fish. One that takes me to beautiful, wild, and unspoiled places, where I meet interesting, friendly people. That provides lots of good, healthy exercise and an occasional fine meal. That relaxes and empties my mind, removes all the stresses and distractions, and gives me a simple, unquestioned goal and purpose for the day. That draws me closer to Nature and a real world that is being rapidly undermined and destroyed. Finally, one that heightens my senses, and floods my emotions with life long memories, a treasure chest of bittersweet and happy reminiscence for the years to come. Who needs further soul searching explanation? After all, what is life if not a search for balance, timing and beauty? Casting a fly is not so dissimilar, is it?

CHAPTER 2

Limestone Trout in Cape Wrath

'Tired, but too full of pure exultation to settle down for the night, I sat and gazed out over the silent hills until it became too dark to see.'
David Paterson 'The Cape Wrath Trail' 1996

My initiation to the limestone trout lochs of Durness, in north west Scotland, left much to be desired. Friend, writer and well known local fisherman, Bruce Sandison had long told me that this was real trout fishing for real trout. I presumed this was a euphemism for toiling away for hours on the off chance of an occasional large wild fish. You know, the one per week that someone else always catches. He had also made it clear that this was fishing for hardened experts, (another euphemism, for demented lunatics).

So I found myself heading north, certainly no expert, in fact having hardly ever fished a trout loch before, let alone the limestone clear lochs of the connoisseur. My experience was more of fishing for stocked rainbow trout down south, or for half-starved, semi suicidal little brownies in the peat lochs of the north. I was used to the Guinness-like waters of the hills, full of little, dark fish. Now I was confronted by crystal clear, almost green-tinged limestone waters, where the bottom can be seen feet below, but the fish cannot. And yet they are there, green-backed, yellow-finned, silver-flanked – beautifully camouflaged and watching your every cast, doubtless with disdain if fish have such a sense. Oh yes, and weighing two to three pounds apiece.

The drive north from Edinburgh, up the A9, then over to Bonar Bridge and Lairg, and finally onto the single track road over the heather and peat moors, is a journey of continual visual delight and mounting expectation. What salmon fisherman can resist stopping the car over every bridge and peering into the Tay, Spey, Findhorn and other rivers en route? Has it rained? Are the waters clear? Are the clouds black? This time the drive took us a full six hours, with many a stop. They should have special road signs along those winding roads that hug leafy river banks. Not to warn you about the meandering road, but about the errant fisher-drivers as they lean over to gaze into the river, usually only just remembering to steer the car at the same time! And why are bridge walls or road crash barriers always at exactly the height that obscures the view of the water flowing below?

The steep, wooded hills of Tayside gave way to the higher, barren moors of Speyside, and then plunged across Cromarty and Dornoch Firths into the rugged rock of the far north. All trees were banished, blown into stunted, cowed bonsai shapes by the wind, as the scenery grew wilder and huge lumps of grey limestone thrust up in glacial carved shapes. The ground changed from black peat bog and brown-purple heather, to greensward and flowers. You could feel the move from the harsh and barren to the softer and fertile – and, far more to the point, from stunted little fish, to glass-case specimens. If you look up by Loch Dionard, underneath Foinaven, you can watch the pair of golden eagles quartering the sheer rock face, and the limestone waterfall tumbling down the side. The loch is pitch black, and a more remote or beautiful place to fish for sea trout would be hard to find, but the streams feeding the fledgling river below alternate colour between those of the usual frothy beer peat stain, and those that are sparkling clear off the limestone.

Arriving at the Kyle for the first time presented quite a view. The River Dionard meandered its way through the golden sands out to the almost Mediterranean blue sea. The hills tumbled down green and rocky to the water, and the white beacon of the Cape Wrath Hotel signaled food, a cool beer and a freezer soon to be filled. So I presumed. In fact, the arrival was perfectly timed I thought. I fully expected Bruce to appear smiling and welcoming with a ready Lagavullin to restore the energies after such a lengthy drive. Well, he was there, but no whisky in sight, and a most alarming expression on his face. I hurriedly did a mental check – had I left the car lights on or off, had someone dyed my hair green? Was I in the right place?

Yes I was, but on the wrong day. A day late in fact. Naturally, the weather had been benign that day – as we sat in the car whilst we should have been fishing. Apparently the fish too had been in generous, sunny mood – the last day that week that this was to be true as it turned out. This was hardly an auspicious start. I still blame Bruce for starting a week's fishing on a Saturday. Still, ever the gentleman, he raised hardly an eyebrow. The next morning the wind veered to the north east and thick grey clouds lowered.

Bruce kindly offered us the choice of fishing Loch Caladail, perhaps the jewel in the crown of the Durness lochs. The water actually was green tinged. You really could see the bottom, and it was very pretty drifting down towards the distant hills. Well, it was as long as you didn't approach too close to the little island where the arctic terns were nesting. Like fighter jets, they would scramble, soar, swoop and release their bombs with unerring accuracy right on your head.

As predicted, the wind rose, as did the waves. By early afternoon we had abandoned ship and were huddled behind a dyke eating soggy sandwiches and cursing the weather as white horses foamed down the loch. Thank heavens for a fine bottle of Chateauneuf which salvaged some of the day. But worse was to come. On venturing forth again, I decided that a brilliant tactical change was what was required to seduce these obviously over educated trout from their element. So I daringly decided to put on a sunk line. I had a new 'loch style' fly rod, ten and a half feet long, light and whippy and perfect for drawing the bob fly through the waves. Unfortunately I was not used to such long, fine tips. As I threaded the line through the top ring, I gave a tug, and my new rod was instantly transformed into a ten and a quarter foot bespoke number. If that was not enough, the spool catch on my somewhat ancient reel gave way so that the spool fell off. Luckily it landed in the boat – I suppose I should have been grateful.

So much for that first foray on the great limestone lochs. We had not seen a sign of a fin above or below the surface all day. We had been blown off by teatime, arrived a day late and now I had a rapidly crumbling array of tackle. Life could only improve. Still, the angler is ever the optimist, and after a hot bath and sustaining dinner all was well. I sidled in front of the fire ready to dream up a completely different scenario for the next day, amply helped by a relaxing dram that I was about to order. Oh the fickle powers of a fisher's self delusion! After all, the failure to outwit a creature with a brain the size of a pea must not be over-dramatised, and a peat-smoked Islay malt does slip down a treat beside a crackling peat fire.

Or at least it might have done, had mine host allowed such craven self indulgence. Unfortunately he was of the opinion that, a day late, plus a day blown off, such opportunities as there were to extricate said fish from watery element should, and could, not be wasted. And it just so happened, as I tried to warm by the fire, that there was a marked lack of external noise above the gently sizzling peat. No wind howling round the rafters. No rain battering on the roof. In fact, just the sort of evening when the big fish come in from the hundred foot deeps of Loch Borralaidh to feed in the shallows. And where was this great loch – about fifty yards away. Now the thought of leaving the fire, the warmth, cosiness and chat, and heading off into the eerie dark in cold, clammy chestwaders on a wild trout chase, was less than appealing. But then you know how it is, just supposing you didn't venture out, but took the soft option and went to that nice welcoming bed? The next morning at breakfast you would be confronted by a voluminous trout, displayed for all to see and all slackers to regret. It would, of course, be the only decent fish of the week too. Somehow, the comforting dram and hot water bottle could wait.

I didn't really have much of a choice did I? So I muttered to myself as I tramped across the field, noticing that the wind was not quite as soft as we had calmly assumed inside. Wading out I was lucky to remember to do so very gingerly. Chestwaders lead to temptation which often ends up in a wetting, especially at night after a festive dinner, and there was a sharp drop off a few yards out. Staying firmly put, I lifted up to cast. Splosh. No, not a huge trout just in front of me, but my reel landing in waist deep water at midnight. With a furtive look around I was relieved to see I was alone and so I started fishing with the landing net. Reel retrieved, I decided to strip off a couple of yards and stuff it all down my chestwaders and be done with it. The rod, shortened as it was, still managed a respectable cast and I awaited the big event.

The first, pleasant surprise, was an arctic char, a beautiful, orange flanked rarity from the ice age. They shoal in the depths but, as Bruce had said, come up for air at night. I had never seen, let alone caught one, as they are indigenous to only a few deep lakes in the Scottish Highlands and Lake District. This treat alone would have been adequate recompense – to catch a new and so pretty species of salmonid is a chance indeed. And then I hooked the bottom, solid and immovable. Until I felt a thump, a distinctly live thump. Not a good moment to be waist deep in an unknown loch with a broken rod and reel by now situated down a trouser leg. As said, cover of darkness does have its many advantages. I was pleased that there was no-one to witness me as I splashed around the loch, frantically trying to keep pace with one large and angry fish. After all, with the reel around my feet, I had no spare line with which to let the beast run! At one stage all went dead and I felt that awful, bottomless sinking feeling that the fish had snagged me. In hope more than anything more cunning, I just kept the rod tip up and pulled. Eventually a head shaking tug at the other end removed my fears. I have on only one other occasion felt a fish go down deep and be completely immovable. That was a twenty pound plus salmon in Iceland that was eventually to join the sad but colourful pagent of lost memories and rueful 'if only' wishes. After all this commotion in the eerie blackness, I almost ran back to the hotel in a state of huge excitement with my first Durness trout. Over three pounds of it, the slightly farcical nature of its demise being conveniently forgotten. It had been caught, of course, cruising the drop off from shallow to deep on the west shore at night, just as and where I had expected it to be…

Since that fateful night, I have often returned to Durness and its beautiful, if often uncooperative, trout. One loch has become a sort of obsession, little Lanlish, in the middle of the mainland's most northerly (nine hole) golf course. It is small, easy to wade, and contains vast fish. The hotel stairwell is adorned with various monsters well into the teens of pounds, and even in more recent times eight pounders have been taken. It is a loch where the fish either rise all over, in front of and behind you, and take nothing, or where you would swear there was not a fish in it. It is frustrating, tantalising and bloody difficult! And on those all too rare days when a fish does succumb, it will be three to six pounds. This is not an exaggeration – but it only happens about once a month.

It is partly because it has such a reputation as a dour loch, with a once in a lifetime chance of a monster, that no-one wishes to fish for the prerequisite lifetime in order to catch one. As a result the place is usually left alone to some of the worst slicers on the tee. Or off it – it is a fine place, in waders, to search for golf balls if the fish are, as usual, playing hard ball. In fact the only real sport I ever had there was, again, at night. The wind dropped and I was left in the middle of the south bay surrounded by the most extraordinary sound. It really was like an army of ill-bred children slurping their soup – a massive midge hatch and rise. And yet I return, in weather foul and fair, always with new hope; with a new fly; a different weight line; a better angle of cast or speed of retrieve, and still this most damned of all lochs beguiles me! I have tried all manner of wet flies, dries, fry imitators, up, down, deep, slow, fast... What do these large fish nourish themselves on one asks?

I strongly suspect the answer is fry. There are, even in the worst weather, hatches of delicate little yellow-green lake olives, and many an imitation (in all life stages) has been ignored. The fish, when finally caught, are often full of small silver fry, not luscious upwings. Messrs. Halford and Marryat might turn in their graves, but I suspect that a fry 'fly' is far more effective than a dry one. When a dry does work it needs to be big, a hopper or daddy long legs, to arouse their lordships' interest and appetite. Of late I have even compounded the crime by fishing a fast sink line on Caladail. This is neither delicate, easy nor pleasant, but in conjunction with a fry on the end I think it achieves the ultimate object. You have to get a real imitation of the actual food down to where the fish are feasting, rather than being sidetracked by the occasional rise to more apparent, and prettier upwinged flies. It is easy to forget that old truism, that a fish will not grow big by expending more energy in catching its food than it receives from eating it.

Somehow, Durness never fails to deliver something out of the ordinary. The last time I was there I spent the morning in a coin phone box trying to call Holland and Singapore. When I finally did manage to set off for Lanlish, I found a car had driven off the road into the sea. It had literally flown through the air in front of some appalled, and very kind, German tourists. The saga turned out to be something to do with sharp Gallic temper, adultery, jealousy and attention seeking. Just what you expect in a tiny rural community on the North Atlantic coast. Fortunately the driver was not seriously injured. Nor were the fish that day, but then that came as little surprise. At least in September, if the fish wont rise, the wild mushrooms usually will, so a fine meal can still be gathered.

But sometimes it works, you learn a new trick, and it all seems worthwhile. You are fishing in unspoiled surroundings for truly wild fish. No stocked, tail-less, mouth-tattered fish, but descendants of the vast fish that the Victorians angled out and glass-cased up. As free, wild and native as the wind. Some say that the extraordinary silver colour and airborne fighting characteristics of the Durness trout links them back to an original sea-run strain, and some of the lochs were I believe linked to the sea. Here, for a modest price, you can fish with the terns, mergansers and eagles, for wild fish, and learn. Isn't that the point, rather than fishing 'below yourself' by routine? Just to take a few predictable, statistically guaranteed fish, without taking any risks or engaging the brain. The first loch trout I caught on a dry fly, and the first on a fast sink line too was on Caladail. My best fish at night was on Borralaidh, and I have witnessed the most amazing nocturnal hatches on Lanlish. These little incidents all form a rich part of the fisher's growing tapestry as they slowly weave their way to maturity, confidence and competence. And, above all, humility, both in the face of such a beautiful, ancestral prey, and one so wary and difficult to catch in such a well suited environment. To enjoy the firm, pink flesh of a Durness trout with a fine, minerally white burgundy is a rite of passage, and a great pleasure, both in the catching and the eating.

One of the most memorable, and one off, events on the learning curve happened one brilliant sunny day in September on Caladail. The weather was unseasonally warm, hot even. We had been beaten off the River Dionard by the low water, total dearth of fish and hideous abundance of midges. Caladail simply dazzled in the sun, an almost azure blue reflecting the cloudless sky, as if sprinkled with sparkling diamonds. It was plainly a ridiculous day to go fishing anywhere, but at least a fine suntan and some unusual photo opportunities beckoned. As we pushed out, I rolled a line off the stern of the boat. The thin leader turned over and positively glistened in the sun, looking as inconspicuous as a hawser. Time for routine going through the motions only. But there was a steady breeze and light ripple. I donned sunglasses and we fished away, fruitlessly as expected. As we ended the drift, Bruce suggested that, as always, I fish the 'turning flee' on the row up the loch.

Now for those that don't know this minor tactic, it is, on its day, a real winner. You simply row the boat upwind, easily said if you have a bad back and always sit regally in the stern. Meanwhile the stern rod throws a longish line perpendicular to the boat, at right angles in fact. Holding the rod straight out and low, parallel to the water, the flies are swept round in a sinuous, accelerating curve. It is just as they begin to turn and speed up, like an escaping prey, that the fish can take – hard. It is, when it works, exciting stuff as the fish will scream line off the reel in one massive hit and run. Keep the drag set low and hang on. On this ludicrously bright day, it worked a treat. Not another fish was touched on the normal wet fly or by the other boat adrift. We took four perfect trout, two pounds apiece, like peas out of a pod. Each take screeched out onto the backing in one long run. A lovely noise! It also, by the way, raises salmon and sea trout. I remember one mad fish, again in a heatwave, on Loch Hope, that took off for the far shore and finally smashed the line, leaving both rods and even the normally garrulous gillie speechless!

I suppose it is the challenge, but I know that I will continue to fly from Paris to London to Edinburgh, hire a car, and motor six hours for a crack at that four or five pounder that undoubtedly awaits me – one day – in Lanlish. Whether this makes any sense to the reader I do not know. I type this on a portable computer, jet lagged and unable to sleep, at three in the morning in Houston, a whole Atlantic away. But to me the image is clear. I can almost feel the brush of the fresh air and gentle rocking of the boat; the arthritic creak of the oars and the sentiment of hope and excitement. Suddenly, there comes a jerk on the rod and rattle of the reel; the clipped, semi-hushed, semi-quavering excitement of the voice as battle is described and a successful end yearned for. The fear of that sudden slack, that split second when reality defeats optimistic hope and the fish is gone. It is this emotion, this picture that the writer, that I, need, and struggle to convey. I can only end by quoting Ransome "thinking about fishing in winter…what is it but 'the spontaneous overflow of powerful feelings; it takes its origins from emotions recollected in tranquility'. But that is Wordsworth's definition of poetry".

CHAPTER 3

A Stick and a Springer

'He comes in from the dark sway of the sea; from lonely reefs and wrecked ships hairy with weed. A wanderer of the ocean returning to spawn in the river of his birth'
Hugh Falkus 'Salmon Fishing' (1984)

The River Don flows into the North Sea almost next door to what used to be the most famous spring salmon river of all – the Aberdeenshire Dee. It is smaller, much cheaper and more accessible than the mighty Dee, and famed for its wild brown trout which are some of the finest in the U.K. Whilst its august neighbour has seen a much publicised and controversial collapse of salmon stocks, the Don still enjoys a spring run, that almost lost pinnacle of the fly fisher's hope and desire. The autumn sees hefty fish, to twenty pounds and more, even in these troubled times. If that were not enough, a six pound wild brown was taken there on a dry March Brown in April 1998 at Monymusk and three pounders are nothing unusual. Few rivers offer such quality fish at such affordable levels.

One sunny May a decade ago, I drove north, inexperienced and with a grand total of one salmon notched under the belt, in search of that most wonderful of all memories. The colours of the rolling Scottish countryside were amazing; an emerald lushness mixed with a generous dose of yellow, a lime-green effusion of spring. The roads were tree lined avenues, endless tunnels of leafy beauty, rustling, dancing and flickering in the breeze. It made you want to breathe in, fill the lungs and freeze-frame life, banishing the greasy black petrol grime, dirt and noise of London for ever. My destination was Bridge of Alford. Of course as soon as I reached that stone arch over the river, I parked the car on the verge, and leapt out to peer over the parapet, both upstream and down. I had no notion of what a normal water level should be, or whether it had rained recently. I wondered if any springers were in the river or still out at sea, were holed up downstream in the tidal depths, or had already run straight through upriver on a flood. But still it was great to be leaning over a bridge in

Scotland on a Sunday, with a whole week's salmon fishing to come and not a pessimistic thought in mind.

Of course, ignorance is bliss, or it hides bad news, at least for a while. A beer and quick research later provided the information that the river fished best when the bottom, triangular buttress of the bridge pillar was under water. I hastened out to look. No, there it was, clearly in view, high, dry and a good foot above the placid stream. Oh the negative power of a little information, be it right or wrong! Somehow the stream seemed to have shrunk, and my hopes with it. What had, an hour before, seemed a delightful prospect, now seemed a foregone conclusion. It was spring, the season that in the past used to offer the most sought after fishing of all, for plentiful, white-silver beauties. But, these days, the spring fish are almost gone, a glorious relic, and the water was dead low just further to diminish my chances. Naturally it wouldn't rain that week; the fishing was doomed to long days of flogging a trickling, empty stream, not a salmon in the lies, not a real hope in the heart. I cursed the lack of rain that had ruined my week, a long, weary five hundred-mile drive up from the City, (these days a half-hour's drive from Aberdeen airport seems an easier way to travel). Once again the salmon fates had dealt me an uneven hand.

Still, a keen young salmon fisher takes more than that to be dissuaded. The arrogance of youth, or of inexperienced hope soon springs back. When arriving at the Forbes Castle beat on Monday morning, I was pleased to see water, okay not much of it, but water nevertheless. Of course there would be fish, it was just a matter of finding them. The keeper insisted on small black flies, a Stoats Tail of preference. You are always told to listen to local advice on flies, which seems obviously sensible. But with salmon fishing, I wonder. We don't know why a salmon takes a fly. Whether it is due to aggression, to some reflex from parr feeding days, or to more recent oceanic feasting, nobody knows. Theories abound, and the ability of supposedly learned fishing experts to credit fish with logical thought processes when they have a brain the size of a pea (the fish, not the experts) is staggering. Anyway, whatever it might be, I doubt that fly pattern matters much. Perhaps in certain conditions of water colour, light and surroundings, one shade may show up more than another. Maybe red is better for annoying stale cock fish in the autumn (surely a good reason for not using red flies?). But of one thing I am certain – if everyone is using a small Stoats Tail, then every fish in the beat will have seen more than plenty of them, so I would suggest that anything that isn't small and black stands a better chance, if just for novelty value.

Once the keeper had ascertained that I was not a real city slicker, egg thief or mad trophy hunter, he led me across a field and pointed to a tall, thin, almost bare firtree. Atop, hardly visible, was a messy bunch of twigs – an osprey's nest. As we looked up, two magnificent birds could be seen soaring way, way up on the thermals, mere specks of majestic wingspan. Who could be so stupid as to refuse them a parr or two, and, for that matter, who could seriously pretend to defend nature and the environment purely for their own selfish purposes? Isn't it a somewhat sick, spurious practice to protect one species at the expense of another just so that there are more of them left for you to hunt and kill?! If nature was left in balance we could surely afford to enjoy the sight of mergansers, ospreys, and otters whilst still being left with an abundance of fish to chase after. After all, they are hunting to survive – we are doing it for fun.

The fishing was lovely, a streamy beat with rocks, fast currents and the odd deeper pool. Admittedly the river was low, but this made wading and covering the water that much easier, and there was still a continuous flow over what looked like the lies. The streams were, perhaps, too thin, and the gliding pool tails likewise, but one pool stood out as a serious, maybe the only, possibility – Craigpot. The river flowed through a rather canal-like, slack stretch, which was full of fly life – trout water I presumed, not that I managed to raise any. It then turned right and gathered, narrowing into a fast, white water rapid, foaming between rocks and boulders before gushing out into a deep, round pot. The main stream could be seen as a standing wave as it slowly dissipated into the blackening depths of a grand holding pool. There was a swing bridge over the top, fun to bounce over, and even more fun to stand on, look and ponder. I tried desperately to work out where the fish would be. By Wednesday night I had neither touched nor seen a salmon, and hope was fading fast – that pessimistic Sunday prediction on the bridge was looking unpleasantly correct.

I had read that in low water fish lie in the faster, better-oxygenated current at the very neck of a pool, preferably alongside a drop off to darker, safer depths. The neck of Craigpot looked just the ticket – right up where the rocky torrent emptied into the main pool. The surrounding water was deep, and the stream strong and well aerated. As far as I could guess, this looked the place.

There were only two drawbacks – a steep, wooded bank behind, and that raging rock strewn water in front. If I could guess where the fly should swing, just how was I to propel it there? I had read and reread my Falkus bibles, and had learned to have a horror of drag. The only serious cast would have to come from mid river, directly upstream of the supposed lie, at a narrow angle made mainly downstream to reduce the skating drag. There was a convenient rock that looked like the perfect casting platform.

Thus enters the stick. Without it I would never have bothered. But a third leg, a properly weighted wading stick, gives you the Star Trek effect – to boldly go where no man has ventured before. Again, textbook stuff, I went out after dinner, waiting for the sun to slip behind the trees, the shadows to lengthen and the salmon catching chances to rise as the light faded into a dusky orange glow. It was a daring plot. As with all such ideas, it seemed a lot less obvious in actual reality, in the twilight, peering into the pot holed white water. Still, probing with the stick, I edged out to the rock, determined to get there, even if a wetting ensued – it was, I thought, not really dangerous. (This was stupid – fast, shallow water potted with the odd deep hole and a few nice head-hitting rocks is surely as easy a place as any to come to a sad, early demise).

I then made my first mistake, not fatal I am pleased to say, (but you already knew that!) – I clambered on top of the rock. It made casting and line control so much easier. I had tied on a large Hairy Mary, neither black nor small, but all that stream surely called for something a little brighter and bigger for the fish to see, to cut into the water a bit and to swim reasonably across the flow. Whatever reaction or memory a salmon fly is supposed to trigger, a small size ten or twelve Stoat Tail in that strength of current would look unnatural and out of place, even to the most intellectually challenged fish. On about the third cast there was a huge tug, and I was fast into my first Scottish salmon. It was only my second on the fly, and my first springer – so the stakes were high. They promptly doubled, then tripled. Oh yes, I had forgotten to mention the tackle – a seven weight ten foot single handed rod, and a cheap trout reel with almost no drag and only fifty yards of backing. Perfect for sea trout, but woefully inadequate for a large salmon in a fast stream. A twelve-foot double handed 'grilse rod' and decent salmon reel would have been perfect, but I didn't possess such extravagances! The fish set off into the gloaming, the reel revolving and emitting a high pitched, rattling whine as never before. I stood in horror as the backing knot ripped and bumped through the rings and the line continued to zip out. After seconds I could see the reel spool about to appear, with maybe two or three yards of backing left. I could not believe my good and bad luck. I was immovably stuck, perched on a rock in mid torrent, attached to a demented whale with trout gear. In the dim, shadowy distance way below the swing bridge, a big fish leapt. In my semi dream-like, semi nightmare-like amazement, I wished I could hook one like that. Only slowly did it dawn on me that I had.

Now, had I been really well prepared, I would, of course, have measured the pool beforehand. From the rock to the sill, where it shallowed right out to a few inches depth, was, I later estimated, about seventy-five yards. I had thirty yards of fly line and fifty of backing, so what was I worrying about? Obviously the good Lord of fishers had a vivid sense of humour, but, overall, a decent sense of fair play. Fish generally don't like to run out of their own pool tail over a very shallow sill. Oh, if only I had known that, but I guess it would – with the comfort of hindsight – have spoilt the fun, or the tension at least. Three times that mighty fish ran to the very sill and hurled itself into the air, a shower of spray in the sinking greyness; and three times I looked at the reel spool and waited for the inevitable break. I should have done my maths. Eventually, the fish still on, I managed to pump it back up, yard by yard, hope, almost belief, increasing inch by inch.

Now I said I had made a big mistake. Being perched high on a rock is great when casting, but not quite so good when faced with a large, played out salmon drifting, dragging and pulling downstream well below you. Especially when your only landing implement is a small trout net. The first scoop got a large head in net, until a sullen flip of the mighty tail left me feeling even more powerless and desperate, and the fish back in the water. Nobody would believe this story of the big one that got away, the pain would be too great – a lovely springer on the fly half in the net, so close, and then gone. Would I have the spirit, the courage to carry on, to fish again for salmon knowing that I may never again have such a fine chance? I scooped once more, a sort of wild, mad lunge, and the head went in. This time I hauled up and grabbed the beast to my chest, in a lunatic, defiant bear hug. I stuffed the rod down my waders and stood there, the net in my left hand, the fish body embraced by my right arm. Its tail flopped in my face, my heart beating like a drum symphony, body and arm shaking with excitement and sheer disbelief. It would have made a fine picture. I suppose the adrenaline surge must have done something, for I don't normally manage to walk on water. I just stepped off that rock, my wading stick drifting aimlessly below me as I had both hands rather full, and simply charged for the bank, white water, pot holes and boulders regardless.

Seventeen and a half pounds (important, those halves!) of firm, silver beauty.

CHAPTER 4

English Chalkstreams

'I come around the bend and see the fairy boats sailing down, and the great head-and-tailers, black against the white-blue water, crossing and re-crossing, lazy and infinitely graceful.'
H. Plunket Greene 'Where the Bright Waters Meet' 1924

I must confess immediately that I have fished few days on the hallowed chalkstreams of southern England. My first foray was an inexpensive one purchased through a fishing club, the second the generous gift of a client. To draw conclusions from such a narrow experience may seem hasty, arrogant and ungrateful, and perhaps I am about to leap to premature, unfair conclusions, but the contrast was profound. I also have to plead ignorance when it comes to fly recognition, which is hard enough in English and quite beyond me in Latin. Classical education at school somehow left out the finer points of ephemeroptera or trichoptera, and I always was at the bottom of the science class. Thus I tread the banks with a woeful lack of knowledge on the life cycles of pale wateries or the mating habits of an iron blue.

In fact, the first trout I sought on a dry fly was in Devon, not on a chalkstream at all. The Teign was the tiny moorland stream that meandered gently through my childhood. In its lower reaches around Chudleigh it is a fine, typical West Country sea trout river, but not known for its brown trout. Still, they are there, wild, undernourished and small, struggling to eke out a stunted existence in that peaty, acidic environment. But do not mistake size for age or cunning – a half pounder down here is a fine fish, and an old, worldly-wise and worthy capture.

Anyway, 'George', as he was christened, took up residence in the pool just below the house. If I strolled down the road on the right bank between ten and eleven in the morning, when the sun sneaked through the narrow gap in the leaf canopy overhead, he could be seen quite clearly, finning quietly just upstream of the trailing branches beside a semi-submerged rock. Every morning, whilst idling away the daylight hours until the serious night time sea trout fishing could begin, I would pop down and check on George from the roadside. I would mentally mark down his position by the tree and rock, wade across the river, and flick a dry fly into that tiny gap. You could hardly see him from the left bank as you actually fished, so the road sortie was a confidence booster just to reconfirm that he was still in residence and dining. When wading, all you could see was the dimpling rise form, but his lie was easy to mark. Once the sun moved round and the little pool was pitched into darkness, he seemed to disappear into the obscurity, not a fin, or rise to be seen.

But in that one, sunlit hour, I would pitch the whole contents of my dry fly box to him. He was not, it has to be said, a trophy trout, though at ten to twelve inches he was a venerable old fish, with very particular tastes. As a real fly would drift over, it would disappear in a business like suck. As my artificial drifted over (drag being no problem, mercifully), you would see a shadow rise, drift downstream, neb under the fly, and then sink back. About once a morning he would actually go for it, like lightning, and I would react like an overexcited tortoise, and that called an end to that day's operations. On the third day, I hooked – or pricked him – on a tiny black gnat, but he escaped in seconds. The next day I was back to London.

That was a good 10 years ago, but I still remember and relish that three-morning stalk. In the end, I lost, honestly beaten by a half-pound wild Dartmoor trout, but seldom have I had so much fun with a fly rod. Shortly thereafter, I took a day on the Lambourn, which runs into that sacred chalkstream, the Kennet. It was a beautiful piece of water, shallow, gin clear and full of trailing fronds of weed and equally waving tails. But whenever I approached to make a cast, there would be a puff of silt and the fish had bolted. On my knees, from way below, the mere raising of the rod tip was enough. It was September, so the fish, wild browns, had had all season to learn, and once again I was dumbfounded. They were bigger than their Dartmoor cousins, weighing maybe a pound or so, but just as wary and just as difficult, (and probably half their age). I eventually managed to take a couple of grayling and one undersized brownie, but that was all. As I walked home along the river, I marvelled at its tranquil, pastoral beauty, and those small fish, sedately feeding in midstream that were so visible, so desirable but, for me, so uncatchable. Round two to the wild brownie.

By round three I was overawed, invited down to the River Itchen no less. A river that I had often pub-lunched by (with nearby family), and cast many a covetous eye upon, but never a fly. I had frequently wandered down its willow-clad banks and watched those bigger browns hanging effortlessly in the pristine waters. Now I was summoned, as a supposedly experienced fisherman to the real thing! As I alighted from my host's sports car, my heart sank at the sight of the thatched cottage with its manicured lawns sloping right down to the river edge and chatty keeper. What a terrible place to foist my ignorance and inexperience upon! I fidgeted nervously and looked at my fly box warily. Rows and rows of tiny specks, shop bought dry flies. I was not quite sure what they all were, but I figured Halford would forgive me from over there on the neighbouring Test. They were proper imitative, traditional dries after all. But not for long – I think he must have turned, groaning in his grave as I was handed a huge Grey Wulff pattern. Not quite the modest, blushing dry fly I had envisaged. I wandered to the river and just hoped I could put the fish down unobtrusively – unwatched by either the keeper or my host.

By lunchtime I had caught four trout, the biggest scaling four pounds, and another of three. They were, at least, browns, not rainbows, but the fight had been that of a wild fish of half, or a third, the size. They were full tailed, quite reasonably conditioned fish, but flabby and stocked. All I had to do was fashion a halfway decent cast, (the Itchen here was pretty small and placid), lob out this vast fly, and a willing trout the size of a lifetime specimen would oblige. Yes, it was mayfly season, and the afternoon mating dance was a delight to watch, but this was a sad, sad apology for a day on one of the world's great chalkstream trout rivers.

Of course one should not be snooty. Even Halford, that supposed stickler for rules and finesse, stocked trout. He may have only cast the exact imitation to a known riser, but the rise was not always wild. But this – a river, or a beat, filled with stupid, oversized sacks? On the Test it is even worse, corporate clients queuing up for first ever fly casts and hauling out huge, fat, flabby rainbows between champagne flutes? How can a heritage be so abused, nature so abandoned and human greed so pandered to? I am afraid that the sight of stocked rainbows in the Itchen or Test, or Loch Leven, just seems to me an abuse of the environment, of the fish and of the fisher. If it is so important to catch lots of fish at all cost, go mackerel fishing. If size is the thing, chase marlin or tarpon. But if dry fly fishing on a natural chalk aquifer is the desire, whatever the price (and I do not expect or assume to be able to afford it) why not leave it to nature, and wild trout, all be they only a pound apiece? As for fishing pressure, there are thousands of put and take fisheries that offer easy access and ready takers, and at a fair price too – so why change a natural fishery into a glorified, overpriced put and take?

The desire for instant gratification surely has no place in fly fishing anyway – in fact it is the very antithesis of the contemplative person's gradual learning approach towards acquired skill. Turning the river banks into a commercial fair is equally sad. I do not expect to be able to fish the Junction Pool on Tweed in October, or the Helmsdale or Naver, or drink Chateau Petrus, but I do expect all of those pinnacles of their art or sport to remain what they are – the very best, the zenith of quality. Of course not everyone can fish the Itchen and Test, or the Dee and Spey – they would be overcrowded and fished out in months. I do not wish to stray into the heated political minefield of the private versus public ownership of fishing debate. To me it makes no difference who or what the owner is, but do we really have to take the lowest common denominator, ironically doubling the price in so doing? Must we turn the banks of what was once some of the finest trout fishing in the world into a pantomime jamboree – for both the novices on the bank and in the water? We should have more respect for the timeless beauty of the water meadows, their wild flowers and wild life; the purity of the chalk aquifer (let me not even mention the destructive horror of over abstraction); and finally the sanctity and integrity of the native fish stock. Man's greed for money and leisure pursuits should not be allowed to destroy that after two millennia.

Loch Caladail – a two pounder on the "turning flee".

The most tantalising trout loch in Scotland – beautiful Lanlish.

All thanks to a wading stick. 17½lb springer on the Don.

Chalkstream idyll or nightmare? The Itchen.

CHAPTER 5

Irish Surprise on Lough Corrib

'Irish boatmen, to a man, treat their clients with the utmost respect, even when it is the last thing they deserve. There are times when a bash on the backside with the wet blade of an oar would be more appropriate'
David Street 'Fishing in Wild Places' 1989

Fishing stories (or dreams?) are like Hollywood movies, often predictable, mildly incredible and finishing with vast fish in the net after epic struggles. So when I had the chance one August to fish the fabled limestone waters of Lough Corrib, I was prepared for all those huge wild trout on Green Peters that I had read so much about. Strolling across the croquet lawn into the delightful Currarevagh House at Oughterard was exciting proof enough – the walls were littered with enormous salmon-sized wild browns and the lough was a mere couple of hoops away. An early morning wake up (however tired, what angler can sleep when a new fishing prospect dawns?), and stroll round the gardens showed a sea of glistening flat calm dotted with islands panning out way beyond the blue hydrangeas and orange tiger lilies of the shore. All in all a beautiful vista, though it would have been much improved had it not been viewed through an opaque cloud of voracious midges!

A rapid retreat and large breakfast later, I was standing by the boat jetty and all seemed well with the world. Here I was, having escaped from business in Dublin to the beautiful wilds of Galway, a lovely balmy day stretching out in front of me as full of hope and trouty dreams as the limpid waters of the lough. Hidden in my briefcase was a new six-piece travel fly rod, reel and box of flies. Would loch flies work on lough I wondered anxiously?

As we started the engine and puttered out of the boat bay, the pebbled bottom was clearly visible through the crystal clear water as were the dimples of small, eagerly feeding trout. I could hardly contain my enthusiasm and finger fumbling eagerness as I tried to thread the flyline through the rod rings. Looking up to the distant mountains of Connemara, a wonderful backdrop to this vast expanse of water, I finally took in some of the more immediate detail. Vide a rather bemused expression at the other end of the boat. Incredulous one might say. Checking to see that I hadn't put on different coloured socks (a little known but infallible minor tactic for seducing limestone loch trout by the way) I looked up and grinned rather sheepishly. And then the bombshell dropped on me.

"D' you no' like trolling then?"

Now this is not a good way to start the day with your new boatman. Well, that is to say it is probably a great way if you like trolling, but if you are a wee bit more of a fly snob, this is a trifle diplomatically touchy. I decided that a guarded, half-muttered negative with a smile was the best option.

"There's no' enough wind for a fly, we'd be much better off with the troll".

Well, he did have a point, backed up all too factually by the phalanx of midges, but I have only found myself trolling once (on Loch Naver) and had vowed never again to be so caught, rather like the salmon that day I'd have to say. I must have winced visibly however much I tried to look cheerful. At which my friendly boatman swung the motor round and we headed back for shore. Good God, had I committed such an awful indiscretion I worried?

"We'll just be popping back for the dapping rod then".

Such charming Irish logic was irresistible – if ever you need a stiff breeze it is for dapping! I settled back and we agreed to troll "until the wind picked up", a generous euphemism. I prepared myself for some large lump of fluttering metal, and was not disappointed when a size five Mepps spinner appeared. I was rather lost – I had been taking salmon the week before in Devon on a mere size one flicked upstream in low water, and this large, fluttering chunk of metal looked horribly crude. Still more shocks were to come. Having boat fished many lochs in the far northern Highlands, I am used to bailers in various forms – buckets, half detergent bottles, beaten up saucepans. Frankly, most boats up there need them after the combined effects of Scottish inclemency and the unmaintained, sieve-like nature of the wooden hulls. Corrib boats are in a different league, three thwarted, beautiful clinkered vessels, the finest I've ever been afloat in. So I figured that the large bucket opposite me was following the "Be Prepared" motto of the local Boy Scouts. I was further impressed by the prescient organisation behind this magnificent craft.

Until the lid came off that is. I suppose you have guessed it by now. One could say that this was only a slight western twist to the Halfordian match the hatch principle. After all they were local, hatched on the lough and prolific. Literally. Of course 'hatch' might be stretching the metaphor. Okay, so their wings were, to be brutal, remarkably like dorsal fins. Minnows; in the plural. One and a half per Mepps to be precise. They were impaled on a weighted rig attached to the spinner, and cast, well, dropped, overboard. The line was then stripped off the reel until the whole monstrous bait was trailing about fifty yards behind the boat. The rods were propped up against a rowlock and off we went. On Loch Naver they have a further refinement, whereby they put a specially selected stone, (it must be the right weight), on top of the line. When a salmon takes, the stone leaps up, the commotion arousing the so called fisher from his semi-somnolent state so that he knows a fish is interested, and the resistance-weight of the stone does the actual hooking. One reads masses of contradictory advice on how to hook a salmon on the fly, whether to release a loop of line, drop the rod tip, raise it, play it directly off the reel or just hope for the best, but this stone hooking method is truly original!

Now I am no fly purist, but this was, rather like going to La Scala and finding the Spice Girls on stage (the poor minnows doubling as Madama Butterfly?). Still, the weather and scenery were wonderful, and we chatted happily about when the fishing really is good on fly, and I am a firm believer in when in Rome... After about fifteen minutes, our deep discussion on the horrors of west coast fish farms (be they Irish or Scottish) was interrupted by a definite nod of the rod top. Sudden silence ensued – not that I was excited of course; there is no interest or skill in this trolling business. I was firmly instructed that the fish, as fish it certainly was, had not taken but was merely having a taste, and exhorted to keep my hands off the rod.

About thirty seconds later another there was a deferential nod, but not as yet a full Japanese bow. Getting rather excited by now, I held off. We motored on, until there followed a quick bow, and then a definite genuflect – the rodbent well over and staying there. I am an inexperienced troller, but this was as obvious as a salmon that nudges at a fly cast after cast and then eventually takes with a reel screeching pull. Up went the rod and an angry tugging at the other end metaphored the arrival of a trout. Corrib trout really are as beautiful as the pundits state – deep, butter gold bellied and densely black spotted, with compact head and high shoulder – all that a real, wild trout should be. But they do not show to their best on a stiff, fibreglass telegraph pole. Even when nudging the two-pound mark. To cut the tale short, that morning produced another fish of fully two pounds and an absolute peach of three and a half. In the afternoon the wind rose to a gentle ripple (no, we didn't avail ourselves of the fly rod) and the only interest shown was from a poor pike which was killed and discarded overboard. I was about to comment that the French, (and English in ages long gone, when it was more expensive than salmon), consider pike a fine dish, and they should know. 'Brochet' was one of Claude Monet's favourite meals.

Three perfect wild brown trout, totalling over seven pounds, in sylvan, unspoiled surroundings and unpolluted waters should be enough to sate any fisher. But as I admired their fading beauty (they taste delicious, with that firmness of pink not carotene colour-induced orange flesh), I could not help but regret the mundane and routine manner of their downfall. The skill lies purely with the speed, depth and location of the troll, all of which is controlled by the boatman, not the rod who is almost incidental to the outcome of proceedings. But I have to be honest – the vast majority of big Corrib fish (over 10 pounds) are apparently taken on the troll. This comes as little surprise – as previously described, the stomach contents of a few Durness limestone loch trout from the north west of Scotland caught in the summer during olive hatches show a remarkable predominance of fry rather than fly.

But I will be back. For the midge, duckfly or famed mayfly hatches (early or late spring), when the fly does come into its own, and when the poor abused minnows and foul fuming petrol engines can be left as they should be – in silent peace. But if you want a real glasscase specimen, prepare your trolling tackle and swap upwing for fin.

CHAPTER 6

Where Mountain Goats Fear to Tread

'...over their shoulders peer Canisp, Suilven and Quinag; seen through a distant gap Ben More Assynt hides in cloud. Far to the north there are hints of still more distant ridges, and over all of this the early sun pours golden light. It is a landscape as if from an earlier age of the world: a view to make your heart beat faster, to make you feel that life is, after all, worth living.'
David Paterson 'The Cape Wrath Trail' 1996

Oscar Wilde once quipped that the best place to be in Paris was up the Eiffel Tower, as it was the only place in Paris where that tangle of steel was not visible. The same goes for the Inver Lodge Hotel in Loch Inver, on the north west coast of Sutherland, five hours drive from Edinburgh. It could never be described as a thing of beauty. Functional, very comfortable and imposing, yes, but pretty damned ugly. However, it has three massive advantages. The first is the view, the hotel being perched on a hilltop overlooking Loch Inver. To the west, across the bay, lie the distant Heather Isles. In the morning you can watch the bright red fishing boats steaming bravely out to work across the placid sea as you sit tucking into a huge breakfast. The dining room is surrounded by panoramic windows and in the evening deer come down to graze on the grass just outside them. If that were not enough, to the east you can see the sun rise behind Suilven, the mighty sugar loaf mountain, throwing the heather clad moors into sharp golden relief in the autumn, or a pinky-purple riot of colour in the summer. The evening sunset across the sea can be equally breathtaking as you settle, battle-weary, into a therapeutic dram before dinner. This is the second advantage to be listed, the bar being inspiringly located under woodcuts of the sort of portmanteau salmon that you would catch in your dreams.

In addition to the magnificence of the view and the comfort factor, there is the third and supreme reason for visiting. It becomes almost a nagging, repeat compulsion once you have so indulged. It is just a couple of miles down the rugged coastline – the River Kirkaig. The short drive thither sets the tone. You hairpin down the steep hotel road, bracken, heather and Western Isles all mixed up, and hit sea level. Immediately you turn sharply left and climb up beside a foaming torrent, which drains Loch Culag and with it a few smolts to the sea. It is like one long extended waterfall, and you can only marvel at the salmon's enduring ability to locate and then fight their way up it. The Loch is a picture postcard, and as you round up and over it, Suilven looms into view. Down to sea level again, a quick left turn and suddenly, gliding between the rowans and birch, a perfect, rock strewn stream appears – the River Kirkaig.

This is the lower beat, which runs parallel to the road, offering lovely fly water, easy access and gentle, grassy banks, plus some fine holding pools. However, this is not the main event. To swing a fly across here is indeed a pleasure, but it should, in Kirkaig terms, be left to those a bit more mature in years or just a bit unsteady on their pins. It is a very dilute foretaste of the real thing which lies just beyond the car park. Well, about three-quarters of an hour past it, to be exact, uphill and panting. In summer it is a pretty path hewn out of the rock in places, rising way above the river trickling below. In heavy rain be warned, even the path requires thigh waders as it converts into a strange form of burn. The hike to the top pool, the famous Falls, is worth the effort, even regardless of the fishing. Again, Suilven appears, eventually, as do Stac Pollaidh and Canisp to the southeast, and they mark the finish of the seemingly never-ending ascent. You feel literally atop of the Highlands, high above the glen, the closest you will ever get to one of the golden eagles that soar overhead.

I hesitate to try to philosophise again as to why we fish as too much has been already written by many far better qualified than I am, but surely one reason is to find peace and solitude? How often do you find yourself not just out of sight, but out of earshot of a road; or of buildings; or of any sign of humanity? I have to say that there are few such places that I ever manage to get to, but the Upper Kirkaig is one. As you plunge down the vertiginous banks, you really are far from the madding crowd. Well, apart from one not so friendly welcome – if the wind drops below four miles an hour, prepare for hell in paradise. No, not the bustle of stressed humans, nor the speeding roar of the combustion engine, but the incessant buzzing of myriad midges, in the ear, up the nose, through the stockings, down the back of the neck...

That apart, the Falls Pool is quite a spectacle, as is that of grown men, nets and salmon rods in hand, scrambling down on all fours from rock to rock. Once there, it is like standing in a cold shower. The river drains a series of lochs, Urigill, Cam, Veyatie and Fionn before plunging over a sixty foot, sheer drop – hence the cavernous pool below, carved out of the rock like a miniature Roman amphitheatre. Conveniently, the Olympian designers also threw in a small casting platform, usually about ten feet above water level, and with surely a malicious sense of humour a much smaller ledge just above, or under, water. It is here that you face the first, and only, moment of human stress. You simply cannot fish the Falls Pool alone – apart from the danger of slipping on the perennially wet rock, it would be simply impossible to land a fish, unless you have amazing powers of levitation and twenty pound nylon. So one rod has to perch up high and flick the fly enticingly into the foam speckled run under the far bank, trying not to hook the other designer joke – a small, scrubby bush, way up above the water and thus cunningly out of sight when casting down to the water, but neatly placed to catch the fly's actual trajectory. Meanwhile the other rod, in the event of a kindly salmon taking a fly that escaped the bush, has to scramble down a vertical rock face clinging on to a very unsafe looking rope. Oh yes, holding a large net as well. As the wonderfully archaic guidebook so helpfully points out, once the gillie has netted the fish, he must pass it up to the rod before he thinks of shinning up the cliff to safety himself, and the overexcited rod must take care not to drop the beast on his long suffering gillie's head! It is an enticing place to linger, as the fish have nowhere upriver to go and often jump in a shower of inspiring spray, but it is easy to waste far too much time, rather like a hopeless comedian with a captive but disinterested audience. I have only hooked one fish there, and the look on my erstwhile gillie's face, Bruce Sandison, was one of absolute horror at the thought of the impending descent. When the fish finally came off, I am not sure which of the three of us was more relieved...

To me the Kirkaig is the quintessential Highland salmon river. In scenic beauty it is unsurpassed by anything I have seen in Scotland or even Iceland (in its scale), but it is the mixture of that rugged wilderness and natural beauty with the sheer physical effort involved in fishing that makes it unique. After fishing the Falls, you have to scramble nearly all the way back up to the high path that runs along the top of the glen. A few yards walk along the flat regains the breath, but then you must descend all the way down again to arrive at the next pool. If the river is high, the banks soon become impassable. You cannot possibly wear chestwaders. I tried once and almost expired from the effort, so to continue downstream when the water level is up takes a mighty detour all the way back up the bank, round or through the silver birches, (wonderful traps for a fly or rod tip) and then down again to the frothing water. It is invigorating stuff, sometimes looking over sheer drops down to the river as you slither along the slippery, muddy sheep track through the heather. The fishing is just as exciting, a succession of rapids, falls, rocky glides and rushing streams, a fly fisher's delight and nightmare all wrapped up in one. It is not for the faint hearted!

Of course if you prefer to saunter down the carpet-slippered banks of one of the mighty east coast rivers, gin and tonic in hand, from the fishing hut to a waiting boat, then the Kirkaig is an altogether rude affair. But it is more elemental in its pleasure, not for everyday, sure, but there to purify and sharpen up the fishing soul and appetite when the double Spey cast is getting a little jaded. It is a river for microfishing, not the long, grandiose step and cast pools of a Tay or Spey, but little miniatures, each one separately crafted and needing a different approach. A floater here on the gliding tail, a fast sink in the turbulent neck, a dibbled cast here, a long, mended one there. An endless variation of depth, speed and angle – a river that requires thought, not metronomic long casting precision.

It is the only river where I have developed a specific technique that actually works. This sounds terribly pompous and very clever, but is in fact dead simple. All you need is a pocketful of braided leaders. When I first heard of them I must be honest and admit that I had no clue what they were. But every with-it angler and trend-setting fishing magazine was full of them, so I bought a few, with varying speeds of sinking. Needless to say they sat quietly and unused in my shoulder bag for years, until one day on the Kirkaig. As described, fishing this river is ruled by two imperatives – the need to travel light to stave off utter exhaustion, and to tailor the approach to each differing pool. The combination of the two might seem to be impossible – how can you handcraft your presentation without lugging along a series of different rods and lines, the carrying of which would leave you gasping for oxygen after a few pools? The answer fits snugly in a single pocket.

Continuing this unusual thread of honesty, I will admit that like most things, this revelation only happened by chance. I was sitting lunching with Bruce and Ann by my favourite pool, the Lower Falls. It was late September and a fair rush of new water was coming down after rain, but the colour was golden amber clear and looked just peachy. Yet we had not raised a snout. I had my usual light twelve foot eight weight double handed rod, which I find perfect for mobility and for covering this small, but fast river, and a sink tip to compete with the current. Any heavier, full sinker is just way beyond both my casting and line handling abilities. It sinks behind rocks, lurks deep in the back eddies, and curls into a dangerous cobra-like dervish when you try to recast. No, the bulk of the fly line needs to float. Anyway, as I looked at the froth churning over the falls and hitting the sheer cliff on the left bank, spume flying into the air, I was suddenly convinced that I needed a little extra depth and 'cut'. A taking salmon would then be assured. I announced this whim with great conviction, and was summarily told to go and prove the point.

Somewhat sheepishly I put down my sandwich, knotted on a fast sink braided leader and cast it out. There was no need to change the fly, a medium sized Collie Dog, as I would rather have a lightish fly that plays in the stream with some semblance of life than a hefty brass tube that sinks like a dead weight. By the time I had reached the pool tail, the fly seemed to be swinging down and across in a perfectly enticing arc, but as so often it was me who was impressed, not the fish. I was about to admit defeat when a hefty tug lifted the rod top and my flagging spirits and kindly backed up my hunch. Bruce's face was a picture. I have used braided leaders on the Kirkaig ever since when I have felt the need to change the line profile and depth. It only takes two minutes and I can honestly say that for once the practice does seem to bear out the theory. It is easy, but lazy, to fish with just one line and maybe change fly size, but I find it far more effective to use the leader to change depth as the water shallows and slows down in a gently gliding tail before reverting to a rushing torrent in the neck of the next pool. How can you fish all that with just one line and expect the fly to settle into and drift across the current properly all the way down the beat?

In one pool, the Otter, the river narrows, with a sheer rock face behind you and a delicately placed overhanging tree above. Any form of overhead cast is doomed, and even a Spey or roll cast is lost with the rod top caught up in the branches. But the stream, as it broadens out, is a likely lie. The temptation, or frustration, is to try to fashion some form of cast. This is a mistake as the tree attests. Any impecunious and energetic young tree-climbing fisher could fill, for free, a number of fly boxes. The guardian tree, standing solemn sentinel at the pool neck, is festooned with an ever-increasing selection of new flies and dangling nylon, a sort of perennial Christmas tree to brighten up the seasons.

I must confess that the first time I fished it I quickly recognised its fish holding potential, and just as swiftly added my Willie Gun to the festive decorations. As it had just taken a fish, and was one of only two I had with me, I was upset at my own stupidity. But who says once bitten, twice shy? As a fish rolled below me, I promptly repeated the ignominious performance and generously relieved myself of the twin fly too. Expletives not deleted, I hurried on, humbled again. One attribute of this river is that it brings you back to earth, literally, with a thump as you fish one pool well and think that you are awfully clever, the supreme fisher-craftsmen, the quintessential hunter-gatherer. Not for long... By the way, the correct method, as artfully shown to me by Bruce, is simply to dangle a double handed rod at right angles across the river, strip off some line, let it drift down with the current towards the fish, and then mend it across the stream. You actually never cast, letting the current and line mend do all the work, and slowly the fly swings across the inaccessible lie downstream. It feels a bit like cheating, and you rather wonder if such a simple, 'non cast', can really deceive the king of fish, but it works, and now even I can catch fish there and leave my fly box intact. Salmon, after all, are not too concerned as to how the fly actually gets into their domain, and do not have diplomas in advanced casting appreciation.

Of course, the word quintessential, these days, carries a darker, sadder meaning too. The Kirkaig is a river that used to produce big fish – and a more daunting salmon fishing challenge than combating a twenty-pounder in one of those short, rock filled, thundering falls pools, I cannot imagine. The spring runs are long gone, but even five years ago, June used to produce fish into the 'teens of pounds, but this run seems to have faltered more recently. Let's hope that this is merely due to unseasonable low waters, but I fear this is ostrich-like optimism. If one ignores the rose-tinted nostalgia, the river produces between one hundred and, if very lucky, one hundred and eighty fish a year, in what is effectively a four-month season to six rods. If one is honest, a fair number of these are red kippers caught in the back end. There are some clean fish in September, but they are a metallic gun metal grey rather than the dazzling silver and white of a fresh run springer or summer grilse, and aggressive red cocks are more likely to be the fare. Surely, in this age of rapidly reducing stocks, such fish should be left in peace to spawn? The Kirkaig, due to its nature, has virtually no spawning burns as such, as they cascade literally vertically into the river, so the fish have to breed in the main river. They have nowhere else to go, as unless they replace their fins with wings they can neither ascend the burns nor the sixty-foot waterfall at the head. Red fish are thus left in the main river, very much at the mercy of late season fishers. I wonder if, like so many other West Coast spate rivers, the close season should be brought forward, by at least a fortnight? It is now such a miracle for a salmon actually to survive through to its native river, that any form of threat in the back end, so close to spawning, should be removed. The chance of a fresh run fish that late in the season is slim, and whatever the care taken with catch and release, hooking and playing out a salmon in such heavy waters is never going to do a fish much good, is it? There is also the temptation to fall for that often heard lie about red fish being good for smoking, (which they definitely are not). Better to leave them to reproduce in peace, though the fishery owners would doubtless bemoan the lack of essential income. Still, if stocks continue their current downward spiral, not just on Kirkaig, but on most rivers, the revenue problem will soon be far more serious than the loss of a few backend rods fishing for predominantly red fish.

That much said, there really is no better place to fish. I love the sparkling waters of the Dee, the mighty push of the Tay, the autumnal colours on Tweed, but in a sense they are huge, tamed, well bred rivers, and, let's not forget, largely inaccessible to the average fisher in terms of both rod availability and cost. The Kirkaig is a freer spirit, more intimate, and easy to afford; not the weight of fishing history, or of fish, but unsurpassed in its scenic and flyfishing beauty. Nowhere else do you deserve, and get, such a fine excuse for a hot bath and recuperating drink over a fine dinner!

CHAPTER 7

Scotland's Heather Isles

'The scent of thyme and bog myrtle
is so thick
one listens for it, as though it might be
a drowsy honey-hum
in the heavy air.'
Norman MacCaig 'Looking down on Glen Canisp' 1966

What is it about islands that so holds the imagination? Is there an extra romance in being surrounded by the crashing, unpredictable waves of the ocean, or an added charm in being isolated and cut off? Or is it just the added effort of actually getting there, which, in this age of abundant and easy travel makes you feel that you have, for once, really gone somewhere? Certainly, reaching the Heather, or Western, or Outer Hebridean Isles does involve a trek seldom required nowadays for what is in essence a short journey. Why else would one series of islands deserve three names? True, you can fly from Glasgow to Benbecula, and on a clear day the view over the Inner Hebrides and across the stormy Minch is fabulous. But this is cheating, an indolent even if time saving shortcut. Far better to load up the car and drive to the north west of Scotland, across the bridge to the beautiful Isle of Skye, past the majestic Cullin mountains up to Uig, and onto the ferry to the Western Isles. It only takes a day and is a visual delight, and these days, thanks to European Union grants, a pretty easy drive too. You might also be surprised to see palm trees growing on Skye.

What awaits you in the Hebrides is indeed different. No trees for instance, the savage Atlantic westerlies see to that, unless you count the odd stunted, dwarf bush. Plus an independent spirit – it is the only place in mainland Scotland and the Isles where I have often heard Gaelic spoken as a true mother tongue. There is a savage beauty, be it the rolling blacklands of peaty North Uist, literally sieved all over with lochs and lochans or the mightier hills of Harris. Heading south the scenery softens into the fertile shellsand machair grasslands of South

Uist and Benbecula, a springtime riot of yellow iris, cotton grass and rare orchids, with, if lucky, the rasping call of a corncrake. Solitude, and tranquillity come free with the wind and the desolate open spaces – the Isles are not a cosy place, no softly wooded, shady glens, no sloping meadows of crops and grass, no gentle lowing of cattle, but everywhere the squelch of peat, bumbling of sheep and the incessant, horizontal push of wind.

And with this almost primordial wildness comes – guess what – fish. Of all sorts, sizes and types. For the beginner, the sharp, lightning fast tug of small brown trout in the many peat lochs. The water froths amber in the waves, as you wade across the golden sands as if lost in a sea of dark ale, a curious but pleasant feeling. For the expert, the silver purple arc of a two-pound leaping trout, black spotted, pink fleshed and gorged on shrimp, lustily fed in the rich alkaline waters of the machair fringe. For the aristocrat, the reel singing run of a fresh salmon or sea trout. Sadly this is nowadays often a symphony of silence, undoubtedly due to many factors, including the irresponsible sponsorship of fish farms to sate short-term greed to the long term, and maybe irreversible detriment of the environment. It is noticeable how the sea trout stocks fare differently on each side of the island, and surely it is no coincidence that the fish farms are all located offshore the one side where wild stocks have all but disappeared. Absentee landlords and Government regulators squander the valuable, precious inheritance of several millennia – a tragic bequest to the future generation.

But if you cast aside, for a moment, the sadness of migratory fish abuse, you can still find some of the finest wild brown trout fishing in Europe, easy of access, soft on the wallet and generous to the fishing diary. South Uist is the jewel in the Hebridean crown where brown trout are concerned, and a place where the epithet 'wild' is gloriously unnecessary – it is guaranteed. The island is divided into two halves. The east side is a landscape of peat, heather and dark lochs, where the water broods black, and the fish run abundant, small and hungry. It is to the west coast that you need to go for the cream of the trout fishing. Thousands of years of Atlantic breakers hammering in from the ocean have created a narrow coastal strip of shellsand, in which nestles a series of shallow, lagoon like lochs. Due to this shellsand the water is richly alkaline and the feeding prolific, giving exceptional growth rates to the trout therein. The machair lochs of South Uist, and, to a lesser extent, Benbecula and North Uist, form a worthy and inspiring end to any trout fisher's journey.

Going from one coast to the other you see an abrupt change, the one main road that runs down the island forming a barrier, a backbone. To the east, all is rock, heather and peat; but to the west, just a few miles away, lie the rolling machair green lands, bedecked with wild flowers, happily munching cattle, and crystal clear lochs. The palette turns from purple-brown and black, from deep ochre to green, yellow and white. It all happens in the space of a just a few yards; you could cast almost across it. The great machair lochs are in fact small, easily covered in a day, except the endless Loch Bee, and shallow. They are ideal for boat fishing with traditional drifting 'loch style' wet fly or, my personal favourite method, for wading. It can be a slightly disconcerting feeling, being waist deep in mid loch, but the bottom is firm and safe, and you can use chestwaders like a boat, to navigate around the weedbeds and islands, keeping your back to the wind for ease of casting, and your body low in the water for camouflage. I often wade fifty yards out from the bank, then turn around and fish in towards it. The big advantage of wading over boat fishing is that you have far better control over the depth and movement of the fly, being no longer dependant on the vagaries of the wind direction and speed – no need for rowing skills and a drogue. You can also tailor a 'drift' on foot to follow the exact contours of the loch, only achievable in a boat with a skilled and energetic gillie working tirelessly on the oars. It is a more intimate, personal way to fish, right there in the water, one more barrier between you and the fish's environment removed.

For wading, Loch Bornish is the best as you can literally cover every inch. I have seen some spectacular hatches there of the dreaded caenis, and failed dismally to connect with any of the fish that were gorging themselves on this most aptly named "fisherman's curse". More helpful rises to midge have produced consequent rod bending excitement. Some of the other lochs are deeper, requiring a boat in parts, though on every loch one of the best areas is the visible drop off between the machair and the loch – where the shallow, golden sands shelve sharply into the deeper, darker waters. A wade, or drift, along this easily visible edge can be very productive.

One loch used, in my opinion, to stand pre-eminent - Loch Stilligarry. It is regally set off by the triple ridged backdrop of Uist's highest hills, Hecla, Beinn Mhor and Ben Corodale. It was always a loch full of anticipation and hope, as the fish, though infrequently encountered, were large. I have taken them to three pounds, their silver flanks and airborne fight making me wonder if their proximity to the sea didn't have some extra significance when compared to the more normal, bottom-boring traditional brown trout. I remember fishing after dinner one June evening, (it is light until midnight), and seeing a simply vast shoulder roll at my bob fly without actually connecting. I froze in eager hope and flicked the flies out again, but to no avail. More and more desperately and vainly I scanned the water and cast, praying against all the odds that the big fish would come once more. Eventually even the most delusionary hope faded and it became obvious that the glass case would not be filled this time. My heart beat relaxed and the dream faded into a pleasant reminiscence, and an exciting emotion that I can still recall now. A few years ago the estate released a large amount of home bred small fish into the loch, I believe to boost stocks badly reduced by local poaching. Vanished were the three-pounders, replaced by hoards of hungry half-pounders, and gone the special magic of the place too. Hopefully the infant fish will have grown on by now, and I am told that the loch is now returning to its former natural glory.

The best time to fish must surely be late evening in May or June. The wind drops and the whole of nature softens, flies hatch and fish rise to them in leisurely peace. The sun sets, a distant sinking orange orb sending flaming fingers glowing across the Atlantic, and throwing pink cloud reflections across the placid waters of the loch. The water surface takes on an almost molten metallic hue and viscosity, ringed here and there by feeding trout. A loch that has been windswept and featureless all day, with scudding waves and white horses, and not a fish or rise in sight, is transformed into a millpond of inspiration. The birdsong multiplies, and the chances of a good fish with it. Those who prefer the comfort of the bar, fireplace or bed are simply missing out on nature and trout at their most accommodating.

The wind, with nothing to stop it for three thousand miles, can, surprise, surprise, be a problem, especially as the relatively shallow sand bottomed lochs quickly churn up into a sort of glistening pea soup of sand, algae and weed fragments. However, in such conditions all hope need not be lost at all, as there are all the peat lochs to the more sheltered east side which remain unaffected. If you still yearn for the argent flanks of a machair trout, there are various unnamed little lochans, mere ponds really, between the main machair lochs on the west side and that spine of a road that marks the transit to peat. Being unmarked and unknown, the average angler avoids them – why will fishers only cast their hopes out upon a known quantity? The power of a name, and a supposed status to bestow often false confidence is remarkable. Conversely the poor little lochan just, literally next door, but not mentioned in the fishing records or learned guidebooks is left untouched, disregarded and disdained. Foolishly. I remember being blown off the mighty (but, in my experience dour) Loch Grogarry and strolling up the road back to the lodge past a tiny lochan. It lay in a dip and was thus sheltered, and produced three lovely plump machair trout of a pound each in an hour, and there are fish of twice that size. Due to the surrounding wet, boggy land, it rejoices in the unfortunate name of Pet Cemetery as the odd sheep skeleton attests. Long may it remain unfished and unspoiled, I would selfishly have to say. I suspect mine was the first fly to grace their window in a couple of years, and yet the water is only a hundred yards from the lodge and two hundred from the main road! It is hardly inaccessible or difficult to find.

On a separate occasion, when blown off the main lochs, we decided to explore and found a sheltered, large peat loch that looked promising. It was a sharp change from sandy, easy to wade Bornish to the plunging peaty depths of Loch Clachan, where the water can shelve off sharply from the steep rocky banks. It was in fact the only time that I have benefited from fish farm cages. They had obviously been sited there previously – now gone, but the mooring rings were still embedded in the rock. Being ever on the look out for a good, free meal, the opportunistic little wild brownies obviously saw this as Christmas come to stay, and had augmented their meagre diet with spare fish food that fell from the cages. The result was real wild peat loch trout, but of remarkable size. I took two over the pound, plump as pie, and a third of two and a half! Unwisely I announced the name and location of the loch that night, my vanity playing to the crowd. The next morning looked like something out of Alaska when the Pacific salmon are running. Wall to wall rods, (I exaggerate slightly, but in the Western Isles two is a crowd). I left in a hurry, and can report, with slightly malicious grin, that there were obviously not that many clever fish that had fattened up on the local fish farm stew, as the catches soon returned to just the normal half-pounder here and there.

But cheating the wind by fluking a few overfed trout that lurked under fish farm cages is surely not the point? There is a nasty habit on some southern English reservoirs, where rods tie up to the cages and fish huge pellet 'flies' on high density sinking lines to catch mutant shaped double figure rainbows – a complete inversion of fishing values. That is what our Trans-Atlantic cousins would call 'redneck fishing', the urge to kill as many and as large fish as possible as a measure of success. Fishing on Uist is a more contemplative, peaceful affair, the only savagery being the frequent inclemency of the climate and the headlong plunge of an angry fish.

Still, for those who only covet the biggest fish, regardless of the whys, hows and wherefores, here is a free tip – and, believe me or not, pretty much guaranteed! Nor is it yet another one season wonder of a new 'infallible' fly, or one more 'variant' that adds a flash of modern fluorescent synthetic material to an old pattern and cons us into believing it is an innovation. By the way, regarding flies I am, as you will have gathered, no expert and though I always lug multiple fly boxes to the loch side, I rarely use more than four flies. On the top, the bob fly, I always tie a Ke-He. This was invented in the 1930's on Orkney, another remote northern set of islands, by Messers Kemp and Heddle as an imitation of a black bee. If I have to remove it from my leader it is indeed a black, and usually blank day. The middle fly, the dropper, need only be a Charlie MacLean. It is a scruffy palmered mix of white and furnace/red gamecock hackles with a flashy red tail and twist of silver. Even better, Charlie was a famed South Uist gillie. On the point you have a toss up between a 'wee double' Kingfisher Butcher for the peaty lochs and a Silver Invicta for the machair. That, in sizes twelve and fourteen, really is all I ever needed, though I am sure tackle shops and fly tying experts will be appalled!

But you are still waiting for that golden hint aren't you? Well, the biggest loch on Uist, (Loch Bee), runs west-east, straddled by the main road which runs as a causeway across it, separating the fresh water East Loch Bee from the brackish West. As the tide floods, salty water, doubtless full of shrimp and seafood, flows through a large culvet pipe from the West Loch into the East. Where the pipe flows in, through the concrete causeway, is a slight depression, and just like those opportunists on Loch Clachan, it is an almost certain lie for a two, three or even four-pounder. You have only to hold the boat off the wall and, with the wind behind, deliver a short cast with a weighted fly and the chance of a cracking fish is high, no exaggeration. But it is somehow an almost underhand way to deceive a fish, to cheat on the natural Darwinian size of things, to boost the average weight. To swap the rustling of yellow flags, a nodding sea of brilliant yellow, for the smell of petrol, and hard crunch of concrete is a Faustian bargain with the Devil within. Now you wouldn't do that for a gleaming, wild four pound brown trout on the end of the line would you?!

Looking west to the Heather Isles – Loch Inver at sundown.

Quinag towers over Ann Sandison on the Upper Inver.

The Kyle of Tongue – good sea trout water.

Good friends, good fishing – Mike with some machair trout on Loch Bornish, South Uist.

CHAPTER 8

Icelandic Salmon in the Wilderness

'Few have taken an interest in Iceland, but for those few it is a passion. Its memory is a constant background to what I am doing.'
WH Auden 'Letters from Iceland' (1936)

What do you need to enjoy a truly wonderful salmon fishing experience in an Icelandic wilderness? Well, lots of salmon for starters, some stunning scenery, a few flies, a lot of luck and, sadly the most critical of all, either a stack load of money or a golden invitation. Corporate hospitality has always been something I rather disapproved of. All those over-fed, over-paid fat cats doing what they think they ought to be seen doing, and jacking up the prices for the rest of us humble folk who don't get invited to such indulgent jamborees. Let's face it, many of the corporate clients don't even know what they are watching or doing, the champagne and reflected glory being the main event. Or so I, (perhaps slightly enviously, if truth be told) presumed. Just look at all the City types strutting around the blessed banks of the River Test, crowing about catching newly introduced stew pond rainbows of the same outsized proportions as their ample corporate girths!

So, feeling morally highbrow if insanely jealous, I was somewhat bemused to receive a letter inviting me to pick between a top beat on the Spey, and one of the best rivers in Iceland, both in peak season. Of course, the self examination of my conscience and righteous soul searching lasted about five seconds, and soul to the devil did I sell, double quick. Faust – was he a fisherman?

Landing in Keflavik was an experience. Suddenly, just as I thought the pilot was about to ditch us in mid North Atlantic, a brown strip of volcanic, lunar land appeared underneath the plane. On stepping outside, the first impression was of the cold, the wind and the utterly deserted moonscape. It was, after all, here that they practised the first Apollo landings. Still, on driving into Reykjavik, a city of about one hundred and fifty thousand in an island bigger than Ireland but with only a quarter of a million inhabitants, the gnarled, moss covered volcanic earth gave way to a softer landscape, a profusion of lupins, brilliant in their purple-blue bloom. In the distance the snow still lingered across the top of the fjord. It was a lot more imposing than landing in the average Scottish airport, my usual arrival point for a week's salmon fishing.

The Icelanders are a very pure race, and if white blonde hair and piercing blue eyes are to your taste, they have produced three Miss Worlds! I think it also true to say that I have never met friendlier, more helpful people – even the customs officials were merrily discussing the salmon season. I suppose it is because salmon fishing is seen and valued as a major tourist resource, and closely controlled, there being about twenty top rivers, strictly limited to a set number of rods and a twelve week season. The Icelanders understand the importance of the salmon to both the visiting tourist fisherman and the local economy – we back home could well take note and learn to guard our natural stocks with such sensible care.

The countryside is very different – all lumpy and bumpy, covered in an almost unreal green sward of moss and lichen, with jets of steam issuing forth from the underground geysers, (the name Reykjavik means Bay of Smoke as so called by the first settlers). Having a bath takes, at first, some willpower, as the hot water is actually taken straight from the thermal springs. It actually has to be cooled down, and stinks of sulphur – I am sure it is very healthy for the skin, but it is like being immersed in rotten eggs! Along the road in one valley we came across rows and rows of huge greenhouses, all thermally heated – the source of the surprising amount of freshly grown local vegetables available in this frigid land of ice. In early July the fjords were dusted with an icing of snow, and the river valley carpeted with minute alpine wildflowers in white, pink, and yellow. Further upriver the glaciers looked so soft and white as to be almost clouds sitting atop the valley. The lower river, the Thvera, was broader, and slower, gliding through a lush green plane, past a small, isolated church, with a sharply pointed red steeple, stark, simple and beautiful against the landscape, and once keeping spiritual guard over one of the most famous salmon pools in the country. Of late it had shallowed and filled in, though a rock was put in just below the church and always seems to attract a resident fish or two. But the upper river, the Kjarra, was the real gem, an Icelandic version of the Kirkaig, rushing through a steep valley, then carving through a dark, foreboding canyon, where you can understand the local folklore and superstitions that date back to the savage, heroic days of the Sagas. As I stood on the crest of the hill, a merlin gazed at me imperiously, perched on a knoll not ten yards away, and then soared off across the river with a strange, incongruously high pitched screech. To the right, the Stygian canyon, where the river turned the corner and disappeared between high black walls. The water glides deep, slow and brightest blue and there is a narrow ledge that you can wade along, right under the looming cliffs. To be honest I really found it quite a frightening place, the unearthly silence being sinister, dark and restricting, like some sort of prison, the water suddenly looking dangerous, threateningly deep and echoing, magnifying the seemingly unwelcome noise of a human presence. Downstream the river slowly broadened out, the canyon walls opened and it meandered off, a silver ribbon, to the distant volcanoes and the snowy fjord.

This is Eyjolsfludir, perhaps the loveliest salmon pool I have ever fished, where the river finally escapes from the canyon's narrow, dark confines. It glides along a boulder strewn run, tight under a sheer cliff, water dripping down it like a mini waterfall of sparkling droplets, nourishing the lush green lichen and brilliant yellow flowers that somehow grow out of the vertical, glistening black volcanic rock. The left bank opens out into a large pebbly shore, purpose made for wading and casting, and the water that slips by is so clear that fish can be seen by every boulder as you walk along – moving out of the way when a fish is hooked. It is the only pool I know where you have to look carefully when playing a fish so as not to end up watching the wrong one! We nicknamed it the aquarium, and it never failed to raise a fish and a smile, nestled in amidst the hills, a little haven of tranquil beauty and fabulous fish stocks.

As vehicular access to the Kjarra is so difficult, it really is a wilderness – in three days fishing I did not see a sign of humanity, not another car, person, or plane. Futhermore, if you enjoy a hike and some really wild fishing, but with no floatplanes, and no helicopters, then this is just the place for you. A couple of unusual pieces of tackle are required – a saddle and stirrups. Not that you actually fish from horseback, but to reach the top pools and arctic char lakes requires a fifty minute drive, (if that is the word, more of an extended, excruciating lurch from pot hole to pot hole) by four-wheel vehicle. Even then you still have in store a good hour's walk and finally a three-hour ride on horseback. Now that is what I call remote! Just remember that you have to carry the fish back, and unlike most Icelandic rivers that contain principally smallish grilse, the Kjarra/Thvera has a fair run of fish into the teens and up to twenty pounds (or more). I suppose you take an extra horse for those...

I have to admit that with such fine pools on the doorstep, and a bad back as an excuse, I declined the intrepid trek to the top river. But even just below the lodge, the only way to get to the Mirror Pool was by scrambling down a small stream which cascaded over neatly placed stepping stone rocks, all bright orange in colour. At the bottom some natural hydrocarbons could be seen leeching out of the soil (as one involved in the oil industry I looked with mixed feelings at the prospect of drilling rigs in such a fair wilderness!). The river burst through a series of mini falls, carving out wide, deep pools and then sliding into the next run. The lodge sits high up above the river. Looking upriver you can see the huge dome of the glacier, whilst downstream lie the crenellated ridges of the fjord. Steep rock cliffs tumble down to the cascading turquoise waters, the banks a mat of tough couch grass, lichen, moss and flowers. Just a few feet away, a pair of gyr falcons nest on a narrow ledge, three fluffy chicks waddling along precariously to watch the casting efforts below.

It really is an ultimate wilderness, unspoiled, wild and savage. Snow still forms strange roof-like structures in the clefts, all be it July, like icy tents strung between the rocks. The only noise is the drumming of snipe, that odd treble squeal of the merlin, and the rushing of water over falls and rocks. You add the rhythmic swishing of the rod back and forth, a metronomic line in relaxed expectation, curling across the limpid waters and landing with a gentle splash, to swing and flutter across the stream in probing, searching hope. It is my idea of perfect fly water, not the vast open expanse of daunting big rivers, involving a routine of step, cast, step, cast for miles on end, but a litany of lovely pools, riffles, runs and pots, amidst scenery of rare natural beauty.

What surprised me most was the size of fly used. Icelandic flies are different – being largely prawn imitations (Francis, Krafla, Raeken), with carrot shaped bodies, clipped palmer hackles and thick feelers sticking out behind the hook bend. They look, frankly, ugly and unreal, but work a treat, and make a welcome change from that latest overhyped prawn fly, the seemingly ubiquitous Ally's Shrimp. But the size used was twelve or fourteen, a ten only for the headstreams – and this in cool clear water that in Scotland would be of spring, April-May, temperature. All I would say is that it is advisable to stock up on flies before arriving – it is too easy to be tempted by the weird and wonderful local creations, but like everything in Iceland, flies are very expensive. Books are even more so, (odd in such a literate country), and the price of booze is a horror! If I were to be brutally honest, I have to admit that a Blue Charm, Stoats Tail and Black Sheep did just as well as the traditional Francis and Krafla, but it's so much more exciting to fish a local fly with an exotic name – a pattern as outerworldly and unusual as the steam spewing volcanic landscape around you.

There are times when I think that some people treat fishing as a quasi-religious experience, or as a hedonistic pleasure that should only be enjoyed with severe restraint, and never on the Sabbath! I am not sure how much I would enjoy fishing in Alaska or the Kola Peninsular in Russia, (apart from the wilderness and scenery which I would love to see), as the fishing challenge seems about the same as catching mackerel, and I graduated from that twenty years ago. A dozen salmon every day (note the every, now just once in a while would be fine!) would surely undermine the thrill? When one becomes blasé, knowing that if a fish is lost another will come along any minute, doesn't that rather defeat the purpose of salmon fishing? I don't know – maybe this is just envy, or a defence mechanism to inure me to the one fish a week syndrome we so often have to put up with in the UK. Anyway, Iceland seems to fall happily in between the two extremes. You have to work hard for your catch, physically and mentally. Fishing is regulated by the state to two six-hour sessions a day, from seven in the morning to one, and from four to ten in the evening. It is exhausting, but who needs to sleep anyway, especially with Icelandic nights of midnight sun! Still, with a modicum of skill and effort, action is assured everyday – not a basket load of salmon, but a solid take or three. If you are looking for a balance between the stalking excitement of the hunt and the slightly surprised, thrilled gratification of the take, this is about perfect – for me at least. Fishing such small flies on floating lines is very visual, the salmon slashing and head and tailing at them like huge trout, even more so if you fish a riffled hitch. It is not recommended for those who suffer from high blood pressure!

So has Mephistopheles come to haunt me, and demand his pound of flesh for this corporate sell out? No, not yet. Alas, last year, I hooked one of those real Thvera fish, and after a truly epic struggle and half an hour later, whilst rolling, almost finished, on the surface just by my feet, the great beast made one last plunge, and despite lowering the drag on the reel, the line parted. I would have jumped in after it, but the pool shelved straight down, and the fish just sank slowly out of sight. Faust's lament? Well, now there's an excuse to return again next year. If I am invited, of course!

CHAPTER 9

Bermuda Shorts

'His sword was as long as a baseball bat and tapered like a rapier and he rose full length from the water and then re-entered it, smoothly, like a diver and the old man saw the great scythe-like blade of his tail go under and the line commenced to race out'
Ernest Hemmingway 'The Old Man & the Sea' 1952

Business travel, perceived as so glamorous, but often just a series of jet lagged sleepless nights in routine, faceless hotel rooms, does, occasionally, whisk you off to exotic and useful places. If you are clever, or just plain lucky, this means escaping the damp, grey chill of a north European winter and winding up in a place where the colour of the water is an almost unreal, fluorescent turquoise and darkest sun glasses are a must.

The first time I landed in Bermuda, I gazed at the brilliant blue ocean and was soon transported to another world. The arrivals hall was arched over by a stuffed marlin the size of a small rowing boat. On finding a taxi, my driver and erstwhile guide was a reverend priest, taxi driver and member of the Senate all in one. I confessed that I had no dollars with which to pay the taxi, (naively thinking that an 'international' airport would have cash facilities), which worried him not a jot. He must have then spotted my bemused expression as I wondered if he was either on drugs, or had only passed his driver's test that day. After the get ahead at all costs, be as aggressive and rude as possible attitude of French drivers (especially of taxis), this was quite a pleasant shock – we were crawling around at the speed of an indolent moped. He then informed me that the speed limit was just forty, and as a man of the cloth and government he had to be law abiding! I settled back, relaxed, and began to enjoy the curious mixture of incredibly lush tropical vegetation, flowering hibiscus and oleander hedgerows in vivid primary colours. It was all in odd contrast with the English road signs, quaint village names and driving on the left.

The next day, whilst watching the elegant longtails, (the national bird), over breakfast, I was to go deep-sea game fishing. Now this was new to me. I had visions of Hemmingwayesque epic struggles, and vast fish with amazing spiked beaks tailwalking across the oceans. Reality was rather more mundane. We soon left the sheltered, shallow seas and headed for what was, after all, mid Atlantic. Following the underwater shelf contours to find the fish where they hunt along the drop off to the oceanic depths meant that we were often broadside on to the waves. This made for a bumpy ride – I clung onto the railing for dear life as we lurched up and down, and I am not a natural sailor. As for the fishing, the skipper baited up the rods, swung out the outriggers, set the echo sounder and navigation, and off we went, trailing an array of hardware behind us. I had done nothing but stagger up the ladder to my vantage point, well out of the way. Hour after hour passed by, and still the engines roared, the fumes made me even more sick, and the boat bounced up and down. The scenery was of an endless dark blue ocean, with a few flying fish from time to time to reduce the tedium. It was pretty grim!

Suddenly there was a whizzing noise to shake my rattled bones out of their torpor. The skipper grabbed a rod and heaved upwards in an extravagant strike, yelling at me to descend. I staggered down the ladder as the boat bucked and dipped, strapped myself into the fighting chair, and was handed the rod. So far my contribution to this great fishing event consisted of sitting down. There then ensued a tug of war, much pumping and hauling, and eventually a small wahoo (barracuda cousin) of about thirty pounds broke surface. The poor beast was grabbed and clubbed to death with a baseball bat, and I ascended back up to my post to contemplate my success. It was the largest fish I had ever caught, though truth be told all I had done was reel it in – with the rod, line and hook size employed there was not much the poor beast was going to do to escape unless I cut the line.

This was my sole experience, no pun intended – and the next time I was in Bermuda I declined the offer of a repeat performance. At about six hundred dollars a day to hire the boat, I felt shareholder's money could be better invested. I would rather read a book, or write this, (indeed, as I do, Hamilton Sound stretches in front of me across the oleanders). Funnily enough, friends of mine, non fishers, recently went to some exotic island and decided to try this big game fishing lark for a day, having doubtless watched the Bogart movie, and promptly took a three hundred pound marlin, making my wahoo look truly miniscule! The marlin was supposed to be returned alive, but after a long fight became wrapped in the line and drowned, causing a lot of backache to drag the immense corpse to the boat. No, this is not for me. It is too brutal, and, unless you skipper the boat, completely dependent on the skill of the crew, not you.

Venezuela on the other hand, has lots to offer. Some of the most strikingly attractive women on the continent, the world's tallest vertical falls (Angel), plus the Orinoco rainforest and jungle, where the rivers look like liquid iron, ferrous red, and the peacock bass are huge. But, best of all, is Los Roques, a Caribbean archipelago just forty minutes flight from the Venezuelan capital. Hundreds of islands, white sand beaches, mangroves, lagoons, and...fish. You name it, bonefish, tarpon, snook – take your pick, and all in a protected nature reserve. Now I had heard much about the legendary, reel destroying runs of the grey torpedo. Confirmed Scottish salmon men went weak at the knees at the thought of a hundred yards of backing disappearing into the dazzling horizon. I was warned to keep my fingers well away from the reel, for safety. I have to admit that I had an unhealthy dose of scepticism, no doubt born of an Old World ethnocentric belief that other, 'foreign', fish could not be better, faster, and more exciting than ours. Just as the Atlantic salmon was, of course, infinitely superior to its Pacific cousin...

Still, bonefish were the quarry and I was about to find out the truth myself. The little plane, a flying cigar tube, touched down at Gran Roque 'airport', used in the loosest sense of the word. It was straight out of a B movie. Once customs formalities were completed, we strolled over the endless white sand beach to the boat – which was playing host to a bunch of raucous pelicans, ugly, prehistoric looking beasts. Up above, flocks of what looked like gannet wheeled, banked and dive-bombed in unison. It was an amazing sight, and I wasted a lot of film trying to catch the dive on camera – mass synchronised swimming in the air. Looking at my feet I could see why – the water was positively alive, teeming with tiny little iridescent green pinfry. No wonder those pelicans looked content, scooping up huge beakfulls.

Unfortunately my friend and host William had only one proper set of tackle, so I made do with a six weight rod and a trout reel with a very light drag. After all, I was convinced that these bonefish couldn't be quite as spectacular as the surely exaggerated reports stated. But in Los Roques the wind is mean, and hurling out a beady eyed, heavy bonefish fly on such tackle is a bit circumspect, and I was glad to finish the weekend without an earring. Our local guide was enthusiastic and charming, and spoke precisely two word of English 'casst, cassst' and 'strripp, strrrippp!!' in varying forms of excited crescendo depending on where and how big the fish was that he had spotted. My Spanish ran about as far as gracias and cerveza, so we made a fine pair, (eventually we settled on Italian of which we both had mastery of at least a couple of dozen words, a multiple increase in combined fluency!). Still, language was not the problem. It was eyesight.

I remember those early days on the Teign, as a boy, being taken out with my great uncle, who would spot a sea trout and ask me if I could see it. He would give the exact position, but I just could not force my vision below the surface. Eventually I mastered the knack, and now a shadow on the river bed, a gentle wave of a tail, a glimpse of white mouth, a silver roll of a flank give them away, and I think I can spot fish relatively well. But bonefish were another sharp blip on the learning curve. They are like grey shadows that move at speed, erratically. This, I think was the problem. A cruising trout in a lake, or river, has a preset, predictable path. A bonefish moves at three times the speed and seemingly at random. Spotting them is an art, casting to where they will be in ten seconds time, even more so. At first, Carlos would crouch low, swing out his arm, mutter directions sotto voce and then gradually get more excited as I peered into the crystal waters and saw just sand, wave and mottled seaweed. Eventually, too late, I would see the shadow, manipulate a panicky, over hasty cast and line the fish. The water would erupt into an angry fountain as the fish bolted, throwing alarmed spray up in disgust. It was awful!

Still, Carlos kindly plonked me on a white sand beach – where the bones are far easier to spot than over the mottled weed, and slowly I began to see and cast at ease and in time. When my fly finally landed in front of the target, – 'strrrripppp!!!' – I hauled in for all I was worth, saw the shadow stop, turn and rush forward, and then there was a huge thump on the line. My first bonefish, and yes, all be it a light rod and reel, this fish, all of three pounds, took more backing than any salmonid I have ever hooked. It was awesome. In fact, to be honest, after a while it became a little tedious as the fish would just run off in a straight line and leave me to winch back in for ages, before he would head off again. But it was good fun. In the afternoon as the tide went out, we waded the flats, calf deep, past bright orange starfish and huge pink-pearl conch shells, and the occasional gliding stingray (you need to wear good boots, to keep out the sand and in case you step on a ray or spiny urchin). Here we found tailing fish, like grayling or trout, tipped right up, their sharply forked tails waving like flags out of the water. Suddenly fish spotting became a whole lot easier! Stalking, on one's knees, and correctly delivering the fly so as not to line, or splash and spook the fish was not.

It has a remarkable similarity to dry fly fishing in a way. You spot, hunt and target a specific fish, and the cast had better be good. Admittedly, a Gotcha, or Mating Crab fly is a little less delicate, in name and appearance, than a size eighteen Pale Watery, and I suspect that the pattern may not be too critical, but the presentation is very similar, as is the excitement when (if) the beast is hooked. On a return visit we faced a really vicious wind, which made fish spotting even worse as we had scudding waves to obscure further the subaqueous view. However, this time I was better prepared, with a proper eight weight rod and highly set reel drag, and the backing was kept mainly on the reel, but the straight line speed of a bonefish is still much faster, I believe, than any salmonid, even if the acrobatics and excitement are maybe less and more predictable. William took an eight pounder that put up an epic fight, and we even managed a double hook up, two express trains on at once. Having just spent a couple of days at Easter deep sunk fly fishing the Tay for the almost extinct 'spring' salmon in a snow blizzard, strolling calf deep in Caribbean warm waters under a hot sun for abundant, if ultra spooky, bonefish does have its attraction! Next year I must get a new set of prescription Polaroids...

Icelandic wildnerness – looking down the Kjarra to the volcano.

Heaven – a good salmon off Eyjolfsfludir on the Kjarra.

Express train – a first bonefish, Los Roques.

Pelican brief: Los Roques, Venezuela.

CHAPTER 10

Rebirth of Iceland's Top Salmon River

'When I first visited Iceland as a tourist the starkly beautiful landscape and the evident hospitality of the people drew me like a magnet'
Terry G. Lacy 'Ring of Seasons' 1998

This story has already been partly told in magazine articles, but I make no apology for repeating it. It is a rare tale of hope and success, of massively increased salmon runs and catches, an almost unique glint of light in an otherwise sadly dark age of ever declining stocks. There has been much argument over smolt rearing, and I am no scientific expert. I know that the Delphi system in Ireland also runs a hatchery, though there the reared hatchery stock are separated and removed when they have returned upriver to avoid any risk of interbreeding with wild stocks. On the Ranga, in 1988 the total salmon catch was all of fifty-three, by 1990 the smolt rearing scheme had started and the river topped the whole of Iceland with one thousand six hundred plus. Last year (1998) it was highest score again, but this time with well over three thousand fish – and up to twenty-seven pounds too.

So how do you achieve a sixty-fold increase in returning salmon stocks in a decade? When you catch a bigger fish on the Ranga, a salmon rather than a grilse, there are special lidded boxes already in place along the river on certain pools, semi-submerged in the flow so that with the minimum of handling and moving the fish can be placed inside. The man who masterminded this whole scheme, Throstur Ellidason, will then transfer the fish to the hatchery for brood stock, rewarding the lucky rod with an equivalent weight of smoked salmon or graflax, a rare delicacy. After all that fat, overfed farmed Norwegian gravad lax, with its layers of fat, like white ribbing, clearly visible, Icelandic graflax from wild, lean grilse is soft, tender bliss. In other rivers, ranching has a bad name. Throstur thinks this is because the smolts are just dumped into the main river and let loose. On the Ranga they are held, maybe for weeks, in smolt holding ponds, netted over and grilled off, built just off the main river, with natural river water flowing through. This seems to guarantee a much better return rate, maybe one, or even up to three, percent of smolts actually being caught by rods. If you work out the statistics, say a thousand extra rod caught fish for one hundred thousand smolts, well at ten thousand eggs per salmon...

However, one must be careful. The Ranga's problem is that it is located right next to Hekla, Europe's most active volcano, and Jules Verne's entry to the centre of the earth. All that black volcanic sand stifles the redds, so the natural spawning is very poor – though the river itself, in water purity, stability of temperature and height, and abundance of parr food, is very healthy. All it needed was a little help. Throstur is now moving onto a new venture, the Breiddalsa, and you can bet that returning runs there will soon be multiplying too. Besides, what better feeling is there when you have caught a good fish, than to put it in the fish box and think of all those future smolts, from 'your' fish – and then to sate the palate and senses with some graflax in reward for such decency, (as if that were necessary).

But the real issue is one of genetic purity. As said, on the Delphi system the reared adult fish are taken out and killed after they have returned at the end of the season. On the Ranga it makes little difference as the natural spawning is so poor. The great debate is whether beleaguered salmon rivers elsewhere should adopt the same smolt ranching system to stop the decline in natural stocks. There is no doubt that economically it can, and does work, and that the quality and quantity of returning fish can fill even the greediest fisher's dreams (or nightmares...). But ironically it could actually undermine the wild stocks themselves, thus leading ultimately to the ghastly situation whereby naturally spawning fish were extinct and rivers only survived on hatchery bred salmon, all be they stripped from returning fish. There can be little doubt that even hatchery smolts that are reared only from returning wild fish will not have exactly the same natural genetic imprint as truly wild offspring. As generations of 'semi-wild' hatchery fish interbreed with nature's own stock, honed over the millennia, what long-term trouble might we be inadvertently cooking up?

It is an emotive subject upon which fishery experts and scientists disagree. It is true that many famous rivers such as the Dee and Don have relied for ages on a hatchery to augment stocks. I think the key must be to retain some semblance of natural equilibrium. Smolt rearing can be used to help counter diminishing natural stocks only if it is carried out under tight scientific control and is just one part of an integrated approach that also covers the improvement of natural habitat, spawning redds, acidification, netting at sea and all the other horrors that the salmon faces. It is not, and cannot be, the universal panacea. One thing is for sure, the sands are fast running out, so the quicker we commit proper resources to this crisis the better, rather than the usual ostrich-like, head in the sand attitude that it is someone else's problem, or, worse, the short term vicissitudes of political expediency. In Scotland, fish farms thrive, but will the wild salmon survive?

But I have strayed away from the Ranga and its heartening success story, so let's head back up to Iceland, (where, by the way, there are no salmon farms, no nets and no pollution – and still lots of fish). The west river is atypical of Iceland as its volcanic springs source means it maintains a steady, clear water height and depth all season, gradually reducing year on year as Hekla heats up for the next eruption. It is a large river, but not glacial, the water being very clear and running peppermint blue over the black, shifting sands. The stream is steady and perfect for swimming a fly around, rarely too fast and never slack. The only problem is the prevailing wind, which is, to put it mildly, upriver. The scrubby little bushes outside the main lodge are a useful weather vane, when blown so horizontal that the white undersides of the leaves are showing, you are in trouble. The fish will still be seen plopping about in the Home Pool, (this one pool alone took over four hundred fish in a season), but a Red Francis tubefly blown into and hooked through some painful part of one's anatomy is not yet a definitive Icelandic fashion statement, and it is fly only for the visiting guests…

If the salmon are the main attraction, arctic char, a slash of vivid underbellied orange, are also on the menu, and up to grilse size, plus double figure sea trout, and further up the river, similar sized brownies. In fact the salmon are, in sheer weight, the least impressive, though 1997/8 did see increasing numbers of multi sea wintered fish returning. Now hooking one of those beasts would be fun! It is also a river that offers a wide range of pools. The most picturesque has to be Aerbaejarfoss, the imposing upper waterfall. It is a stunningly beautiful arena to fish in as the river cascades over a huge fall, a thundering mass of sound and spray, carving out a surprisingly intimate black cliff surrounded arena. As you wade across the little black sand beach, the only noise is the crashing water, as it surges, deep and crystal blue below you. A magnificent backdrop for a bent rod and screaming reel! If you head over to the smaller, more remote beauty of the East Ranga, billberries, (or are they blueberries?), grow wild on the rocky banks. You can munch them as you wade along, the sharp escarpment banks being softly carpeted in an almost glowing green. My favourite pools are in fact not the great Home Pool, where success is almost guaranteed, nor the grandiose waterfalls, but the small stretch between them where the river splits round a large island. The right fork is like a typical Highland spate river removed, runs, riffles and pots, to Iceland. It has a far faster current than the main river and poses some exciting wading, and rather than opening the shoulders and casting for distant Hekla, it is a matter of tailor made micro fishing, shaping each cast and each angle to the pool. It is also underfished, which is unusual on top Icelandic rivers in their short twelve-week season where the fishing goes on for twelve hours every single day.

The wildlife is ever present, great northern divers, (loons), wailing their mournful way downstream, or bobbing up, imperious and unafraid, just a cast's distance away. Tiny waders dart and scurry around the shores, their little straight beaks shifting through the mud. Up on the banks, scampering, galloping and cantering up and down, their thick manes flying in the wind, are Icelandic horses. They are, I believe, the purest strain in the world, with their curious fifth step way of trotting. Coming home from the Upper Falls one night, still twilight at eleven, we drove across the flat, black volcanic plain where NASA had practised the Apollo landing. The falls thundered behind us, and in front, the glaciers were clearly visible, white capped in the distance. Whimbrel scattered and flew in the beam from the headlights and suddenly, just coming out to start hunting, a snowy owl hovered over us. There are worse places to be!

Such as the spit below the Lower Falls. It does make a great picture, but is, (now I know why), rarely fished. Basically, the two halves of the river leave the island, regroup and to celebrate that extra rush of communal water they drop vertically over a huge waterfall. Up the right bank is a fish ladder, and as the river gouges a huge, wide, flattening bend, the run up to the ladder can be a great cast – about a rod's length from the bank. Most people wade straight through or past it, but the fish lie just a few feet out, in the bright blue, deep water. However, below the middle of the falls, which are V shaped, is a long gravel/sand spit. From here, my guide informed me, I could fish both back in towards our bank, and cover the other, never fished side - the best of both worlds. It really does make a great photo shot – with the right depth of field it looks like you are walking on water right below an enormous waterfall! The secret is how to wade through the deep bit to the shallow spit, as there is just one entrance where the water is chestwadeable. Fortunately a large rock marks it – but then there are boulders all along, and let's be honest, one looks much like another after a while. So I placed my fishing gloves on top as a marker and, very tentatively, edged out. Sure enough I was not whisked off to an untimely visit to the eternal river in the sky, but attained the spit with relative ease. Feeling very clever, I headed up to the foot of the fall and began to fish. I was a little wary of the shifting black sand beneath my feet and even more so of the very abrupt end to the spit. The sand just literally runs out and plunges almost vertically down – I tested it with my rod. Luckily the water colour changes to azure to mark the edge. As I amused myself in mid river, an astonished colleague, (unaware of the trick), rushed up to watch, thinking I had either gone totally mad or ascended to some higher ethereal plane. On explaining that I was not going to turn the water into wine or part the oceans, he grinned, waved and began to stroll off. In the distance, just before he reached the bend, he suddenly turned and yelled back at me. I had forgotten my gloves on some rock, but I needn't worry, he had picked them up for me. Thoughtful soul, little did he know!

All of this is in sharp contrast to salmon fishing back home. If I look back over my recent efforts, in past years I have fished five weeks in Scotland for salmon, (and I exclude one drought week of Mediterranean sun and low water). All were in September, a time when post equinox rain is pretty assured, and runs, especially after summer droughts, should be also. True, the fish may include a few aggressive red old stagers, but given fresh water, new fish should come up from the sea. In each of the five weeks we had suitable rain and new water. I was the lucky one, taking eleven salmon, of which nine were red and returned. Two clean fish in five weeks – and I was the favoured, fortunate rod. The assembled host of six rods averaged three quarters of a fish per rod week and only a quarter of a clean fish. The scenery, ambience, fresh air, relaxation, and companionship were all great. But was it all worth the effort (and cost)? When I mention to my American fishing friends that I spend several weeks waist deep in a river in driving rain on the off chance of a hit or two per week, (not per day), they stare at me in disbelief. My only answer is that it makes that one fish per week all the more exciting (providing you get it of course). But they are surely right – I am not a numbers man, but paying through the nose for a hard earned, much awaited and anticipated week to catch, if lucky, one or two red fish is grounds for the green couch and men in white coats to be calling...

Yes, I am very lucky; I can fish in Scotland because I love the country, the friends, the glens, rivers and lochs. It is a magical place. I cannot imagine being deprived of a glimpse of Suilven jutting its sugar loaf head above the moors, or of the Dee sparkling way down below Cairn o'Mount, all silvery in the moonlight. Or the black waters of some northern sea trout loch, mysterious and foreboding beneath the cliffs, or an Atlantic sunset glimmering across the machair sands, and Bruce at the oars whilst a large trout grabs the turning flee in a frenzy of reel ripping excitement. They are unforgettable, precious moments that form a treasure chest of happy memories. But I do not have to fish in Scotland to catch salmon. As said, I am fortunate – I can do that, and satisfy the need actually to catch fish, in Iceland. By the way the Ranga has never had a blank week; nor a blank day, nor a blank rod.

Postscript (2001)
Throstur Ellidason nurtured and created what the Ranga is now – one of the world's top salmon rivers. In 2001 the landowners decided to sell the fishing lease to a higher bidder, (hence rod prices will escalate). The greed and ingratitude shown leaves me speechless. His struggles have made them wealthy. I for one shall not fish the Ranga again, and will be sadder for that.

CHAPTER 11

Hope on Hope

'We should, of course, be hypocrites, if we pretended that scenery was the sole inducement; but I can honestly say for myself that the angler has to contend against so many adverse conditions, and must prepare himself for so many blank days, that angling would never have been my passion had there not been that other inducement, offered without money and without price, by nature, in compensation.'
William Senior 'Travel & Trout in the Antipodes' 1879

The sea trout is an enigmatic creature. Fishmongers call it salmon trout, inaccurately, but presumably so that they can charge inflated, salmon-like prices for it. Scientists say that it is really the same fish as the native brown trout and debate which one came first. Was it a greedy, half starved brownie that first figured out that estuarine salt water feeding on shrimps, sand eels and fish would be far easier and more fattening than the skimpy, meagre fare of bugs and flies in a river, and headed seawards? Or a sea fish that decided that the placid, fresh waters of a river would be a better place to rest and spawn? I like to believe the former theory, it seems more logical, and can envisage that golden brown little trout, eking out a marginal existence in some acidic, peaty stream, foraging further and further downstream in search of food. Eventually it must have entered brackish waters and then, finally adjusting to the saline osmosis, headed out to sea, feasting on what must have seemed a parr's ultimate dream of a food chain! It would have been a permanent open season for gluttony, until the spawning urge came with much fattened, and silvered maturity. By now pink fleshed, firm and athletic, the once underfed little brown trout surged back up its home river, ascending rapids, weirs, waterfalls and every obstacle in a wonderful display of natural superiority, fitness and navigation.

All that just to end up poached, skinned and filleted on a fisher's plate with home made mayonnaise, green salad and new potatoes. All because of one, nostalgic urge to chew on a flickering morsel of tinsel and feathery temptation, despite the fact that the digestive and reproductive organs had done a deal and feeding in freshwater was useless, in fact, impossible. It is a hefty price to pay for the seductive charms of a Butcher or a Peter Ross, or for one last giving in to greed! Put that way it's almost enough to make you put away your rod for good. Almost, I said.

Sadly, in much of the west coasts of Ireland and Scotland, a region of unsurpassed wildness and beauty, such poignant thoughts on the abrupt, sad end to so valiant a life are now all but irrelevant, slipping into nostalgia, as remote as the lochs, loughs and rivers that once held so many legions of silver fish. A mere decade ago, sea trout were abundant and often regarded more highly than salmon, and inexpensive fishing could be enjoyed with this most acrobatic of fish either in the lengthening shadows of a darkening, dusky pool tail or the buffeting waves of a mountain encircled lake. Now the waves still roll, chop and froth, but few flashing silver shoulders break through the crests or rise, explosively, to the dap. The streams still glide, the nights still embrace, warm and cosy, the deep black pools, the eddies, rocks and runs. But the silence and calm is no longer shattered into a surge of spray and arcing, airborne grace, the moonlight no longer illuminates the sleek, nervous shapes of silver, the rivers run empty, eviscerated, betrayed and lost. The sea trout have gone. That miracle of nature, that small parr transformed over many miles and many dangers into the most athletic and wild of creatures has been polluted, netted, sea-liced and abused to the very brink of extinction.

Meanwhile, salmon farms proliferate, sponsored by cynical, careless authorities only keen for short-term political gain, votes and cheap, easy fixes. They trumpet the creation of a few jobs in the remote, underemployed areas, whilst unwittingly destroying the livelihoods of so, so many more locals that have for generations relied upon and looked after their fish stocks. Tax payers' funds flow endlessly into foreign owned multinationals, Norwegian oil companies, just to oversupply an already glutted market. But the politicians boast of the new employment opportunities they have brought, whilst the gillies, bed and breakfast owners, hoteliers and all the local fisher tourist support dwindle and disappear. The empty boats and hotels, now quiet and deserted, stand like dinosaur skeletons in the valleys of death. Even worse are the absentee, southern landlords, the syndicates of the wealthy, or the local owners, (who should know better), selling their cheap souls to the devil for a quick fish farming subsidy and some rental income. Short-termism runs riot, this is an income for what? The cages breed over stocked, flabby apologies for a salmon, tail-less insults, not to speak of the chemical and disease horrors of invemectin and ISA. In a supremely ironic touch, the very multinational that may well have inadvertently spread the ISA disease to Scotland (by transporting infected eggs), and has benefited from so much subsidy, is now demanding further millions in help from the Government as they claim that they had to destroy all the diseased fish. I hope they did, though there are many well founded allegations stating that some ended up on the supermarket shelves. Fortunately, just like BSA, official sources stated that there was no health risk to the public...

But it is not the risk to human life that I am most concerned with here. The worst side product of salmon farming is the millions of hungry sea lice that are chemically treated sufficiently to make them drop off the salmon, but not to die. Hence they wait below the cages for the last remaining survivors of the wild sea trout stock to swim by, and then pounce in blood-sucking, life-sapping death. It is an invisible, hoovering death trap. Nor is it just the sea trout that suffers, ask any local lobster, prawn or sea fisher in the bays and sea lochs where salmon farms proliferate. The chemicals and faeces, the delightful detritus dumped and excreted daily into the sea, soon leaves an area beneath and around the cages of utter destruction, lifeless but for the caged fish and hungry lice.

But enough of such depressing diatribes. There are still rivers in Scotland, (especially on the east coast), south-west England, and, especially, Wales, where sea trout still run, perhaps not in the same numbers and sizes as before, but still enough at least to support a spawning stock. Coincidentally these regions have no fish farms. What finer fish is there to seek and deceive? There is much debate as to the relative merits of the salmon and sea trout. I have not caught enough large versions of the latter to comment, but the few grilse sized fish I have taken have been magnificent sport on a single handed rod. What would I give to fish the Falklands, Sweden's River Morrum or Argentine Tierra del Fuego – where the sea trout are all salmon sized? A lot of money for starters, but what sport it must be! What a sea trout may lack in a salmon's stamina it makes up for in gymnastic acrobatics. A sea trout is fast and furious. A salmon will often take and rest still, or hug the bottom – not so a sea trout, which in my experience is all a-run, on the top and in the air. It is a short burst of frenetic, adrenaline pumping excitement. Anyway, why make meaningless comparisons; both fish are unique and magnificent adversaries in their own right.

Of the much beleaguered north west Highland lochs, (one can only stare in mournful disbelief at Maree, once the jewel in the crown, now hardly worth fishing), one still produces fish, perhaps because of its apt name – Loch Hope. Drifting beneath Scotland's most northerly munro, you simply have to take in the scenery, fish or no fish. It is a fickle loch, the weather along its long, narrow, northerly course being the main problem. The first time I fished there was as a guest host to some French journalists, and finer fly casters I have not seen. The French often take a sadly pragmatic attitude to fish, seeing them purely through a court bouillon or au bleu – dinner to be caught, regardless of method or size. Opening day on many a French stream is like wall to wall hardware, spinners, worms, floats and all, even the smallest catch being killed for breakfast. Many perfect rivers are fished out, or almost, but when they do turn out true fly fishers, they are real masters of the art. Anyway, we drifted out onto Hope, in late September, the moors looking like a golden carpet in their autumnal hue, the deer munching unconcernedly by the roadside. The loch was wreathed in an ethereal mist, straight out of one of those over romanticised Victorian oil paintings, soft, swirling and mysterious, Ben Hope towering threateningly above. Alas it was a short day; a drift by the shore of the middle bay produced increasingly choppy waves, the boat becoming uncontrollable at the oars and dangerous. Reluctantly we retreated, the gillies celebrating their early relaxation and a birthday with a phenomenal display of whisky drinking, their noses fluourescing from red to purple, the French staring, amused and shocked, cameras clicking.

The second visit was in August, a rushed affair after christenings in Edinburgh and Inverness, ironically adrift peacefully on a day that an oil rig I had just signed the sale contract for, forty-eight hours before, sank, in flat calm, in ten thousand feet of water. Blissfully ignorant of the event, we again set out, on a drought stricken water that had not produced a fish in a fortnight. I had borrowed light line trout gear, and we fished somewhat aimlessly until a salmon, or, I suspect by its sheer speed a large sea trout, grabbed the turning flee, a Blue Zulu, (a wonderful bob fly by the way). It headed for the horizon, weed bed and freedom, leaving me with a wry smile and broken leader. Bruce then raised, and missed, (not through fault of course), I don't know how many fish – as did I, until the wind whipped up and before lunch we had to hurry for the shore and safety. We sat there for two hours, vainly hoping for a gentler afternoon before accepting the harsh reality and abandoning. If that was not frustration enough, the next visit was pure vinegar in the wound – a flat calm, the boat stranded in a sea of glass, each movement sending out a semaphore of ripples to the wary prey. As we headed back, stretching out the last minutes of the fading day, a laughing, sarcastic zephyr rose up and blew us gently home. For once though, we got the last laugh as a nascent ripple appeared, and there is a burn that flows into the loch just by the boat moorings. Burn mouths are always worthy lies, especially later in the season (as fish run them to spawn). In a fit of hurried excitement as the sun sank on our last day of the season, we managed a couple of leaping fish, both set free in hope that Hope would, next time, be kinder with the elements. I am still waiting...

Loch Dionard, just up and round the coast, gave fishing of similar texture, heavy, tough days of one extreme or the other, of numbing rain and cold, or becalming indolence. My birthday produced, I think, near hypothermia, bare hands having to be warmed over an open gas flame and a bone chill that took literally hours of hot bath and fire hearth to dissipate, (and a medicinal dram or two). All for one fish taken at the very end of an icy day. A year later it was the exact opposite and we were greeted with dazzling weather. It was ideal for photography, and for watching the pair of eagles or the black throated divers. A day made for idling, for tanning in a boat on the pitch-black waters beneath the vertical cliff face of Foinaven. But it was hell for fishing. Once again, we fell into a trap, fishing assiduously the very margins, contouring the drifts around the shoreline, searching the shallows. Any textbook will tell you that these sheer, deep northern lochs drop off very quickly, and that sea trout hold in only eight feet of water or less, so it is pointless fishing across the middle of the loch. On the last drift of the day, in desperation, we floated over the middle, over the deeps. Of course it produced the only take of the day, a wild, leaping fish of good size that finally threw the hook, showing us where we should have been fishing, just as the argocat rattled up the track to transport us home. I have to confess that whilst Bruce (and I) insisted on fishing the shallows, his wife Ann had seen fish move further out and suggested we move further offshore. Not for the first time, male chauvinism and know it all fishing arrogance won the day but not the fish! It was a silent, rough, bumpy, lurching drive back, over the limestone and peat tracks of the nature reserve, past the breeding greenshank – all sullenly unnoticed in the bitterness of abject failure and frustrated hope.

But to my taste, though you have to trade the wonderful scenery, the best sea trout fishing is a personal affair, an internal struggle with the horror movie fears, sightlessness and blackness of a night spent by a river. The water curls, oily and pitch dark between the waders, a distant owl hoots up in the trees and bats flit noiselessly across the river, darting here and there, feeding on the wing. All of a sudden, a duck crash-lands in front of you, magnified in the dark, startling you with momentary fear. The heart beats fast as a sea trout explodes, fins whirring, vertically into the air. The rod top disappears into the inky monochrome, the silence is thick, almost touchable, the rhythmic swish of rod and line being the only indicator of direction or distance. The line swings, invisibly, somewhere out across the stream, the mind trying to imagine the drift, the waiting fish on their lies, the flash of tinsel, the alluring flutter of squirrel tail. Each cast is a probe into the darkness, an antenna groping, feeling for the faintest twitch, or the heaving pull of a reel-strumming take and run. If nothing else, it is exciting stuff!

As often or not, the tug, vicious and mouthed in the dark, somehow, inexplicably, comes to nothing. Time and time again the fly is savagely wrenched and yet fails to get a firm hold. Even when hooked, a quick cartwheel beneath the stars and it all goes slack, the ripples just visible in the dark, ringing outwards in the moonlight. If lucky, you are left peering into the darkness, the line lost, wondering exactly where the fish is, reacting only to the pull of the rod, the changing pressure and angle, a distant leap, a bottom boring run, a hurdling, scattering slash across the surface. You swing round as the fish heads upstream, canting the rod over to sidestrain it away from the tree roots. Finally there is a glimpse of silver, the momentary roll of a white belly, signal to unship the net, fumbling in the dark, and reach out into the water for the fish. Then, triumphant, heart thumping, the lift and first feel of weight, guessing the size as the net is raised, a wriggling, writhing, capture of purest wildness.

I have had a sea trout, of only a pound or so, hooked in my favourite little run into a Teign pool, (scene of that first grilse), head upstream, leap and leave me solidly hooked to a tree. It took me a while to realise what had happened in the dark, as the spring of a branch 'pulls back' when you tug, so it seems as if there is life, all be it rather dull and reactive. To lose both fish and fly to a tree is galling! Another fish in the same pool, bigger but nothing special, ran downstream, leaping, as expected. It then stopped, slowly giving ground upstream as I reeled in, so far all going to plan. As the line tightened, the precursor to another running burst of energy, I was mindful of the tree and deep hole below, and kept a mental eye open for any tricks. The fish promptly turned and headed straight across the river, diagonally at me, throwing the line into a slack loop whilst I frantically handlined in, and then the fish gave one majestic leap. The line went heavy, unusually dull, jerking, and I heard a strange rustling commotion in the bankside grass. The fish had jumped onto my own bank, maybe ten yards below me. Sure enough, as I wondered how to play a sea trout on land, the hook fell away and there was a quick splash as fish and natural element were reunited!

There is nothing quite like night fly fishing for the wild, unpredictable sea trout. I hear optimistic rumours that some stocks are finally recovering, all be it slowly and right from the brink of extinction. I fervently pray that this is true. Hope, both the loch, mountain and sentiment, must spring eternal.

CHAPTER 12

Snake Rolls in the Snow

'It was one of those times that come to all fishers, when we win back something of the vision of boyhood and yet experience it with the deeper gratitude of grown men'
Laurence Catlow (Trout & Salmon 1999)

Spring – time for an April Easter treat. In San Francisco it was hailing, in New York eighty degrees, in Paris hot and sultry, in Scotland, well... Blame all the climatic oddities on El Niño, but some things are predictable. I stepped onto the flight at Heathrow in shirtsleeves, and off it in Edinburgh in horizontal rain and chilling cold. I had been warned that the hotel was basic. That is another thing one can rely upon, the English penchant for understatement. In fact it was friendly, remarkably cheap, and the food plentiful, if not exactly haute cuisine. All in all it was generally fine, except for one minor detail – the heating. Or the lack of it, to be precise. The room, in an extension building that resembled an overgrown Portakabin, had very thin walls. Outside, at night, it was five degrees (centigrade) below zero. Inside, it was not a whole lot better. The bedroom luxuriated in the extravagance of one small, overworked heater. The bathroom was not so lucky. With only four days there, I wondered if I could get by without washing...

It reminded me of chilly mornings at boarding school, years ago, waking up to dress hurriedly in bed, pulling on as many thermals and woollies as was possible without having to get out and actually brave the icy cold. Now I had extra delights – such as thawing out the shaving foam under the hot tap so that it would actually squeeze out of the tube! In fact, school it was – for rather more mature students, and a syllabus that they certainly didn't teach in my day, (more's the pity!) – the Spey cast, single or double, and the intriguingly named snake roll.

It is odd that people will spend vast amounts of money on fishing, buy every latest, overpriced technical gismo on the market, but never pay to go to fishing casting tuition. Never is money better spent – a few days will cost less than a new rod, bring much more fun and undoubtedly increase catches far more than the latest carbon blank. Is it the fear of looking stupid, the arrogance that one knows it all, or just an unwillingness to mix what seems like serious work (or learning) with pleasure? I suspect it is a mixture of the lot, and, in my case, an inability to be by a river without actually going fishing. The idea of standing by a salmon pool, not actually casting in anger, but merely practising, well what a frustrating 'waste' of valuable fishing time. Could I really give up precious fishing days booked, planned and desired for so long in advance, merely to go to school?

I well remember my introduction to the Spey cast. It was on Tweed, at Boleside, in May, a decade earlier. We were two inexperienced youngsters, having just bought new, cheap, bottom of the range double handed fifteen footer rods with no clue how to use them. Avidly I had read every book on the subject, rehearsed the moves in my head, but couldn't bring myself to the embarrassment of standing on the banks of the Thames waving around a salmon rod. These days there are, once again, a few salmon that run through London and up the Thames, for the first time in over a century. It is odd to think that in Elizabethan times the workers went on strike to complain about the endless diet of fresh, wild Thames salmon, and that pike was more prized and expensive! So when we arrived at one of Scotland's better beats on that most historic and famed of mighty rivers the Tweed, we were mightily unprepared. Compared to the small spate streams I had previously fished, it looked huge. I felt very self-conscious unpacking the gleaming new rod and squeaky-clean chestwaders. Apprehension rose further when the gillie, a wizened, sour looking man, appeared clad in full tweeds from head to toe. He asked to see my fly box, full of home tied efforts, and disparagingly scoffed 'ach, they're no Twid flees' and almost threw them away. A more discouraging, unpleasant individual one could hardly meet, and he ruined what could have been a fantastic learning experience for two mustard keen tyros.

As it was, we were frog marched to the Upper Garden Beck pool. He inquired, well, barked, who wished to fish first. My friend had suddenly lagged behind, so I received the honour. I waded out to make my first cast on a major salmon river with a big rod. My helpful gillie suggested that I just roll it half way across Scotland and land it under an overhanging tree.

Oh yes, and I forgot to mention, in a stiff upstream wind. I quaked, lifted, waited and threw – straight into the tree. Once I had repeated this, the gillie grabbed the rod and asked if I didn't know how to Spey cast. On my half ashamed, muttered negative, he made two perfect Speys right under the tree, handed me back the rod, and stomped off. That was his idea of help for the week. What was worse was that the beat was full of beautiful silver flanked, white bellied, firm deep springers. I hooked one and lost it – a regret to this very day. Just to pour salt in, there was a ghastly middle aged woman who had never fished. She was one of those thoroughly unattractive, mono brain celled creatures that demand, and expect full, unlimited attention. She dragged the gillie off, monopolised and muttering, (though he was obviously in awe of the lady, and as meek as a lamb), and planted herself on the boat pool. She then flung a metal devon spinner out and handed him the rod when a bird's nest overrun appeared. In between unravelling her miscasts, a run of fresh fish came in and stopped, parked, right in front of her, (we were in the pool above). She hooked five, landed four and announced that this salmon fishing lark was dead easy and very dull...Not normally a homicidal type, I was sorely tempted!

Thus, a decade later, I was on the banks of the Tay in 'spring'. We were to fish for half the day, and learn the Spey cast the other half. Michael Evans, our tutor and mentor, was a fine teacher and quite remarkable caster. Let's be honest, it was quite sickening, regardless of wind direction or speed, the line just sailed out, effortlessly. Every damned time! Meanwhile, I managed to make every unknown muscle in back, shoulders and arms ache. Still, the Tay was beautifully clear, though running a couple of feet over the banks. As almost always now though, the spring season was a disaster – the worst in living memory. After fourteen weeks of the 1998 season, one of the two alternate gillies was still fishless, and ready to throw a stick of dynamite off the boat, or at least drag a net behind. However, it was exciting stuff, wading out into the Glendelvine Boat Pool, home to the most famous fish of all, caught seventy six years before. Parking the car by Miss Ballantine's cottage was to glimpse a piece of fishing history, to dream in nostalgia of those vast autumn fish of long, long ago, and to relive in the mind that epic struggle. My efforts to emulate her record catch were sadly unproductive, though I did not come away without a fish. Swinging round my large, deeply sunk prawn fly on a heavy rod, it was taken with a savage tug – by a six ounce brown trout. Sixty three and a half pounds too small…

It was a curious feeling, to be looking at the brilliant citrus green of freshly budding spring, the daffodils bright and yellow, waving in the breeze, the cock pheasants strutting around, chests all puffed out. On the river, March Browns were hatching in abundance and floating down in flotillas to the eager rises of hungry trout, (alas there was no break for a few trout casts). Meanwhile there I was practising a double Spey in a snow blizzard. The Highlands in spring, and what a beautiful picture. I finally realised that I had attained a new level of eccentricity, (a polite euphemism), when wading waist-deep in the cold waters of the Tay and trying to propel a fast sink line and heavy tube across an almost certainly empty pool in a driving snow storm – and thoroughly enjoying it! It was lovely to watch the line shoot out and uncurl across the limpid waters, (sometimes), and then cut down and into the river as it sank slowly round. I could imagine the mobile fibres of the long, trailing wing flickering, beguiling, in the current, hopefully just past a springer's nose. As for the snake roll, it is a wonderful cast, a sort of exhibitionist lasso, pause and tap – and due to the high line speed it positively leaps across the waters, (well, in theory at least). It is the sort of cast that I will sneak off and practice in private, well hidden from prying eyes. Once mastered, and with the wind downstream over my left shoulder, (I need all the help I can get), I will nonchalantly saunter in front of the lodge and whirl the line, dervish like, above my head and then flick it prodigious lengths across the river. Or something like that.

Anyway, forget the dreams, we need to get back to the dull, frigid reality, that dark green line probing around the dips, runs and hollows of the Tay; deep, slow and enticing. Once again, many years on from that first, long lost salmon on the Eachaig, I hooked the bottom. Yes, with the river flowing feet up and fast, I had hooked the riverbed. Eventually the truth dawned with a thump - that fly simply could not get anywhere near the bottom out there in this depth and push of current. I was fishing below where a burn flowed in, over the ledge into the deeps, in fact just where I had been told the fish, if fish there were, would lie. Tentatively, enquiringly, stupidly, I lifted the rod, half fearing, half hoping, and yes, the bottom moved. The first springer for Donald, the gillie, after all those fishless weeks? Well, I leave that one to your imagination and my dreams…

CHAPTER 13

Salmon Therapy

'Thus have I proved that the sport and game of angling is the best means and cause that brings a man into a merry spirit, which according to the said proverb of Solomon and the said teaching of medecine makes a flowering age and a long one.'
Dame Juliana Berners 'The Treatyse on Fysshynge with an Angle' circa 1496

I was never a great sportsman at school. Keen and determined, yes, but always the best of the second team rather than the first. I guess my fishing is largely similar. But the one sport that I did take to, at university, was rowing. I can well remember my first regatta, at Reading, my mother excitedly yelling encouragement from the towpath, but at the wrong boat, and when we did actually race by, the bow side crabbed and my seat jammed, leaving us way adrift and disconsolate. It was hardly an auspicious start to a short 'career' that ended in a, (for us), glorious qualification at Henley, (to lose in the first round), and then for me a rapid descent into the abyss when my back was injured. At first it was diagnosed as not a big problem - I would be back for the races in a few weeks. Then it was delayed to the next term, until as hope dimmed and the painful reality crept in like a reluctant, grey winter's dawn, I finally accepted that my days in a boat were over, and switched to coaching, screaming up and down on a bike yelling encouragement and advice. It was 1982, year of rampant British xenophobia over the Falklands war. It might have been the greatest year since 1961 (my birth) for Bordeaux, but it was the worst for me.

But I fished on, here and there, without great problem, until 1990, when I decided for the first time to go down to Devon in May. Traditionally, sea trout are thought to be summer prey for fly-fishing at night, and if large quantities of increasingly small, school fish are what you want, this makes every sense. But I hankered after something bigger than the two-pound mark, which seemed to be a sort of natural size barrier on the Teign in July, dropping even further in August with the 'harvest peal' runs. So I thought I'd go earlier, and try for the big fish of spring. It was a revelation, the wooded banks tumbling down to the river in a riot of bluebells, a purple carpet of delicate beauty. The grassy banks were covered in little wild flowers, all shades of pink, orange and blue. The river had a little more water in than the habitual, over extracted summer low and, for once, looked pristine, almost lively. Birds nested, new life sprang up and somehow the chance of a bigger fish seemed very viable.

I have already regaled the sad tale of the lost salmon, my line breaking and my treasured first spinner and springer being lost. I, of course, rushed to the shops, cursing my own stupid laziness in not changing the old line, but it was too late, and the poor fish, mouth festooned with hook, would not come again. In fact a similar sized fish was caught a week later in exactly the same lie. There was no trace of my spinner, but as there had not been a drop of rain in between times, and no fresh fish had run, I strongly suspect it was 'my fish'. That night I went down to the river with a grudge, unfairly transferring my own shame and anger to the liquid stream in front of me. I sat on the bank, on a convenient grass verge, and watched and waited, as I had a hundred times. Slowly the shadows darkened into a universal grey, the leaves on the far bank blurring into oblivion, the first bat flapping across the sky and a mighty splosh announcing that one of the treasured spring fish was indeed in residence. It was my last night, and the previous three had only produced one fish, just under the two-pound mark, a small fish for spring and a disappointment to my greedy hopes.

I took a last gulp from the hip flask, squinted at the river, and went through the usual routine – net unleashed and extended in readiness for the big event, fly wetted and checked. It was a fine, cloudy night, retaining some heat from the day and avoiding those depressing billowing clouds of breath, harbingers of difficult sport. Almost hesitantly I waded in, somehow it seems rather brutal to shatter the calm of dusk turning to night by wading, the deepening night seeming to amplify every move and the ripples caused. I tiptoed across the pebbly shallows, the water lapping at my ankles, and stopped opposite the last tree and above the still visible white stone behind me. In position, I measured and pulled off eight arms length of line and flicked it out. I aimed diagonally across into the shadows, still just able to see the pitch of the line as it landed, knowing that the fly was within a foot of the far bank, swinging across the narrow stream of popply water. I convinced myself, talking out loud, that this was to be it. I had seen a big fish jump, the night was soft and balmy, and I had the right fly on, a simple mix of squirrel tail and silver tinsel. Desperation and desire mixed to form an illogical belief that this had to be the night, I had caught many fish here before, so why not now, in spring, for the big fish? As I could just feel the line pull round, I breathed in quickly, a little excited by my own meandering thoughts and dubious self-conviction.

Confidence, merited or not, is surely the key to success? It separates the journeyman from the 'lucky', the envious from the envied. But not this time, or was I to remain on the wrong side of the fence, always peering over and up at the finer catches beyond? The run in produced nothing. I crept down to the big corner tree, straining into the dark to make out the last branchy silhouette, and cast just beyond and under it. The water here deepens and slackens, a narrow line of frothy bubbles from the incoming stream conveniently marking the main current and lies. Again I cast out, counted to five and slowly pulled three arm lengths in, trying to feel the fly across the water, lifted and re-shot it back. Distant road lights glimmered across the water, another fish lunged across the surface and hope beat fast in my chest. Still the fly drifted, dragging across the angle, surely visible and attractive to a waiting fish? I shuffled gently down a couple of yards and cast again, now below the tree, where the river bed flattens out from the deep hole, shelving into a long, slack, canal-like run, uninspiring perhaps to an inexperienced eye, but the cream of the pool nevertheless.

My conviction was beginning to falter. If nothing took here, the best lies were passed. The chips were surely down. Suddenly, in a yanking lunge, so was the rod top. This was no take and responsive strike, it was a manic burst of activity, a screaming run off the reel before I could even react, a series of spray-flying, silence and surface smashing leaps. I tried to remember that this was the same as a normal pound and a half fish, but bigger, that was all, same technique, same deal. The fish careered about with a vengeance, a weighty pull that I was not used to, a speed of activity that surprised me, an extra force of resilience. But eventually the strain wore, the endless arc of rod and line sapping the strength, the leaps and runs diminishing, more of a dull weight than an active, lively pull, a roll on the surface and a great, curling bag in the net. Four and three quarter pounds, not large by some standards, but a perfect, square tailed example of wild, spring beauty. In an extraordinary hour or two, three more fish followed, two to the net, one to eventual freedom, before the mysterious switch was thrown and the river went lifeless.

It was a heady walk back home that night, and a restless sleep, eager to be up early and proudly display the lucky spoils, to admire at length and in daylight the streamlined silver forms. What a delightful feeling to snuggle into the warm sheets, tired but content, and reminisce on the evening's wonderful fortune, to thrill to the nocturnal epic.

The next day I was just stripping the bed before leaving when my back went. Cruel fate wrought revenge for the previous night's over indulgent generosity. I staggered, bent over and crab-like, to the car. A month later I was in the Western Isles, a holiday booked and eagerly awaited for months and a chance to meet Bruce Sandison for the first time. When I did, he looked kindly but shocked upon the rather pathetic fisher that hunched, slowly across the moors. Any idea of sitting in a boat, with no back support, at the mercy of the bucking waves, was gone. I tried to fish from the bank, where the wading was easy, in short bursts. Every hour or two I would rest, laid out on the soft heather carpet, staring up at the sky, feeling the rain slap down on my face, my glasses sprinkled with blurring raindrops. It was a strange way to spend a holiday. My first trout, a lively pounder on Benbecula, came in pouring rain. As I tried to net the fish, I realised that I could not bend over to reach the tail fly with the net. Worried, with the golden flank just out of range – a would be first fish not to be lost, (especially under the circumstances) – I improvised a sort of curtsy, a truly deferential way to net a trout, and also, not quite so pleasant, to ship a wader full of water!

It seemed obvious, as the second orthopaedic operation seemed to make little appreciable difference, that my days as a budding salmon fisher hurling prodigious lengths of line across the vast pools of a Tay or Spey, were numbered. Frankly this was probably not a great relief to the fish nor loss to me having seen my prior casting and catching efforts! But it was a sad blow nevertheless, the Ashley Cooper, Falkus and Oglesby bibles growing dusty on the bookshelf, those pictures of famed pools and dream sized salmon fading into an even more unattainable unreality. I looked at my fly box rows of neat salmon flies, all ranged by size and pattern, those simple approximations of exotic, evocative names, now resigned to frustrated premature retirement.

I continued to trout fish, eventually in boats as well as from the bank, and without any bizarre netting ceremony, but not for the big prize. Until September 1994, when Bruce convinced me to head up to the, at that stage, unknown wilds of the far north. I figured that if I could catch trout and sea trout with a nine foot rod, surely I could manage one a foot or so longer? As you will hopefully have read, the Kirkaig was rather a robust assault on my lack of vertebral confidence. Still, what better place to take the plunge than the deep end? On that first day I clambered, slithered and waded ever so gingerly. Looking at that little fly in all that rushing dark water, it seemed highly unlikely that a salmon would take. I felt humbled and had to cling on to my few memories of former luck to boost my confidence. I still feel the same at the beginning of any salmon week, and I suppose that when the surprise and delight is gone and I actually expect to catch a fish, then I will need to move on to find new challenges and leave the rods, and fish, in peace. Luckily, such self-assured conceit is still a long way off.

But as the sun faded I came to the last pool on the beat – Hazel. It is easily accessible by the path, a typical piece of Kirkaig mini perfection, the river hurrying along and emptying out from shallow rapids into a widening, swirling pool, straight out of the textbook and obviously fishy even to a first time visitor. Half way down it a sudden, short sharp grab wracked my senses and left me palpitating and wondering. It must have been, but no, surely not? After all those years I just couldn't be sure, and as I walked back home, with tired but happy step I struggled to rationalise. Was I kidding myself, or had a fish really stopped the fly in all that confusion of currents and waves?

The next day, as the water rushed over the Lower Falls and swung into the sheer, rock cliff left bank, I sneaked across the stepping stone rocks to a perch in mid river. (Yes, I did it again, breaking all the rules of watercraft and safety in my eagerness to catch a salmon). Once there, I cast into the far current. The line swung briskly round in the sparkling white froth, a myriad exploding minuscule bubbles, and this time the take was accompanied by sufficient head shaking to leave me in no doubt that a vital force was at the other end. My back was suddenly forgotten as I somehow scampered back to the bank, rock hopping madly, without falling in or slipping, hanging grimly on to the tugging rod and trying to keep the tip high and cushioned. It was a mini epic as the fish worked rapidly downstream as I struggled to get opposite it. I clambered over the sofa sized jumble of riverside rocks trying meanwhile to stop the fish from washing, broadside to the current, over the rock strewn tail of the pool and into the rapids below, in which case evident curtains loomed. Unaccustomed to such strength of water, and of fish, I had to heave with what I thought was daring brutality, jamming my hand down on the reel in an effort to stop the endless drift downstream. With maybe only a yard left until the rapids, I finally, crudely, dragged the fish back into the pool proper, got below it and to the waterside and concluded affairs in a less hectic fashion. After six years, and much back stopping disbelief, a salmon finally graced my net. It was also my first catch and release, being on the red side, but a happier soul would have been hard to find. Aches and pains seemed as ephemeral as the sunshine, an ode to the joy of catching salmon.

More were to come. On the last day I had to fish the Upper Inver, a broader, gentler river running down from the postcard-pretty multi ridged backdrop of Quinag and Assynt, an almost indecently stunning sculpture of wind and rock, of ice age and giants. But the rain, which had rendered the Kirkaig an unapproachable, unfishable torrent, had also left the Inver a high and wide proposition. Not one for a single hander, unless you happen to be a caster of Olympian skill or can walk on water, two skill sets I sadly lack. The old fifteen footer still resided, by chance, fate or obstinate hope, in the car boot. As it was the last day, and a fish was already under the strengthening belt, I felt it worth the risk. Looking back on it now, it all seems so ridiculous, many thousands of double handed casts and rivers later, but at the time it was quite a decision. It was the same when I first got up after the operation; I can remember being terrified of walking. If someone were coming towards me, I would stop on the pavement least they bump into me and break me in two, a ridiculous over-sensitivity to an unreal, presumed fragility. Unfortunately surgeons never seem to explain this.

The fish continued their recuperative, healing aid to my medical self-confidence. In recognition of such, (okay, let's be honest, they were red cock fish), I gently slipped one more back, and released another even earlier, a minute or two after being hooked (unintentionally of course). In a modest way it seemed quite a bonanza. My salmon fly boxes were restored, vindicated and brought back to life. The dream, hope and excitement was revived, the salmon lifeblood coursing again through my veins. I forgot the seemingly offhand platitudes and placebos of various surgeons, the almost shockingly uncaring 'if it hurts take some paracetemol' post operative advice, and indulged in a far better cure – a wild salmon in a wild land, a natural treatment of far greater, and more pleasing efficacy!

CHAPTER 14

Kindred Spirits

'To her fair works did Nature link
The human soul that through me ran;
And much it grieved my heart to think
What man has made of man'
William Wordsworth 'Lines Written in Early Spring' 1770-1850

My mother much enjoys regaling the story of when she picked up two scruffy youngsters from Reading Rock Festival, after three days of camping. With what I suspect might be just a touch of parental poetic license, she says she ordered an instant disinfection, fumigation and bath before dumping us on the overnight sleeper to Glasgow. Mike was a schoolmate, and we really were brothers of the angle, growing and learning together in a wonderful innocence of eager incompetence. Enthusiasm conquers many things, but not fish, well not in our case anyway. He also had the unfair advantage of being a Scot, all be it educated down south, and having wealthy forbears from the brewing industry which made him financially less dependent on the fates than most of us, and, best of all, his family owned the Argyllshire River Eachaig.

I used to love the long trek north, being slowly lulled into sleep by that rumbling, rhythmical rocking motion of the train, dreaming of all those fish and opportunities to come, eagerly awaiting the early morning knock on the door as the steward brought refreshing tea and biscuits. It was a gentle way to build up the momentum and anticipation, increasing as we took the little Clydesdale train down to Gourock and then the ferry across to Dunoon. One could sense the fish getting closer as the hills sprung up steeper and leafy deciduous gave way to fir and pine. I can remember seeing the lodge for the first time, in awe, a huge house backed by a high wall of massive rhododendrons, the rain dripping noisily off the large, dark green foliage. Our transport to the river was precarious, the two of us balancing on a moped, like some weird spider, a jumble of waders, nets and rods sticking out. I think we only fell off once, and with traffic levels considered heavy if we saw another two cars in a morning, we came to no harm.

Nor, in the main, did the fish. But there were many epic tales of daring do, Mike once hooking a salmon on a size fourteen Peter Ross in the cauld (weir) pool. This was great, but there is a ledge that drops off sharply into maybe eight or more feet of water, and more important, which hides an old tree-trunk. Not surprisingly, Mr Salmon promptly availed himself of this aid. Undeterred, Mike stripped off and leapt into the cooling waters, but his swimming talents were less than the salmon and all he gained was a soaking and a good yarn. On another desperate evening I remember throwing stones at a recalcitrant fish, until we realised that it had long gone, and the 'fish' at the end was merely a stake post. If only we had owned a reel with proper drag, but doubtless we would never have had the courage to use it properly. I am sure most novices lose salmon, (I certainly did), by being so nervous that they let the fish play them and not vice versa, until the inevitable happens and the hook hold wears loose. On the other hand I have seen a mad Californian steelhead fisherman in Iceland, a man of experience, and a walking tackle shop, lose fish after fish in a row by either breaking or pulling them off. I sometimes wondered how he found time to fish after choosing which of the five rods and countless line densities and profiles to use. He was so thrilled with the express train stopping state of the art drag on his incredibly expensive Bogden and Abel reels that he seemed incapable of actually adjusting the thing down. His rod would be hooped into, literally, a U shaped loop, and it says much for SAGE rods that he only broke one. He was a tackle manufacturer's dream and nightmare as he continually broke rods which were all replaced for free, whilst he muttered bitterly about unreliable, faulty tips.

Somehow for us the learning process was very slow. At the time there was a manic expert who fished the Eachaig frequently. He never offered any advice or encouragement, a sullen, selfish man, and every time we arrived at a pool the telltale Jaguar would be parked nearby and the only taking fish in the pool already on the bank. Its lilac silver flanks would already dulling to a burnished gun metal as rigor mortis transformed living beauty into inert death. He once took fifty pounds of sea trout out of the cauld pool in one night, killing the lot, probably to sell. We also had internal family competition, as Mike's brother was just old and favoured enough to fish elsewhere, on Ballindalloch on the Spey where he was taught to Spey cast by the gillie. He always seemed to take three fish a week whilst we struggled to lose one between us. But it was great fun, fishing what was then one of the finest sea trout rivers in the U.K., with fish into the 'teens of pounds, not that we ever breached the four-pound mark. We certainly tried though, fishing all night long, watching the sun drop softly behind the hills, hoping that the temperature would sink sufficiently to dissuade the midges from biting but not the fish. We might grab an hour or two's sleep staring up at the stars and then start up again for the morning rise, to the gentle bleating of awakening lambs. If that was not enough, and the tide was right, we would then rush off to the Sea Pool, scene of one of our more enthusiastic but less inspired moves. Knowing that sea trout take best under cover of darkness we had the brilliant idea of fishing the Sea Pool at night. It was an odd sensation as the river flowed into the Holy Loch, home then to a US Polaris submarine, and as we fished down the river the Polaris station was all lit up in mid loch, orange lights glaring threateningly across the waters. Well, I said fished down. That was not strictly accurate. One rather important detail that we overlooked in our cunning plan was the tide, which happened to be flooding. If you have ever waded out into mid river, at night, and found the river actually beginning to flow upstream, and then realised that the water between you and the bank was now deepening and deeper than your waders, well...

Our last visit was a sad affair, in the mid eighties. Already the salmon runs were disappearing, sea trout were not as plentiful and the family had sold the river to timeshare for a relative pittance. The old house was unkempt and empty, uninhabitable, the roof leaking, the massive Aga cooker cold and silent, the rhododendrons looking like a latter day hippy in need of a haircut. Even the steady drip of the rain seemed depressing. We eventually convinced an absent owner's agent to rent us his chalet for a week, and headed off for the river. It was to be an all night sea trout session, but the fishing, (or was it just us), wasn't up to it. Whispy grey mist curled up from the river and hung like a low bank hugging cloud, and the water surface ran heavy and unbroken. It was leaden, the fish flat on the bottom, no doubt pinned down by the plummeting air temperature and falling barometer. It was truly hopeless. We headed back to the car, and drove home in the freezing dark, the car heater working overtime, windows all fugged up and steamy, to find that we had lost the chalet key. We rushed back to the river, and searched the banks with a torch, but, of course, found nothing. We were left with little choice but to sleep in the car and then find a way to get in the next morning. Eventually we found a small neighbouring boy who clambered through the bathroom window and broke the front door lock from inside, an expensive little game which he found hugely entertaining but we did not. They say history repeats itself, or is it just growing senility, but I did almost the same, locking my hire car keys in full view on the car boot shelf last year in Caithness. The local police turned up with strip of packing binder and had a competition to see who could break in first – it took two minutes to get in and unlock the door. I pretended not to watch…

After the Eachaig we graduated to a November timeshare week on the Nith, scene, for once, of heart warming amateur triumph. We were on the Closeburn Castle beat, as always the youngest rods by a goodly twenty years, and trailing around behind a casting instructor from Aboyne on the Dee. Effortlessly he swept down the pool, projecting remarkable lengths of line, arrow straight and true, across the waters. We were equally impressed by his converted tackle box which housed a range of drinks and glasses including home made sloe gin that restored feeling to the numbed extremities after a long frigid wade, though doubtless dulled the thinking parts at the same time! We plodded and splashed behind, using Mike's special technique, the 'upstream heap cast', employed when trying to hurl a solid brass tube fly on fast sink line all day became too much, and the spinning rod was brought out. But we took the only two fish of the week, much to the communal chagrin of the experts. Who says fishers are a companionable, friendly sort – rubbish – there often lurks beneath the smiling exterior the competitive, green-eyed desire to catch both more and bigger fish than anyone else. Ah well, it was beginner's luck no doubt, and I took my fish on the last day just as the meadows glowed beneath a Turneresque orange wash, a molten sunset illuminating the fly line as it snaked across the river. It was lovely to fight and beach a clean fish in the very last days of the season, like the glowing embers of a fire smouldering before it finally goes out. The next year we returned for the same week and fished for precisely three hours, the river a muddy brown forest of leaves and detritus, the burns washing millions of autumnal fallings into the river with each passing, daily storm. It drove us to the bar and the Upper Tweed, where yet again a weak reel drag and terror set in and left me watching a large fish cavorting in the air a good eighty yards below me, my fly line drowned and slack. By its acrobatic, exhibitionist display and speed I suspect, to my horror, that it may well have been one of those very large sea trout that run the Tweed in the back end – I hope not, but I will never know. Yet another lost fish etched indelibly on the memory, in a cartwheeling shower of spray.

The Tweed was also a shock, but for all the wrong reasons. The locals, or some of them, seemed to presume that being born next to this mightiest of rivers gave them a God given right to harvest the late run salmon, red or not, by any means they wished. When first we fished, up at Walkerburn, we were bemused by the technique, a lot of rod top motion but otherwise a very static approach. We thought it must be some local form of 'induced take' over known lies. Alas it was nothing of the sort. The 'fly', the hideously named 'Walkerburn Angel' is none other than a weighted bunch of treble hooks, a deadly snare. The line was ultra fast sink, and the lifting motion was to yank the hooks into the belly of a salmon. It was utterly disgusting, and brazen. On Saturday, when the local Association 'fished', we gave up – the riverbank was a procession of foul hooking locals. Did anyone do anything? I believe that steps have now been taken, and fast sink lines banned, but I wonder. On another occasion, as we were heading home in the sunset, we saw a pair of figures lurking, crouched by the riverside, just where a small island split the stream. We returned early next morning and pulled out a gill net with two five pound sea trout, both fresh fish trapped by the gills, alive but half suffocated. We could do no better than put them speedily out of their misery. It was an interesting little island, the sea trout running up the narrow inside, (hence the net), but the salmon for some reason taking the main stream. I waded out to fish the far side of it in a just rising water – another lesson well learned. It only took half an hour, but on returning the river was up six inches and the flow ferocious. Fortunately the inside run was only a couple of yards wide, but it is the only time that I have been swimming in chestwaders.

If salmon fishing was a character forming waste of time, (why is it that anything bad is supposed to be good for you, can't we just admit it was lousy and we wished it had been better?), trout fishing was a lot of fun and activity. Everywhere around there was nature, in unspoiled, wild beauty. I think we have saved at least four sheep, stuck in fences, in peat bogs, on highroads and one prone, Monty Python-like, on its back, legs in the air, weighed down by all those future Pringle sweaters, cable knitted to the ground and unable to rollover. Left like that, a sheep soon gives up the will to live and dies – but you'd be amazed how heavy a fully laden woolly is, and how reluctant they are to be helped. Nor do they ever say thank you, usually just giving themselves a good shake and sauntering off with that usual aimless expression. I suppose the word sheepish was coined for good reason. Much more frightening, like a Hitchcock remake, was an impromptu lunch left on an island in South Uist. I had inadvertently placed it right next to an arctic tern's nest. Bravest of birds, so fragile, and yet so well travelled, from Africa to Iceland, it swooped at me so low that it actually hit the hood of my fishing jacket. I fled at full speed waving my net above my head – it must have made a great sight! Seagulls are far less courageous, they fly low across the water at about head height, but then bank and rise way over your head at a very safe distance, making much noise and dropping their bombs as they go.

With my bad back, Mike was always, tirelessly and uncomplaining, at the oars. But as we drifted across the lochs and years, we began to drift apart, separated largely by the rigid social mores, the inflexibile strictures of British society. Mike was hardly a rebel, but he had perhaps more of a wild, free nature than most. He would have made a great manager on a Scottish sporting estate. As it was, as we all were, he was herded into undergoing one of those farcical multiple guess examinations by so called job consultants. They pigeon holed him as an accountant to be, (as they did most people), and a more inappropriate career would be difficult to imagine. As it was he did struggle through a year of bean counting exams before flunking out, and I can remember him rather shiftily, embarrassed, replying to the usual fireplace questions in various fishing lodges of 'Oh, and what do you do?' Frankly, who cares anyway, such idle small talk may lubricate the wheels of political correctness in boardrooms, but has little place when on a week's fishing holiday. After that he headed off travelling, then panning for gold and teaching diving in Honduras.

We met once a year to trout fish, but the fire place interrogations became more awkward, and ever more extravagant answers concocted. Our conversations centred more and more on the past, on nostalgia, on what friends we had been. Meanwhile I was making a perceived success of a career in multinational business and I suspect Mike thought that I too disapproved. I tried not to, and didn't, but the stress and responsibility differences between a life of relative drifting ease and one of corporate deadlines did begin to tell. As he began to age and feel a social outcast, and I to feel that I had no right to judge, our fishing fortunes seemed also to make a patronising assessment – all the fish, and especially the big ones, came to my end of the boat. Even when fishing the same flies, the two-pounder would always seek the gainfully employed KeHe, not the 'idle drifter'. It, of course, became a vicious circle, and, as said, confidence is all. Without it the casts are, imperceptibly, not fished out with due care and attention, just a little too fast, eager to get on to the next one as you know this one will not catch anything. The eyes and senses drift off to the scenery, to the horizon, just when a fish does boil. Then the rod at the other end of the boat, just a few feet away, and with the same fly from the same shop, bends and bucks and kicks as another good fish rams the point home.

Post-prandial sorties, which take the most discipline and self control, were the worst. After a long, often elementally and mentally harsh day of wind battering nothingness, it is all too easy to slide into thirst quenching beer, food comforting wine and soul warming malt. It is far harder to go it easy, to remember that the wind may drop, the flies just might hatch at dusk and the best chance of a rise is yet to come. It is a battle of future hope over current indulgence. We would set off, and I well remember that fateful day of the tipless rod, with the reel down my waders, as described earlier. The last I saw of Mike was seeing him striding across to the boat clutching a fine bottle of Islay malt whisky. I am sure he had an enjoyable evening, but he missed out on the main chance, asleep behind a dry stone wall. In fact poor Bruce, our host, was so worried, that after celebrating the fish, 'wetting its head' as customary, he set off in search of the still missing Mike. Kind man, he walked around the whole loch at midnight, or later, to check that he was safe. As Mike snored away, well hidden, the heavens opened, and the welcome at breakfast the day after was a touch damp! To fish at night takes clinical efficiency, and the slightest alcohol induced dulling of co-ordination ruins the timing and ends up in frustrating birds nest tangles, the soft night air ringing with expletives and flickering torch lights. Just when the big fish are slurping audibly right in front of you...

Our last week summed it all up. Bruce and Fiona Armstrong, the charming television and media personality, were giving a BBC Scotland radio broadcast, and looking for a suitably verbose third party they roped me in. It was rather odd to be standing aside a Caithness loch with a furry microphone stuck under one's nose, trying not to sound too pompous and to answer the questions without a string of pausing 'umms'. Mike, of course, set off on his own, no doubt musing that all the so called experts and corporate celebrities, (Bruce would like that description!), were in a cabal together. When the day ended, I looked for him, saw no one, and presuming he had caught an early lift home, I jumped in the car and drove back to the lodge. Needless to say when I got there, there was no Mike. Poor friend, he was away round the corner of the loch and spotted me drive off, watching the tail lights of our friendship disappear into the distance. It was two years ago, (I did, of course, hurry back as soon as I realised my mistake and pick him up), and we haven't fished together since. I wait for a call, and did receive one cut off message on the answer phone, but no more. Good, understanding fishing companions, (and boatmen!), are hard to come by. Perhaps, like the salmon, our day is done, but, equally, I hope not.

CHAPTER 15

Escape to the Wiltshire Avon

'This almost unchanging English scene, with its red and green rolling hills, holds a romance that wild rocks, and wild rivers, or snow-capped volcanoes could never give you. It has a gentleness, and an unostentatiousness that is like the English character. An imperturbable scene, which fills you with contentment.'
Negley Farson 'Going Fishing' 1942

Work has two great raison d'etres. It pays the bills, and it heightens your awareness and appreciation of beauty and relaxation when you can escape it. The geography of this book's creation would need quite a global map, being largely written in drearily similar hotel rooms at antisocial jet lagged early hours of the morning. Generally it was in some far flung city, hoping to find the usual tea and coffee maker to keep body and soul vaguely alive until room service opened, checking the time difference to see if I could phone the office. At such moments it seems an unreal, stressed and pointless existence. But then I get away, and the difference is palpable, like a plant that you have forgotten to water and come home to find all a-droopy, leaves hanging curled up and limp in a sad refrain. They look pathetic in an almost human sense, but one good soaking and the transformation is remarkable, you can almost see the sap rise and the chlorophyll perk up. The more I work, the more I find myself fishing, partly because it is relaxing, and leaves no time spare for diverting thoughts back home, but in a more positive sense because I just appreciate it that much more. I notice the crest of a ridge, the freshness of the air, the limpid purity of the birdsong in a way I never did when working in far easier times a decade ago. Perhaps the computer has a positive effect on the aesthetic senses after all!

So when I touched down in Gatwick airport for a long weekend, I looked hurriedly out of the plane window and was dismayed to see the flags flapping noisily and horizontally. I was supposed to be in Scotland on the Dee for a day, but my plans had fallen through at just a week's notice, and I had been left to find a replacement in a hurry.

May in France is a blessed month of short weeks, and I had been driving down the dreaded A6 motorway for one bank holiday Friday whilst ringing every number I could find advertised in 'Trout & Salmon' – for once praising the merits of the mobile phone! But the wind looked very iffy for delicately casting a size sixteen dry fly, and you could surely guarantee it would be straight down river!

It was particularly pleasant, in a perverse, gloating manner, to be up early and driving along the M4 against the traffic, watching the gridlock of uniformed, sheep-like commuters flocking into the City in the opposite direction. Slowly the cement and tarmac gave way to open fields, as I drove past the old concrete bowl of Queen Mother Reservoir where I had spent so many hours as a kid fishing sunk line lures for all too rare rainbows. Will I ever repeat the hushed excitement of that first fish, taken deep, deep down? In fact, if truth be told, I had put the rod down in the boat to net, slightly enviously, a fish for a friend, having had no time to reel in the line. When I picked it up the line pointed straight down into the depths over which we had drifted and there was an almost unbelievably lucky, much hoped for tugging at the end of the line. What a triumph to take proudly home – all three-quarters of a pound of newly stocked rainbow, green backed and pink striped in its naïve, greedy ignorance.

Back on the motorway, the green fields stretched into bilious yellow rape seed, and then began to lump and hump up into the rolling chalk downs of Wiltshire, the ploughed, open ruts looking brownie-white in the sun, purest of filters for that crystal aquifer below. I had no idea what to expect, but as the car stereo reached a glorious operatic crescendo in a sinuous, climactic duet which set the skin tingling, I looked up and saw an 'Iceland' refrigerated truck in front of me as I turned off, surely a good omen? Up and down the quaint, winding hedged by-lanes of rural England, the houses were all of weathered old rusty red brick and thatch, the gardens with immaculate, neat flowerbeds. I finally crossed a bridge proudly sign posted River Avon. Well, perhaps there is a tone of ironic sarcasm here. It had been a record wet April, (at last, enough water to feed the sprinklers, car washes and dishwashers for a few weeks at least), but the bridge was more of a hop than a long jump, the river a grandiose name for a yard wide trickle. I tried not to be too disappointed; this was, after all, a lovely day out in the countryside. I was to fish the upper waters of what is, much further down, that gracious chalkstream, the Hampshire Avon, historical training ground of Frank Sawyer and his famed Pheasant Tail Nymph. It was to be, I hoped, a cheap source of wild fish within a couple of hours of London. In fact it had cost a mere thirty pounds, (mere being in relative terms), and I had booked just a week earlier, even though it was in peak season. I could hardly expect a fisher's paradise, could I?

As I turned into the pub car park to meet my host, such level headed thoughts were wavering. The husband was away, and his wife, a charming lady, knew nothing about fishing. I was allowed to wade, but she had never heard of nymphs, or fly names, so I just decided that upstream dry it would have to be. Better safe than sorry, and English chalkstreams are not the most relaxed, democratic place to break the rules, even inadvertently on the headwaters! The beat was on one bank, a few hundred yards of a rather wild field, the banks a nicely overgrown mix of lush foliage and not so friendly stinging nettles. The river was, I was delighted to see, about six yards wide, flowing fast and pretty clear, with lovely bright lime green fronds of weed, swinging aimlessly, nymph-full in the stream. It was three to four feet deep. Unaccustomed as I am to clear water fishing, I could not see sign of a fish, nor rise, nor hatch, and the scudding wind, (yes of course it was!), didn't help either. I handed over my money rather wondering what I was in for, and trooped off to start.

As I sat on a rustic, thick hewn wooden bench sensibly placed by the water, the air was full of hawthorn flies. Of course, it was their season – I had seen the hedgerows all white with hawthorn blossom, as if dusted with snow, and the easiest to recognise and name fly of all was swarming over them, (but not over the water, not a hungry brown neb appeared). They are rather alarming creatures, or would be if bigger, black and hairy with huge trailing, tarantula-like legs, a Hitchcock fly if ever there was one. Naturally, if I had thought about it, I would have tied some up, with those distinct legs they are easy to mimic, but had I? I scurried through the box and found one Black Hopper, not quite an exact imitation, but remarkably similar. As I struggled to tie it on to the thinnest three pound fluorocarbon leader, (a mistake, fumbling fingers and indelicate handling do not suit such gossamer nylon), a fish rose. A distinct swirl of expanding rings, only ten yards away, aside but not under a lovely weeping willow. Fingers fumbled even more. Creeping along on my knees, I aimed, with perfect length and pitch, but just one mistake – the wind. Not really fair for a first cast – a malicious, viciously timed gust and my one and only impromptu hawthorn imitation joined the willow in inseparable embrace.

I was beginning to have fun. I went for a size fourteen Irresistible, as much for its confidence inspiring name and, (let's be honest), ease of visibility as any more deeply thought out logic. I bent my way along the bank, trying to peer beneath the rippling surface. But each time I got close enough to spot a fish and raise the rod, there was an insulted flick of a tail and puff of chalk dust and I was left trying to imagine a trailing weed frond into a flickering caudal fin. I had been told that there were no rainbow hued interlopers here, or overfed stocked browns. The fish, such as they be, were as nature had created. I continued my regal fish putting down parade up the bank and finally, in a wrist jerk reaction more used to thick nylon, broke off into a fish. On my knees I cursed, but it was, at least, progress, all be it a disgrace to leave a fish swimming free with a hook in its maw. I tried to programme my brain to remember this was not eighteen-pound nylon on the Tay and a one-inch brass tube.

Up ahead, there was a splash. Oh, that delicious anticipation as the fly, high and dry in its lethal disguise, drifted down and over. Splash. Flick (this time). Wriggle. Yes, it was a wriggle, not a thump. About six inches of trout came sliding by, and a rainbow at that, (though perfectly finned and lovely, quite wild in look, a beauty in fact). Ah well, it was still an advance of a sort. By lunch I had three more, but all the same – where were the wild natives, or was I fishing in the wrong place with inadequate skill (perish the thought)? I sat down to munch and ponder. Around me the nightmare flies buzzed, goldfinches flitted by with brilliantly flashing yellow wing bars, and warblers and cuckoo competed in song with the incongruous thump of military shells and the explosive rattle of machine guns. Salisbury Plain was just behind me and the army was training. It was the one drawback to such a peaceful idyll. I decided to change tack. I had, on my rather too apparent travels, spotted the odd real fish, (as they had me), and seen a few more purposeful rises on the far bank glides. Furthermore, I was allowed to wade. In such a small river it seemed ridiculous, but I figured I couldn't put down anymore fish than I had in the morning…

So I slipped, as heron-like as five foot ten of human flesh can try to be, gently into the water, and, hugging the bank, started to fish blind. I flicked the fly to where I had seen fish or rises before, or where I guessed they should be, in the narrow channels between the weeds, by the bank, under the trees. It was pleasant not to have to ache, bent double, up along the steep banks and be stung by the nettles. I realised my mistake – down here, in the water, I could creep up far closer behind the fish and still be invisible, my position well below their window. I stopped spooking fish, and with shorter line and faster strike, started catching them. A hopeful, speculative cast just above a willow on the far bank disappeared in a quite gulp and a three-quarter pound wild Avon brown trout kicked the rod tip down. It had a small head, sharp teeth, highish shoulder and a speckling of red spots over the burnished flanks – a lovely sight. Seven more followed, some a hand span in miniature, the best a pound, quite an exciting fight over the glistening weed, the fish running downstream towards the tree, snags and freedom. An added bonus was a couple of grayling, actually out of season, but in perfect condition. In fact they were the hardest, most powerful fighters of the day, that sailfish orange tipped dorsal fin erect, their sides a melange of metallic grey and iridescent markings. I was pleased to see them alive and well, left in peace as they should be, not exterminated as vermin as on some trout only stretches. I kept the best trout for a delicious lunch, and slid the rest back. It was a delightful day's fishing for wary, natural sized fish in a wild, unspoiled place. It was seven years since I had last fished a wild chalkstream headwater or tributar (that day on the Lambourn), and my score had improved I am pleased to say!

The next day dawned even sunnier, and I exchanged the M4 for the M3, heading a few miles further south. The more delicate intermingling of yellow flowering gorse and silver birch slipped into the long green pastures and water meadows of Hampshire, the copses carpeted with an almost ethereal, smoke-like mist of bluebells hanging over the ground, a blue-grey mantle, straight out of the set of Giselle. Surely the M3 is the most beautiful of motorways, and yet so close to the built up carnage of London. It was, again, just a great spring day to be out and about. I felt distinctly like Toad sitting in his car, thoroughly contented with both himself and the world. Even better, I was bound for more prestigious, (and expensive), waters – the Itchen. The Test was five times the price of the Upper Avon, and full of stocked rainbows. Being booked for months ahead, it was not an interesting option, financially, or sportingly. The Itchen was stocked, but 'sensibly' with appropriate browns I was informed. As I collected my licence from the archetypal English upper crust salesman, I hoped so. The only other rod might be 'a charming fellow, the General'. I looked at my scruffy jeans and imagined some tweed and tie, gin and tonic type, his posture, humour and lifestyle as stiff as his split cane rod.

The river was much the same size, a little broader, but shallower, rather weedless, (it was just ahead of the weed cut) and slower flowing – drag being far less of a problem. The banks on both sides were mown, nice bridges and little river-watching benches thoughtfully placed, and a wooden fishing hut and fish book at the ready. It was all so easy going, cosseted and unchallenging. Unfortunately, so were the fish. Between a pound and a half and two, they stuck out like the proverbial sore thumb. Unlike any wild fish, of which I saw none, except a sad, murdered and discarded grayling, curled up and floating downstream, thrown away as vermin by some mindless rod further up. Now you will have gathered that my prowess as a dry fly fisher leaves a lot to be desired, not really my forte as it were. I had been told that the rules were strict – kill the first four fish, then leave. Obviously my day's training at UpAvon had done wonders for my technical skills. In three hours I had risen a dozen, hooked six, and try as I might to shake them off, four were lying, sickening and plump, in the fish bass. Should I stop – it was only lunchtime? It seemed ridiculous. As it was a lovely, balmy day, (with no military orchestration), I ambled up and down, not bothering to crouch and crawl, casting as I fancied, sometimes even roll casting out an idle line left handed – and fishing slack, with no line control and no strike. I rose many more before thinking I'd had more than enough of this farce and headed off for dinner. Almost apologetically I handed out the fish to eager, hungry family, muttering that they were not the real thing, the flesh a lurid pink compared to the pale, off white cream of the wild fish, a symbol of both their and my disgruntled embarrassment and sadness. The Lower Itchen is a lovely river, pure water meandering through the prettiest of banks, but sullied perhaps forever. I will search out the upper waters, the Alre, for what it was once like, wild and free, but of the supposedly prime beats further down I am twice bitten, twice shy, fish and freezer aplenty, but with no desire to return.

CHAPTER 16

The Ultimate Elixir

'Fish are allured not on account of the close resemblance which the artificial hook has to particular insects but from other causes of a different nature. These are size, motion, form and colour'.
Tom Stoddart in 1847

Let's be honest – what do you really need to catch a salmon? Well, first of all you must be possessed of adequate casting skills and deep wading technique. Then you should have an understanding of water dynamics, plus knowledge of the water temperature, depth, speed, clarity, and air pressure. All of that is before you even think of choosing the correct size and pattern of fly? No, come on, I said be honest. What you need is simple - money, contacts and luck. Then, and only then, need you worry about all that technology, expertise and fishing skill. Put it this way, place the world's best fisher in the wrong river at the wrong time and guess what they will catch – a lot of excuses and a bad temper. Now plonk an absolute beginner in one of the prolific Kola Peninsular rivers, or Iceland in August and what will you find – 'beginner's luck' aplenty. Of course I am being partly facetious, but the one absolute sine qua non when salmon fishing is to have some fish in the beat – and that is, I'm afraid, down to contacts and money (plus luck) more than anything else. Which, of course, makes it a mug's game (or a wealthy mug perhaps!).

That said, there is no doubt that, over the long haul, an expert will of course prove his worth compared to a less experienced rod on the same water. But does the fly pattern matter when salmon fishing? I have to think not. After all, we don't even know why a salmon takes a fly in the first place, and literature abounds with a plethora of theories, many anthropomorphic, some scientific. They range from memories of parr feeding habits to sexual aggression or territorial defence. Arthur Ransome, sitting in a London hotel during the war watching US GIs chewing gum, suddenly thought of a salmon's desire to exercise the jaw muscles and have a good chew. Every fishing magazine comes up with a 'new' infallible pattern, but I can't help wonder what is really new under the sun, except for ever glitzier, space age materials and more outrageous names. The Victorians shot nearly to extinction many an exotic species to adorn their colourful, artistic creations, but I dare say they, or the straggly, dowdy old Spey flies of long trailing grey heron, would be just as effective as today's ubiquitous hairwing and fur patterns.

It is a modern day arrogance to think that we are being innovative. Aelian's 'Natural History' mentions a Macedonian fishing technique used on the River Astraeus to tempt fish with 'speckled skins'. They used a short rod and tied crimson wool and cock feathers to a hook to imitate a waspish sort of hover fly called a Hippouros. This, believe it or not, was written in about 200 A.D. If we leap in the time machine to the Middle Ages, a Bavarian manuscript in the abbey of Tegernsee lists over fifty types of fly employed in fishing for numerous species including all the salmonidae. Three centuries later, during the English Civil War and just after Shakespeare, Dame Juliana wrote here famous 'Treatysse on Fysshynge with an Angle' and gave a dozen trout fly patterns. Amusingly, even then there was much debate as to whether you should fish up or downstream, so maybe we have not advanced so far in the last three hundred years after all! At least now we have more choice – in days of yore the direction and presentation of the fly was mainly dictated by the wind, not by the whim's of the fish or fisher. Least you should think that the sacred Test was the home of the dry fly, it seems to have first appeared there in the late 1880's, whereas it was in ply elsewhere a good forty years previously – and as far afield as in Philadelphia! Finally, if bucktail salmon flies are considered modern, they were used by American bass fishers in the 1890's and for salmon on the Restigouche in Canada way back in the 1920's!

Doubtless size and presentation matters far more than pattern, though even there a scan through the average fish book in any lodge or hotel reveals a mind boggling and theory-busting array of successful hardware, from metal spinners and heavy tubes to light doubles. A salmon in one pool will respond to a drab, small Hairy Mary on a single hook, whereas in the pool below one will be caught on a heavy metal spoon festooned with trebles. If you then throw in differences in line profile and flotation, the plot thickens to curdling! I suspect that fashion is the number one dictate, followed by the magazine editors' need to sell copy. It is that universal desire of mankind – the never ending search for the ultimate elixir, be it as philosophical as the stone, as ludicrous as the key to eternal life or as mundane as the perfect fly. Fortunately we haven't discovered any of them yet!

Trout flies, I will admit, are different – after all, the little beasts do actually feed, and though they may have been munching away on pretty much the same plateful of bugs for centuries, at least we have something to aim at and imitate. Even here though, you have to wonder at the reasoning capacity of an animal with a minuscule brain that relies mainly on instinct for survival. Can a fish really count just how many knotted legs our fly has, especially as the image is reflected upside down in its shimmering window? Cynic I might be, but I doubt a fish can tell whether the body, sorry abdomen, is correctly segmented. Naturally, the largest trout have a classical education and would no more dream of rising to an incorrectly Latin named subspecies of the genus ephemeroptera than they would of dancing with a mayfly with one tail too many! I have the greatest respect for the modern, expert fly tiers, in seeming direct lineage from Halford, though I dare say they would decry the link, as their imagination and skill in finding and weaving new materials into the most intricate, life-like semblance of an insect is truly impressive. As is the expert who can spot, identify and name in at least two languages, one dead and one alive, any speck floating by on the surface twenty yards away.

I have to admit that I have not the scientific knowledge, dexterity or interest to be so exact. Somehow it reduces a subtle, natural art form to too much of a human science for me. I remember once, years ago, leaving a stray fly by mistake on top of my desk at home. The cleaning lady tried to swat it, much to my delight as I arrogantly revelled in the deceit. It was a pretty inaccurate approximation of any real, living creature, and with a strange hook sticking out of it, and you have to query how such a very generalist fly could delude a human with a brain many thousand times bigger than a fish. I am sure the answer lies in the expectation. It was summer, bluebottle flies were around, and a rough imitation in the right place gave the casual eye enough stimulus to engender an instinctive response – splat. Or, if we take a more hopeful fishy metaphor, slurp. Now transfer this to a much smaller brained creature that is feeding in a fast flowing, watery environment and needs to eat in order to survive, and surely one's chances are much improved?

I am sure that this is the key – to have the right impression of the right form of life at the right time and place. Therein lies the skill, not the exact perfection of the fly, though this may be an added delight if one so aspires. Certainly when I have been dry fly fishing for wild trout I have usually found general flies of the right size to work a treat – perhaps due to the fact that I fish in fairly low rod pressure, remote places? I guess that on heavily fished, catch and release public waters the fish may get a lot warier, though I still wonder at a fish brain's ability to assimilate all those patterns. I would venture that it is more an awareness that all that floats enticingly above is not food rather than a specific 'Oh, dear, another size fourteen iron blue, don't they realise that the naturals are size eighteen today and have six, not ten legs?'

The Irish and Scottish lough/loch traditions have an interesting variance from the southern lakes and rivers where closer imitation is the norm. In Ireland, lovely great straggling flies, all trailing hackle and wing, cut and plough through the waves to bring up those magnificent silver and black spotted limestone trout. To the north east, across the Irish Sea, the Scots ply their Mallard, Grouse and Teal flies, or the flashy Butchers, none a specific imitation of anything, though I have heard of a Butcher being described as a copy of everything from a hatching midge to a fish fry. The latter is obvious, the former less so. On turbid, dark, peaty waters I always like to include some gold and orange in a fly, be it for native or sea run fish, and on clearer waters something more dour, dapper and silver. A Silver Invicta does sterling service as both a fry imitator and a rising sedge pupa (again, a rather broad-brush approach – Cezanne rather than Vermeer).

As said before, I think that the fry rather than the fly may be the real key. Should we adopt the Latin name for the minnow to give credence and credibility? From live trolled and impaled minnows on Corrib, to equally plump limestone trout in Durness, the marrow spoon as often shows fry as fly. I have become so convinced of this that even I have tried to be vaguely inventive, or at least thoughtful. Tubes of foul smelling epoxy resin have been bought and mixed, rather like Macbeth's witches brew, and shaped into deep bellied, silver scaled fish shapes. I wait to see if the fish book and freezer will groan in approbation! Of course this may seem more akin to spinning than true flyfishing. Halford tried, in 1886, to sum up dry fly fishing as '...presenting to the rising fish the best possible imitation of the insect on which he is feeding in its natural position.' If you submit the word 'feeding' for 'rising' and 'food' for 'insect', haven't you just about described and legitimised fishing a fry imitating lure?!

But I have another confession to make, charlatan that I am. A while back I was, on a dismal, wet Sunday afternoon, dreaming of seemingly distant days afloat and wondering if I couldn't pass some time to create something effective, if not exactly new. I liked the fuzzy, mobile, pulsing form of the Irish 'dabbler' flies and decided to tie a sort of modified, more Scottish version with the materials I had to hand. It was a type of mallard and olive dabbler fly. I sent it to Bruce Sandison and named it after him, for all the kindness, hospitality and effort he has put in over the years, at the bar, home, loch and oars. The inauguration ceremony was to be in Caithness, on Loch Toftinghall, after the impromptu radio interview with BBC Scotland. The fly thus had an august birth – on radio and press, as it soon appeared in The Scotsman. In fact, Bruce fishing 'The Bruce' was indeed, fittingly, the first to christen the fly and so earn a bottle of champagne in celebration.

I would like to say here that like the scratch golfer playing with his boss or his top client, I intentionally miscued into every bunker to ensure losing, but my Pinocchio nose would be hitting the wall! I failed dismally, and couldn't raise even one damned trout to the new pattern, (though I did to others). Anyway, I thought little more of it until I received a call from Mark Bowler, editor of 'FlyFishing & FlyTying' magazine, asking for the killer pattern and an example, saying that he was being pestered for the design. The tackle shop up there also asked if they should start to produce it for sale. All of this because of a few wee trout caught and one article in The Scotsman! I have to say that I hope that it has brought endless success to the eager readers, because for its brilliant designer and creator it remains a rather miserable disappointment! Not the elixir after all...

CHAPTER 17

Norwegian Spruce

'Every water has its secrets. A river or a lake is not a dead thing. It has beauty and wisdom and content. And to yield up these mysteries it must be fished with more than hooks and for more than fish. Strange things happen to the enquiring fisherman. Nature meets him halfway on his adventure'
Zane Grey 'Tales of Fresh-Water Fishing' 1928

Mention Norway to any dreamy eyed fisher and what image do they come up with? Mountainous snow topped fjords towering over a vast white water torrent of a river, rushing over rock strewn rapids and holding salmon of simply enormous size. I remember talking just a couple of summers ago to a rod just back from the Alta, (no, unfortunately not on its river banks but in London) who said that during the peak season the fish still averaged over twenty pounds. It is probably the most exclusive salmon river in the world, but even on such hallowed ground, hydroelectric schemes have wrought havoc with the salmon returns. Now, alas, with commercial netting, fish farms in every fjord and the latest killer, gyrodactalus salaris, such one time reality has often become merely a nostalgic pipe dream.

The stocking densities allowed in Norwegian fish farm cages are far higher than in the U.K., and the water exchange in a fjord is much less than in the open sea. The result is a deadly combination of sea lice and fish excreta swilling about beneath the cages – a fatal welcoming embrace for returning salmon. Recently the collapse of fish stocks has seen commercial netting stopped, but rivers have now been infested with the gyrodactalus louse. The only solution is to poison the whole river, thus eradicating the killer louse but also all fish in the river, adult, parr and fry. It is a desperate solution, the hope being that the smolts which are out at sea, and are still healthy, will come back to ascend a clean river and start to spawn and restock it. The recovery period is measured in several years, and the roll call of famed Norwegian salmon rivers, such as the Laerdal, that are closed well into the next millennium is tragic. So far the louse has not spread across the sea, but for how long I wonder?

But salmon are not the only worthy quarry in Norway, and it was for trout that I was to search in Norway, and what surprises you can find. Business usually takes me not to the wild north coast of salmon fame, but to the tamer south, to Oslo. It is a lovely city where my first daylight view was of a tangerine sun rising over the pine trees, throwing an orange glint across the snow, the boat moorings sticking out into the frozen fjord like an icy skeleton. Beautiful and relaxing, but as you have guessed a good four months too early to pack a fishing rod. When I returned, in June, it was prime trout season, and the Norwegian capital offers a varied choice of trout fishing within easy access of the city centre at minimal cost. All you need is an inexpensive licence from the nearest post office and off you go. Perfect for a business trip where you only have a few hours to spare. Besides, it is difficult to secrete chest waders and a fifteen-foot salmon rod in your briefcase, whereas a six-piece travel fly rod is easily squeezed in!

For the very busy, a short trip to the famous Holmenkollen ski jump, clearly visible on the outskirts of town, also offers a lake full of trout, but is crowded. A couple of kilometre's walk, or cycle, brings you to three good trout lakes near Gronmo, (the city garbage dump!), but again they tend to be heavily fished and the trout are wary. I decided to hire a car and head off for thirty-five minutes to the Skellbreia forest lakes of Ostermarka, in the hills above Oslo. My travel directions were somewhat sparse, but all I had to do was stop the car in the middle of nowhere and ask any passing local I could find, and I received a friendly response in perfect English. As an added bonus, the drive along the side of Oslofjord was spectacular, and well worth a look.

I found my Mecca after a forty-minute walk up the forest trail. The path was like one vast air freshener, bracing and heady with the scent of pine, spruce and fir. The lakes had unpronounceable names, but were translatable as the large and the small. The first one I came across looked pretty large to me, but as an even bigger one stretched out next door, I figured that this had to be the small one – this was Norway after all, and if the rivers and salmon were of such epic proportions, why not the lakes too?

There was a conveniently placed rock, the size of a large car, that had tumbled down to the lakeside and sloped perfectly to allow me to lie back in the sun, swallow a cold beer and sandwich and survey the placid waters in front for sign of a rise. And so I did, thanking Odin and his fellow Gods for creating such a lovely lunching spot, but not a dimple did I see. On finally venturing forth with rod and line I caught only a perch, a vivid memory of childhood, those orange fins and dark green back with zebra black stripes, the skin leathery to the touch, the dorsal sharp and erect. Perch are tasty, as are most carnivorous 'coarse' fish, but for some reason the British disdain to eat them. I moved on, confused as to where the small lake was. Twice I tramped across the peat bog between the two bigger lakes wondering if either I was stupid, or the map, or my kind local advisor who had tipped me off to fish here. He had said the lake was small and round, and full of free rising wild brown trout of modest girth. As valuable fishing time was disappearing, and I was getting frustratedly keen to wet a proper line, my temperature and temper began to rise. Where the hell was this stupid lake? Just finding the place was becoming quite an epic saga in itself.

It was also somewhat iffy going underfoot, the ground being in fact a sort of peat and moss crust, about two feet thick – rather like walking on a frozen river or lake, but more springy. Below lay the inky black depths of peaty water. One step I sank knee deep, which seriously slowed my advance and enthusiasm! But in the middle of this floating crust was a hole. It was round. About twenty five yards in diameter. I could see the ground just stop and drop vertically into eight feet of watery blackness. Could this diminutive hole be it? I felt rather silly casting into a glorified round ditch where even I could hook the far bank without a double haul, but why not? A yellow bellied, red spotted trout agreed. As did another – this one an honest three-quarter of a pound. I began to take this place more seriously. How could such a tiny hole in the ground produce so many and such decent fish? Where did they spawn? Where was the food? Was there some underwater connection to the two bigger lakes? To cover the whole 'lake' only took twenty minutes. I would release half a dozen fish, (often early – their reactions were far too quick for me), and then go to fish the real lake for an hour before shuttling back for more Lilliputian fun and action. Overhead the clouds darkened, glowered and lightning, just like the fish's reaction to a fly, streaked across the sky. It was then that I realised that I had forgotten my waterproof trousers, so I stood watching my jeans from the knees down turn darker and wetter as the forest scent mingled with the hot electric smell of the storm. It was one of those unreal little cameos, a moment of weird perfection and unexpected beauty. In the distance the sun reappeared over the forest, bathing the far off moor in glorified spotlight whilst I still stood in gloomy, Stygian darkness. The rain punched bullet holes into the lake surface, the trout down, all activity ceasing until the sun and fish began to break through and rise again. It was as delightful as it was unexpected, and makes me wonder about all those tiny lochans you drive past in the Highlands and Islands and never fish, presuming that they are too small to support decent fish. I wonder how many golden bellied opportunities are thus wasted?

The next day, Sunday, I headed off early for more, this time eager to work the bigger lake where I had lost a couple of fish at distance that had pulled the rod tip down in more earnest, weighty fashion. The big lake was difficult to fish, the banks being steep and tree-clad right down to the water's edge. Wearing only wellies it was impossible to wade and difficult to switch or roll out any decent length of line without eventually festooning the trees with an ever growing assortment of Scottish loch flies. I suspect that the locals may have been rather more Catholic with their choice of lure, and have to admit that there were times when flicking a small spinner out from beneath the branches seemed an attractive option. Still, a fly rod was all I had, and being typically dark peat waters, I used a team of three traditional flies just as I would in Scotland, all gold flash and orange to show through the water. It was comforting to flick out my usual assortment of KeHe, Black Pennel and something flashy, a Butcher or Dunkeld into the Guinness-like waters, just as I would in the peat lochs of Scotland. Happily the technique worked just as well. In the evenings when the wind drops, the lakes flatten down to a glassy millpond calm, and delicate casting and small dry flies come into play. But the rise-swallow-reject motion is so fast, a tiny splash and a circling ring across the mirror calm, that I was usually left cursing at my own inept slowness and wondering just how to speed up my reactions enough to be able to hook these sprightly little trout.

Still, my general approach was raising interest, especially at the end of the lake where the trees finally gave way to a thirty-yard stretch of blissfully free-casting bank. By some querk of Norwegian hospitality the trout were rising here as well as off the nearly unfishable forest shores. I am sure that back home they would have avoided the easily fished treeless bank and only cocked a snout up in the impenetrable backcast reaches where they would have somehow worked out that they were safe! So I had work to do, experience to garner and ready little wild trout to catch. Maybe not the glass-cased salmon of a lifetime (I couldn't afford the stuffing and mounting, let alone the fishing rental), but not a bad perspective after all? I set off with happy tread, all be it uphill, with step and spirit as buoyant as the moss and peat underfoot. And if nothing else, driving home from the hills towards Oslo was a special treat. As I rounded the crest and turned down, the placid waters of the fjord came into view, dotted with tree clad islands, looking peaceful and calm in the setting sun, a perfect backdrop to a gentle, enjoyable day.

I strode on, and as I rounded the corner to my lunch rock, the whole scenario took an even better, unexpected turn as a lovely pair rose up before me. Now I had said that the lake seemed only to contain perch, and, no, these were not trout, but they lay within easy casting range and were as fine a catch as you could hope for. Two lovely blonde Norwegians, taking in the morning sun, topless and free. As English as an Iron Blue, I didn't know where to look, (okay, let's be honest, of course I did but was far too embarrassed to leer in amazement), so, staring stolidly at my feet I trudged by, wondering just what other surprises lay in wait for me in this mystery land of beauties amidst the Norwegian spruce.

CHAPTER 18

Lies and Female Lingerie

The trout in yonder wimpling burn
That glides, a silver dart,
And safe beneath the shady thorn
Defies the angler's art.
My life was ance that careless stream
That wanton trout was I;
But love, wi' unrelenting beam,
Has scorched my fountain's dry'
Robert Burns 'Now Spring has Clad the Grove in Green' 1759-1796

Fishermen are notorious fibbers: lies, damned lies and fishermen you might say. Just as the American footballer has almost inhumanly broad shoulders, so the angler has an extra long bicep thrown in, just so that he can stretch out the arms into that expansive one-that-got-away measurement. It's the same as Pavarotti after the high C at the end of the sleepless aria 'Nessun Dorma', arms out wide, beaming grin – how could you possibly not believe? Like the best charlatans, fishers are perennially economical with the truth, whether they are boasting of the size and number of their catch, or divulging the exact location of a secret hotspot. One gillie told me that he sent one particularly obnoxious guest off to the fastest, deepest run on the beat, where the wading was awful and the fishing even worse. Naturally he enthused to the rod that this was the one and only lie for the day (true – but he meant lie in the sense of a salmon resting-place of course!).

I well remember the one time that I was fool enough to be honest about a 'hot' fishing spot. I have already regaled the story of the fish farmed trout loch in the Hebrides that bred a few unusually large fish. On releasing the name, the next morning was truly combat fishing, wall to wall with KeHes, Black Pennels and Invictas. It was worse than Alaska on a bad day when the silvers are running. As my favourite spot was already tenanted, I decided, in an unusual flush of altruism, to pass on the fact that just behind the rock out there lurked a two pounder. Yes, just there. This was purely due to the fact that I had fluked three fine fish the day before, and a beautiful three pounder on the Monday, so the two day week was, up until then, one where the fish had been as overgenerous and wild as the wind. I was simply basking in reflected glory, and an already healthy freezer compartment. Also, just possibly, I quite enjoyed lecturing the poor assembled host, (who had not been so fortunate), on how to do it... What was that about pride coming before a fall?

The man in situ was a charming retiree, and it was to be his last visit to the Western Isles before his ageing limbs gave up the unequal struggle against the knee deep heather, foot sucking peat bog and jumble of rocks. I wished him well. His first cast was met with a slurp and a thump, his rod top jerking up and down like some teenage headbanger. Here the real fun started – and not just in the water. You know what it is like – you are safely ensconced on the bank, quite comfortable thank you, watching a fisher grapple with a large beast and, and as he gets more and more excited, he makes more and more of a hash of it. What do you do? Sit back with malicious, mean grin, or try to help and run the risk of being an unwelcome, know it all interference? Or, God forbid, do you chance the ultimate recrimination – being the cause of a lost fish? Let's face it, I have been on the other side often enough! In this event, there was no issue. The angler was in complete control, yelling out in an ever higher pitched, excitable voice, that it was only the take that mattered, and that he didn't mind at all if the fish came off. Like Hell he didn't! It was his largest trout in years, and he would have probably shot me to get it. When his collapsible, folding net did just that – neatly netting the fish and then generously depositing it back into the loch, I didn't know whether to laugh or cry, to stare nonchalantly in the opposite direction and pretend I hadn't noticed, or to wade in with a large, comforting net. It weighed two and a half pounds, and we all breathed a huge sigh of relief.

Anyway, I am about to be honest again, and yes, my motives are as pure as the driven snow. I am about to release the exact location of 'That Place'. Willing readers, you should be honoured. It is a loch, of limestone, on the North Atlantic coast of Scotland. Whoever named the place either had a vivid sense of humour, or had maybe tried to extricate the local finny inhabitants. The exact location is Durness, (try adding an extra O after the D, it becomes so much more descriptive and poetic...), and the finger of rock and limestone that curls out towards Iceland is called Cape Wrath. I rest my case.

Others call it Loch Caladail, but to Bruce and I it is 'That Place', a sort of Hibernian curse, only to be mentioned with Holy Water and crossing of the chest. Otherwise you might be doomed to fish there, day after day, wave after wave, long, bleak, row back to the boat-mooring bay after grim, fish-less day. Of course, as you have already read, it is probably my favourite loch. I mean that – anywhere. But just to help those who suffer from similarly obsessive or delusionary behaviour, let me describe my descent into the pellucid, green water embrace of this most fickle and heart breaking of lochs. Lie back on that comfortable green couch, and let me begin.

My first visit was back in 1992, and I really was a complete beginner at traditional Scottish loch fishing, stroking a team of three small, gaudy and straggly flies through the waves. I struggled to keep in tight line touch with the flies in case a fish should take, whilst not dragging them unnaturally off or through the surface into the air – brown trout are not flying fish. Of course all of this was conducted whilst bouncing aloft the waves in a Highland 'breeze'. The sort of gentle Arctic zephyr my grandfather would have termed 'bracing'. It is so easy to watch a master of the art merely roll the flies out, lazily raise the rod tip and somehow hold them for ever in the wave tops, like some emerging or escaping creatures restrained by the surface tension. It all looks so simple, until you try. If all this were not enough, I had the beady eye of Bruce Sandison watching over me, kindly acting as expert guide, boatman, raconteur and waiting netsmen. And wait he did! Seldom have I strained so hard to keep the line, all ten yards of it, and flies under control.

You can wince visibly, but in silence, whilst pulling gently at an oar to keep the boat on the perfect drift and well placed for the fishers' comfort. I began to realise this. Usually it was when a small, to me indiscernible, hump, or splash rose up in the water in the vicinity of my flies. Perhaps just a subaqeous glimpse of light, a tiny flash of turning flank. Bruce would quietly ask if I had felt the fish. Felt it? Half the time I had not even realised that a fish was there at all. It was a tough immersion into the rigours of limestone loch fishing. Still, someone up there was being kind, and the rite of passage was relatively short. Half way through the morning, just under the sheer cliff face at the top end of the loch, a fish of just over the pound, (small for Caladail – probably young and greedy), slurped up and grabbed my KeHe. It stuck fast, and that Orcadian fly immediately gained a permanent place in my fly box annals of history and on the top dropper of any cast.

That was all for the day. The wind blew pretty softly from the northeast, but it was cold and unfriendly, rapidly cooling the water surface, and a dazzling sun did not help. Funnily enough, as an initiation, it was a pretty user-friendly day, the fish rising to the odd natural fly and also to mine – though I think they really were rising 'short'. This is usually a feeble excuse, but sometimes it does seem to happen – that the fish will swirl at the flies without actually touching them. You can use smaller or larger flies, fish faster or slower, change the angle of drift, in fact do whatever you like, until you eventually have to admit sullen defeat and give up. Why or how, I don't know – if I did, I guess I'd have to write a book about it!

A year later I returned to the loch, keen after my limited success to score again. We fished twice, and on both days a gusting, freshening north westerly had us blown off by lunchtime. The wind and waves scurried down the loch as if in a hurry to dislodge the island and hurl it onto the bank, whipping up white spume and showering the lee shore with what looked like shaving foam. It was hopeless, and we could only cower behind the dyke, in relative shelter, and listen to the wind howl and the rain thump down on our rainproof jacket hoods, a thundering percussion with woodwind accompaniment. Yet just down there you knew there were beautiful wild trout, with delicate apricot fins, backs of glistening avocado green, black spots and silver flanks. They have been there since the last Ice Age. In fact, it is quite interesting to see how the fish from the four lochs, all within a mile of each other – have evolved differently since the glaciers carved and gouged out the lochs and left the trout marooned in each one, all those ions ago. Fortunately, the little stocking that does happen from time to time is strictly controlled – the fry taken from native fish from each loch being reared separately. The best I have ever seen caught on Caladail was a mighty four and a half pounds, and on Lanlish was over six. (You might note that the Microsoft spell-check comes up with 'Languish' at this point. Maybe Bill Gates really is omniscient after all!).

The lucky catchers of both these lovely prizes were beginners. We have all sneered at beginner's luck, (when we are the expert), or, (when we are the tyro), rather self-consciously claimed it as the obvious and only reason, or excuse, for our undeserved success. But I wonder if there is not more behind it. Why do beginners, and women, catch so many and such large fish? Learned scientific professors and expert, famed fishermen have written semi- technical literature stating that it is the pheromone effect that is behind the fact that the female sex that has caught all the largest salmon in the UK. It is remarkable what scientists can find research grants to subsidise and what publishers will print! In fact, though I cannot comment on the scientific basis of the pheromone attraction, I believe that the biggest fish of the lot, Georgina Ballantyne's off the Tay, was taken on a natural bait that was surely put up and fished by her father off his rod. When one reads the evidence, it is stated that a male hand dipped into a fish pass or ladder will stop the fish swimming up it, whereas a female hand seems to encourage them. This does not quite tally with the fact that I am sure that it was her father who handled and baited the rod. Can a salmon in the mighty autumnal waters of the Tay really scent a female pheromone from an eighteen-year-old girl floating up above in a boat with her father? When I sea trout fish at night on the Teign, I wade out until I am a mere ten yards away from the fish, and stand heron-still. If and when I catch a fish, and decide to keep it, it is dispatched on the spot, put in my fish bag and my hands rinsed off right there in the river – literally just in front of the fish's noses. It is surprising how often another fish will take on the very next cast in from same lie.

Still, if I can't help somewhat cynically debunking the pheromone theory as mere book-selling sensationalism, (and nothing wrong with that), I do think that women, and beginners, share some 'luck' in common which does have a logical rationale behind it. Look at the average male salmon fisher. What does he pride himself upon? His ability to wade chest deep, (without life jacket), in roaring waters without being washed away and his facility to cast further than anyone else. Such is the macho ego. But how can you really control the drift and presentation of a fly thirty yards away? Hooking a fish becomes even more haphazard. Besides, how many fish actually lie under the far bank? If I had a salmon for every time I have seen a fisher either wade through the lies or land his line heavily over them, (rather than his fly or leader), I would have an endless freezer full.

When the fish do not oblige, the male expert is quick to find a host of excuses and to head back, rapidly, to the bar to drown the unfairness of it all. The beginner, or female rod on the other hand has no such crutches, but persists on, with a thoughtful, delicate approach. They are not hidebound by received conventional wisdom and dogma, nor spurred on by a thoughtless desire simply to wade and cast the furthest. Is it any wonder that women are so often such skilled practitioners of what is more of a thinking art form than a mechanical bravado test?

Of course, that still doesn't explain why those damned beginners caught those fabulous Durness trout and not me. There is no justice. Some men have been known to take pieces of ladies underwear with them when fishing, to add the magical pheromone allure to the fly, (well, at least that is what they say). Such seeming perversion certainly raises eyebrows if not fish. But then, perhaps I am not the best man to talk. At about the same time, I could be found, of an evening, giving fly casting lessons in the Bois de Vincennes, just on the outskirts of Paris. This might seem pretty mundane, and so it seemed to me. Being part English, I little realised that I was rapidly falling for my willing trainee, nor that her sudden desire to learn to cast a fly and go fishing had any ulterior motive. I naturally just presumed that I had aroused her sensible interest in the noble art. The locals did look a bit bemused, sauntering across the parkland with dinnertime baguette under their arms, to find a couple trying to catch fish in the middle of a grassy field in the woods. Doubtless they just presumed this to be another example of the eccentricity frequently exhibited across the other side of the Channel. I suspect that they were even more taken aback when they noticed that the man was tying up the woman, in full view, with a rod bag. She just wouldn't keep that shoulder in and use the wrist, so I promptly tied her arm to her side. For once, just once, perhaps the locals thought the 'roast beefs' were not so staid after all.

But enough of this French diversion, the olives were still hatching and the trout not rising way up north in That Place. Since that week spent at Durness, and that lucky nocturnal catch described earlier, I have returned for the odd day here and there, capped by that marvellous triumph with the turning flee and four peachy fish in the boat. Their pristine beauty was nicely captured on film, (without ridiculous, grinning captor I am pleased to say), and appeared in various magazines. That was undoubtedly a mistake – one self satisfied slap on the back too many, and I have struggled ever since. I suppose that is the reason for my obsession with this most unpredictable and difficult of lochs. I am still striving for that four pounder. It is a place that demands thought, plotting and execution and that, just sometimes, hands out handsome rewards that make all those long, miserable fish-less days fade in the memory.

The last day was typical. As we arrived, I eagerly peered out of the car window to judge the wind and wave. It looked, from up on the road, pretty benign, a gentle westerly blowing sedate, steady ripples across. Down at the loch side it looked a little less inviting, but still hopeful. One thing that I am certain of is that this loch produces far more fish in warm sunny weather, and that cold, gusting winds send the fish well down to their gluttonous bottom diet of shrimp and fry. You read that west and south winds are supposed to be good, though as this blew straight off three thousand miles of Atlantic, it carried an icy edge, all be it May. There is usually a cocky fish, of size, that rises just beyond the boat-mooring bay just as you tackle up. Usually I cannot resist – as soon as the rod is up, I hurry, crouching, to the waterside and rapidly extend line out to the rise. Unfortunately I also forget in my haste to look behind me, and the high grass and mottled limestone white-grey rocks have claimed many a new leader. This, first cast of the day, before even getting afloat and with a large fish guzzling away just ten yards in front of you, is a lousy start! The fish also tends to welcome you home – this time just as you have pulled the boat up the bank and taken down the rod.

Anyway, this time, not a nose appeared, as Skues so beautifully put it, not even an underwater wink. We pushed off, and once past the headland into mid loch, the full force of the weather was felt. Time to zip up, batten down and sweater up. As always, regardless of the weather, delicate, gossamer winged yellow-green olives were hatching sporadically, as bright as the lime green grass around us. But there was not a sign of a rise, not a dimple in sight, except for the odd diving dabchick that left a surface swirl that could be mistaken for a large trout if you tried hard enough, or if your glasses lenses were too blurred with the rain. By lunch, still nothing, and serious rain had joined the meteorological outlook. But Caladail always produces something out of the ordinary, every visit – another of its attractions. Whilst idly chewing on a damp sandwich we noticed that the raucous black headed gulls and sleek, elegant arctic terns were going absolutely mad in mid loch. At this time of year the island is literally covered in nesting birds – it is the embodiment of the word cacophony, the noise is incredible. It is also a miniature rock garden, a small glimpse of what Scotland must have looked like before it was over-run by omnivorous deer and sheep. There are bushes, bonsai-like windblown trees and wild flowers in a riot in primary colours – free from the marauding grazers and beautifully unkempt.

Meanwhile, its temporary residents were swooping, dipping and circling in an orgy of feeding the like of which I had only seen with the pelicans in Los Roques. It was time to abandon lunch and set afloat. Of course – and this is dead true – having fished all morning with not a fish in sight or a single rise to a hatching olive, I had adopted cunning pre-plan number two and changed my line to a fast sinker. As I was only up for the weekend I had brought just my one travel rod, so there I was drifting through a swirling cloud of screeching gulls and surface hatching olives with a fast sink line. By the time I had changed back, and put on all manner of dry flies and emergers, the excitement was fading and we had seen all of four rises. One was ten yards dead ahead of me, Bruce yelling at me in nervous anticipating excitement to whip a fly over – difficult when it is twenty yards away and the whole line sunk ten feet down! I stripped line in like a wailing dervish, lifted up to cast, but we had already drifted over the fish.

That, put simply, was that. The rain, just to hammer the point home, worsened and began to seep through everything. Clothes, damp and clammy, began to stick to the skin. Glasses became so rain spotted that I could only squint through in a blur. The westerly droned on and knuckles chafed as fingers turned red. It was time to admit defeat, to renounce all that closed season of hope and return to a warm car with heater blaring! We sat and steamed and wondered why.

As we slowly thawed out and drove home, I peered out of the fugged up car windows at the scenery, the almost Caribbean white sands of the little beach coves, the lush green limestone grass and the rugged brown heather, all aflame with lurid yellow gorse cascading down the slopes. We were so glad to be in the shelter and warmth, and away from that frigid, unwelcoming loch where the fish were so dour. It had, truth be told, been a pretty uncompromising day – a euphemism for miserable. All my long thought out plans, new fly patterns, known drifts, varied depths and general intellectual musings had, once again, failed to outwit that little scaly beast with so small a brain. I was left humbled, cold, disappointed and slightly irate.

It is only a forty-minute drive from Durness back to Tongue where we were staying. We rounded past the ugly fish cages in the once beautiful Loch Eribol, where the local sea trout lochs are now deserted, and as we crossed the Kyle a golden eagle was soaring above the house. Already I was, yet again, pondering just how to catch the next trout, and, yes, looking forward with growing impatience to returning to That Place. Who knows, maybe next time, I'll just sneak in some of that enticing French lingerie into the fish bag…

CHAPTER 19

High and Dry – Expertise on the Rocks

"There is a lot of amiable fantasy written about trout fishing, but the truth is that few men know much if anything about the habits of trout and little about the manner of taking them...I have fished for trout since I was a boy and I admit I still know little or nothing about them. Indeed this is one of the special fascinations of pursuing them. Perhaps it is also the beginning of trout wisdom.'
John D. Voelker (aka Robert Traver) 'Trout Madness'

There is nothing worse than know-it-alls. Well, that is unless they are actually right. The trouble with the published word is that it seems to convey upon the author a mantle of superior knowledge, a spurious authority. After all, don't you generally believe what you read in books, (this one excepted, of course)? The very fact of having had something appear in print suggests that you know what you are writing about. This is how politicians survive. Now I might add quickly that in my regard this is not at all the case – I fully admit to more literary than angling competence. I hope I am better at sculpting a phrase than turning over a leader...

When I first started to write, I was just thrilled to see my name in print. I am sure that the circulation of 'Trout and Salmon' magazine must have doubled that month as every member of the family was cajoled, encouraged or plain bullied into buying a copy. Friends and relatives had coffee tables loaded down with issues casually displayed, open at the appropriate page. It was a harmless ego boost, but what do they say that pride comes before?

While basking in my newly found literary, expert fisher status, the phone rang. The caller had recognised a photo in my article. It was of his local sea trout river, the Teign, and he had spent many frustrating hours failing to extricate its wily inhabitants from it. I had just written chapter and verse on how it should be done. As I was thus an obvious, if self-professed, guru on the subject, would I be willing to pop down to one of the better, private beats and show him how to do it all at his expense? Now this came as somewhat of a shock, as the article was based more on common sense than any special intuition into how best to seduce recalcitrant fish. But my bluff was called, and as I was about to be down in Devon anyway, what could I do but rise to the occasion?

A week later, I drove off up the valley road in the growing darkness, the broad afternoon sunlight dropping and softening into the rustling shadows. To the local pub, which was mistake number one. If ever you plan to meet a complete stranger, a pub car park is logistically as good a place as any, but not if you then intend to plan your campaign in the beer garden. The local brew is quite strong, and as I was rather new and nervous at this game, and wishing to be sociable, I returned the rounds and four pints later we headed off to the river. As I write this, Paris is awash with drunken football fans, (it being the World Cup), and I am sure that to them four pints is a mere warm up before getting serious. But they don't have to wade out in the pitch blackness on an unknown stretch of river and demonstrate how to catch fish.

Mistake number two was to arrive in total darkness, a pint too late in both senses. No chance to look over the beat, work out where the fish might be and, more important, where those innocuous looking trees were that at night would suddenly branch out into huge, octopus-like fly-catchers. It is a little known fact that trees grow at night. And as things always come in threes, my final error was to be over-confident and fish a dropper, tying on two flies instead of playing safe with just the one.

So I waded in, a little gingerly, bleary and hesitant as my expectant host waited for my pearls of wisdom to be cast upon the darkening waters. In fact it was not so tough. The pool was a typical one, a deep, slow-flowing stretch boarded by trees, and the presence of fish was amply demonstrated by the continual jumps of hefty specimens. The almost viscous surface of the oily waters was flung into an effusion of spray and whirring fins as sea trout after sea trout launched into the air. The cast was an easy one, and the fish were there, all I had to do was put the art into practise. The odd bat flitted by on soundless wings with that rapid, darting flight, an owl hooted up in the valley and I settled down to serious business.

It was textbook stuff, just as the article had said. In such slow reaches, a slimly tied fly with a mobile marabou wing was just the ticket, cast across under the trees and retrieved slowly back. I had been expounding on the fact that the usual sea trout tackle as suggested by eminent sages was wholly inappropriate, the ten and a half foot rods and heavy lines being better suited to salmon. Here a light outfit was better able to keep the fly alive in the slack water, necessitating lots of movement and some false casting. Just to prove the point, a fish wrenched at the fly and the reel blurted into a screeching spin, a ringing endorsement of my status as a true professional. I was beginning to enjoy myself! For about fifteen seconds that was, until all went horribly limp and a thudding silence yelled out the question as to what had gone wrong. The cast had parted at the dropper knot, leaving the poor fish trailing both cast and fly, and my beery self-importance somewhat tarnished. Being broken is shameful, but leaving a fish so handicapped due to a badly tied knot is really a disgrace. I never fish after the pub nowadays, and always tie my flies in the bright, sober light of pre-cocktail daytime.

I muttered some feeble excuse and my willing tutee seemed suitably impressed that the theory and fly really did work, even if the execution left a lot to be desired. And so we fished on, but as usual the midnight curtain dropped to close the first act and usher in a long, silent interval. The fish had gone down, the water now slipping by uninterrupted, energy, hope and enthusiasm all sinking with them down to the gloomy depths. I tried everything, switching to my favourite wake lure, a silver-bodied hook with a crude fish-shaped body/wing of ethafoam on top, that carves a nice furrow across the surface. On some nights it will bring up fish from the bottom when all else fails and can be the most exciting form of night fishing, fish attacking the lure like a magnified dry fly. If the moon is out you can see the wake snaking across the river until it explodes in a splash of silver scales and flying water. But not tonight. Not a fin stirred, everything except me resting in peaceful somnolence.

I was feeling pretty weary, but realising that my kindly host expected his money's worth, i.e. a whole night of action, I wondered what to do to stay awake and, hopefully, entice a fish to take. I headed down to the deep hole above the weir, an obvious holding lie where I presumed the fish would be quietly relaxing after their earlier frolics. I could visualise their serried ranks, nose to tail, a small shoal of silver beauty hanging just above the pebble-strewn river bed, tails waving gently in the easy stream. My only hope was to make eyeball-level contact, as they were not going to rise up for a floating fly at this late stage. Much as I hate fishing large tandem lures on sunk lines, it did seem to be the only viable option, and I had to come up with something.

The trouble with sinking to their level is that if you overdo it by a few inches you end up stuck fast into the rocky shelves above which the fish lie, and playing a riverbed at two in the morning is, frankly, pretty pointless. Fortunately darkness offers a perfect screen to shroud such incompetence. Meanwhile the night drew on, all of nature slipping back into dreamy apathy until the eastern sky began to change to a monochromatic greyness. The riverbank and tress looked out of the mist, a smoky veil wafting off the river as dawn crept into the valley. It was if the very earth was steaming, a cloud rising up and enveloping the emerging features of the landscape. Birds chorused the start of a new day, but it was a cold, damp grey awakening, and the fish did not rise up to join them.

When the air temperature drops well below the water, and thick mist rolls off the silent stream, it is time to pack up and go home, but we were not finished yet, so I strolled off downstream where the main river cascaded over a mini weir. It formed a miniature waterfall, the water coursing in and out of a jumble of rocks that bordered it. As I reached the river below, by which time I was out of sight of my colleague who was still determinedly flogging away, something caught my eye. It was just an odd disturbance of water coming from the rocks beside the fall. The water should have been just tumbling down, but in the misty gloaming I could just discern something waving at me. I hadn't even bothered to bring a rod with me as I thought it so hopeless, but I hurried over to find a sea trout that had miscued its jump over the weir and landed, nose first, in the rocks, firmly wedged. As a fish has no reverse gear, and its tail was in thin air, there it stuck, but with some macabre sense of humour there was enough water running past its snout for it to breathe and stay alive. I hastily freed the errant victim into the river above. As I did so, a much larger tail appeared just above. Now this tale, if you'll excuse the pun, is quite true, and I have stood by a much larger weir downstream in December and had a salmon land at my feet, high and dry on the concrete bank.

Anyway, I grabbed this tail, pulled hard and a healthy grilse came out kicking and wriggling rather ungratefully. I strode up over the weir and released the fish, thinking that this was indeed a strange morning, but happy to be able to help one of these valiant creatures on its epic, obstacle-ridden spawning journey upstream. It is not often that my best fish of the week comes by hand!

A minute later my host came running up, rather breathless and wide-eyed. What on earth had happened, had I just put back a salmon? And where was my rod? Nonchalantly, with the knowing look of the expert, I nodded an affirmative, adding casually that a fine sea trout had just preceded it. You know, the morning rise is often as good as that first hour of darkness, of course you need to change to the appropriate fly and line density, with the proper angle of presentation, but basically it's pretty obvious. The grilse was a fresh fish, but a bit small, and I like to do my bit for stock preservation. Dionysian status restored, I started to stroll off, but honesty got the better of me, and I admitted the truth, pointing out to my incredulous amateur the secret fish lie amidst the rocks.

CHAPTER 20

Dreams Turn to Nightmares

'Also, you must not be too greedy in catching your said game as taking too much at one time...which could easily be the occasion of destroying your own sport and other men's also.'

Dame Juliana Berners 'The Treatyse on Fysshynge with an Angle' circa 1496

Daydreams: I wonder just how many pleasant hours I have whiled away musing upon large fish, spectacular scenery and epic struggles – and how many hours of office time have been happily spent escaping from the stressful drudgery of emails, faxes and corporate politics. Of course my boss might not quite see this as returning maximum shareholder value, but who cares, you need some measure of equilibrium to restore sanity from time to time!

As a teenager, sitting in a small bedroom thirty miles west of London, with the nearest salmonid a good hundred miles away, dreams were largely as good as it got. The real thing was unattainable – distant, expensive and far too complicated. I could only read, voraciously, every book on the subject, gaze in envy at the photographs of Norwegian leviathans or Scottish peaks, and then return back to school and swoop fly patterns for Latin syntax and irregular conjugations. Most books, naturally, deal with the so-called great and good, the famous four rivers of the Scottish East Coast, where catches were enough to hook the reader's attention both in terms of quality and quantity. Of course this makes arresting literature, but is rather a vicarious pleasure – who, after all, gets to fish the top beats of Tay, Tweed, Spey and Dee in prime time? Besides which, as a beginner, I had neither chestwaders nor double handed rod, and even if I had, I wouldn't have known what to do with them.

I therefore also searched out books on more humble fare, and especially on the sea trout, the one fish that I did manage to bump into on occasion, each summer down in Devon. If there was one river that stood out, it was the Border Esk. Not only was it supposed to be one of the finest rivers to fish, it was also imbued with ages of bloody history, acting as the border between England and Scotland, often crossed by marauding armies and pillaging clan raiders. Indeed, the most famed pool of all, the Willow Pool, has the border running straight down the middle of it. The story goes that the ever religious Scots, obedient Presbyterians to a soul, would bc praying fervently away in the local Kirk of a Sunday, as fishing for migratory fish is banned north of the border on the day of God. Meanwhile, the heretic Sassenachs would, on their southern side of the border/river, be merrily casting away. Incensed as they were, (more, I suspect by their inability to fish a good rise than by any more pious thoughts), the Scots would line up on the north bank and hurl stones into the river and at their English counterparts, where no such Sunday fishing ban applies.

A few years later, I was scanning the classified ads in a fishing magazine with a view to taking an impromptu week's fishing. It was August, I was working in the City, and needed to escape the regimented ranks of grey buildings and even more grey people. An old coaching inn caught my eye, again a throwback to the distant past, when the only way to travel north was a long, bumpy coach journey, with regular stops to dust off the aching passengers and refuel or change the horsepower. I had images of low ceilings, gnarled, darkened old wooden beams, the creaking of coach springs and the thud of hooves. Even more to the point, this particular coaching inn was in Canonbie, right next to the Association water of the Border Esk. As I chewed on a city sandwich, and glanced over the tedious sea of computers, insurance wordings and policy files, that old teenage dream took over. It was all too easy, a short phone call and I was connected to that far off world of sparkling waters and nightly epics.

Why is it that so many hotels that feature, prominently, fly fishing as one of their principal attractions, have no-one on the staff that has a clue about the actual river or loch that they lease? My call was transferred to the bar, where a lunching angler was asked over to give me an up to date report. He excitedly mentioned that the fishing was just great, and that they had caught over forty sea trout that week. Overeager to hear what I wanted, and not enquiring further, I hastily booked for the next week and hurried home that night to prepare for the coming assault. I rushed to the bookshelves and read every page I had on the Esk, rummaging through fly boxes to check that every conceivable pattern was there, and fiddling over the vice to create a few more. At long last, a sea trout fisher's idle dream was to become reality, as all those pictures and words merged into the sinuous curve of an arched rod, the dramatic parabola of a leaping fish, the rattling note of a straining reel. I was going to fish the Border Esk.

The drive north is long and tedious, a succession of traffic jams, spaghetti junctions, the industrial wastelands of the Midlands, as ugly and flat as the local accent, and an endless, exhaust-fuming procession of trucks. One long series of leapfrogging overtaking manoeuvres, cassette after cassette on the car stereo competing with the droning whine of car engines. Only when the Lake District appears does the monotony lift, the dull colours of manmade construction, cement and tar giving way to the rolling greens and ochres of the fells, land of poetry, flowers, lake-deep char and, of course, babbling sea trout streams heading seawards from the hill tarns. Hope, enthusiasm and excitement all rise as one nears the border and the south fades into a five hour long, distant memory.

Nor was I disappointed. Eskdale was unlike any river valley I had fished, the banks high, steep and heavily forested, plunging down to a broad, fast flowing river of rocks, runs and long, shadowy glides. In the nocturnal mind's eye it all looked distinctly fishy. As I drove upriver, winding my way up the glen, scattering rabbits, pheasant and buzzard as I climbed steadily uphill, the water became faster, at Langholm crashing under the road bridge through a rock carved gorge and scoring a deep, deep pot hole out below. There is said to be a car at the bottom of the pool, resting like a mysterious shipwreck. It is invisible from the surface, a dark, rusting lie for the silver shoals of sea trout and salmon that pause on their surging, leaping run upstream, pulled by the magnetic force of nature and the spawning redds. A discarded adder skin lay on the road side, making me a little more wary as I hurried through the bracken in an eager, excited rush to see the river, to study the pools and wait, impatiently for nightfall, for the river to quieten down to a murmuring dusk, the placid, sliding waters erupting into the heart thumping beat of a leaping fish.

There is nothing more frustrating than the long summer days of the north – if you are a sea trout fisher that is. I wandered up and down the high bank of Glenfirra, a pool that was straight out of the textbook, really a fisher's dream, a long, steady glide across the whole river, interspersed with rocks and pots. All I needed was binoculars, as the best viewpoint was high up amidst the trees, peering down into the waters, trying to beat the refraction into seeing the shadowy shapes below, the flickering tails that slowly emerge from the riverbed to disclose the presence of well-camouflaged fish. To be honest, for such fine water, there were precious few to be seen, the odd little pocket here and there, spread out and solitary, but I was still expectant.

Thus, a few, long hours later, I turned the car into a darkening lay by, climbed over the roadside barrier and headed through the trees, the air full of the sound of rustling leaves and the gurgling, rushing waters below. I caught my breath as I stood, feet just in the water, waiting for the first bat to flit by, and the crashing jump of a sea trout to herald the start of serious proceedings. As I slipped out into the river, ready to make my first cast, the tension was palpable – surely one of the most delicious moments of fishing. When all that preparation and expectation is converted into the brink of reality, where hope merges into action, where the line slips between the fingers, pulling gently with the water current, the mind already imagining a more savage tug as the line pulls tight into a fish cavorting acrobatically downstream.

Perhaps I should leave it there, at the daydream stage, as the harsh reality was more nightmarish. I suppose it was a fine lesson in two things – the inadvisability of wading at night in an unknown, fast-flowing river and the absolute necessity for a wading stick. The Esk, here, flows rapidly over long, flat slices of rock, smoothed and polished over the ages into a mid-river ice rink. An unfamiliar river at night, deep in the woods, is always a little unnerving, the owls hooting in a horror movie chorus, strange rustles and inexplicable noises behind you. But trying to balance on slippery shelves of rock whilst struggling to manipulate a long line across a fast dragging stream, well, this adds an extra dimension to the discomfort. I had to concentrate more on staying upright than on the delicate business at the other end of the line, swinging a fly around over those fish filled pots and dips under the far bank, a luring probe in the darkness. It was ghastly! I slipped and slithered, arms out wide, waving to maintain my balance, frightened of the next step in the dark. The waters swirled around me, pushing on my waders, the rubber soles slipping across the rock, an over-hurried cast hurled into the distant oblivion and left to fish itself as I struggled to keep on my feet. Meanwhile, the odd fish would slosh on the surface, just to increase the frustration and magnify my sense of the unattainable.

Eventually I retreated, humbled but grateful to be out, dry and safe on terra firma, determined to practice a wading route in daylight the next day after I had been shopping for a wading stick first thing the next morning. It is gratifying how quickly you can look on the bright side and plan great things for the morrow, with the utter relief of pinecones and earth beneath your feet. But worse was to come. I did indeed drive off to Penrith the next morning and purchase a sturdy, weighted wading stick. Incidentally, it eventually proved to be the long delayed, overdue silver cloud to the Eskdale cumulo-nimbus, when it enabled me to wade out to that precarious rock on the Don nine months later. But on the Esk for which it was bought, it was never used. The elements, as so often, conspired against my most cunning fish-catching machinations.

The pitter patter of rain drops from the eves of the hotel, and from the million leaves overhanging the river, tiny droplets pinging into the rapidly colouring stream, soon became more of an orchestral crescendo as torrential rain scudded across the valley and battered against the window panes. As the clouds darkened and belched out their soaking contents, the river suddenly changed into a seething froth of milk chocolate, surging up amidst the tree roots, clambering up the trunks, a thick, unfishable torrent. This was not the six inch, black-brown summer spate of a Devon moorland stream, peaty-dark but still fishable with spinning rod and clearing in a couple of days to a liquid amber. No, this was a veritable sea of hideous cocoa, submerging the lovely fly streams and runs of Glenfirra, all hope of night fly fishing gone for the week as the river rose a few feet overnight. I trudged up and down the banks, my boots squelching into the sodden turf, the air bedevilled with the incessant pounding of rain on car roof and jacket, the trees like mini waterfalls of water. It was a sorry and frustrating sight, the end of my little idyll.

But the scenario soon took on nightmare proportions. By midweek, the river was settling down, but still way up the banks and coloured, and I was aimlessly wandering along when I noticed hunched figures perched along the bank. They were stationary, but wielding long double handed salmon rods.

At first I thought they must be spinning – but why with a fly rod? Anyway, the water was obviously far too mucky for either. As I approached, I noticed that some had what looked like a small sock slung around their neck on a string. I was bemused and intrigued. This was obviously some arcane local technique. Well, I guess, after a fashion, it was. Suddenly there was a movement, one of the heron-like rods sprang up, twelve feet of salmon rod lifting up and swinging over onto the bank. A small sea trout followed it, dangling on the line, unceremoniously heaved out of its element and dumped on the ground behind the fisher before being bashed on the head and killed.

It was disgusting. They were fishing a bunch of worms, (hence the sock – a bait receptacle), dangling them in the little calm patches of water by the undercut banks where the fish were taking shelter from the flood. When a sea trout was hooked it had no chance, it was simply hauled out onto the bank and slaughtered, a new worm impaled and the process repeated. As I later learned, this was the source of the forty fish a week, and indeed the majority of catches. Fly fishing at night takes a certain amount of skill and determination, just the very fact of it being in darkness at antisocial (pub) hours rendering it difficult and unpopular to all but the dedicated aficionado. Drowning a bunch of worms on a telegraph pole a yard out from the bank in a raging spate when the fish are running, is child's play. Now, I am not a fly snob at all, indeed on slack, slow flowing, tree-overhung rivers like the Teign, a fly is pretty useless for salmon, and I greatly enjoy the challenge of trying to flick a small mepps spinner in low water under the trees and over the lies. The cast must be accurate first time, and the lie known – it may be the size of a bath tub, that's all, and you have just one cast at it, and may have to wade several hundred yards to find the next one. It is a delicate art, every bit as testing and as fun as the fly, and leaving an array of gaudy spinners twirling in the breeze in the bushes and trees after an over enthusiastic cast. I have never fished the true upstream worm, but believe that that too is a technique that needs feel, accuracy and skill. But this bastardised form of worming is totally without merit, an ugly, crude way to kill large numbers of fish, (and worms), and a terrible waste of what are now such precious, threatened stocks of the few wild sea trout that sill remain. It should be banned immediately, and the fish given a chance, when nature rains, to ascend the river in peace.

CHAPTER 21

Twilight of the Gods

'I pick up the routine of the day, wind in the line, examine the fly and walk slowly off into the blue, conscious only that something has stopped inside and that the wheels of articulate emotion have ceased working. Tragedy is supposed to stun, and that is my experience.'
H. Plunket Greene 'Where the Bright Waters Meet' 1924

Klapperflojt – oh, the evocative power of one word, the ability of a few unpronounceable syllables to inflict painful memories. Of course to you it is probably just one Icelandic consonant too many, so perhaps we should back upstream a couple of beats to The Church Pool. Naturally that is the English translation, but to save my computer's spell check from overload (and the reader), perhaps we will stay at that. The pool is, as you will have divined, named after a church that watches over it, a small, pointy roofed flash of red colour amidst a broad, bleak greensward plane that stretches between the wide mountain ridge walls of the Borganes Fjord. It also marks the start of a remarkable trio of short, one rod beats, and fishing that really does take on a quasi-religious overtone, one of hushed reverence and almost ecstatic expectation.

The Church Pool used to be the most prolific, but the sands have shifted and perhaps the incense these days burns a little less. In 1997, the shoals of salmon, like an armour-clad medieval army, pitched their base camp in the beat below, Armortakvorn. As you stride purposefully across the shingle, an almost perfect pool appears, one that you could say had to have been designed by Him above. The water thins and chuckles over the pebbly stickles, then narrows into a discernible run, a veeing downstream wave broadening, rushing and emptying into a deep pool. It then hits a sheer rock faced hillock and doglegs left at right angles into a slow, deep run. You simply couldn't design an easier place to fish. Or, it would seem, a more accommodating place for a river-running, weary salmon to hold up.

It is difficult though to work out whether this is really paradise or purgatory, or one of Dante's infernal circles somewhere in between. I fished there for two three-hour sessions and took three gleaming white-silver, sea-liced fish to fourteen pounds each time. Heaven you might say, but I wonder. The expectation was so high that anything less than a brace was treated as a failure. To me it took the edge off it a bit; it became just a bit too predictable, too routine, a little too easy. Yes I know, chance would be a fine thing and you must gasp at my ingratitude to the piscatorial ambrosia eaters who sent me to such a divine place.

In fact it does have its Stygian side if you ignore a few basics. The fish lie fairly high up in the stream, just off the edges of the fast current – pretty obvious and classic really, any beginner's guide would point it out. But the temptation is to wade and cast too far. All you have to do is stand well back and gently flick maybe ten yards of line into midstream and swing it round across the current edge, and, thump, a live, pulsing force is attached, throbbing and tugging the rod down. It is a place where chestwaders and Spey casts are anathema. After all, on a windless day and with the nearest tree requiring a backcast of several hundred miles, who needs fancy distance casting? Impressive for the ego, but not for the fish, who understandably seem to object to having a hefty fly line dumped on top of their heads, rather reducing their enthusiasm to snatch the small fly attached thereto and swimming far away behind their tails. One unfortunate soul, an experienced hand who knew the river well, momentarily forgot that he was fishing not just casting, and caught precisely nothing on what was one of the most prolific Atlantic salmon pools in the northern ocean. His casting skill is undoubted, but was not best suited here. Meanwhile, I quietly mentioned to my host, Magne, that a further off approach and shorter cast might prove, perhaps, more useful. The Norwegians' humour, drinking capacity and sense of fun was as keen as their fishing, and they promptly returned with the requisite ration of a leash of fish, beaming happy. After all, let's be honest - it's no bad thing to help your hosts' catch statistics if you wish to be invited back the next year!

If we now drift a hundred yards downstream, you find an almost facsimile copy pool – Klapperflojt. A solitary rock pokes out of the water to mark the head of the pool, once the most famed of all on the river, but like the ecclesiastical run up above, now rather deserted except for the odd nostalgic resident. In the lodge there was the usual array of photos of grinning humans hoisting aloft a variety of dead beasts, the poor fish looking a little past their prime, (much like the fishers it has to be said). A few were of interest purely because of the generous size of the fish caught, well into the twenty pounds, unusually big for Iceland. I glanced up enviously, but thought little of it. The Gods were being munificent, but not that much!

Thus having taken my fill from Armortakvorn, the beat rota switched and I moved down apace, keeping the same small, size ten treble fly, twelve foot double handed eight weight rod and thirteen pound line. An outfit that had proved itself admirably capable of propelling a small fly into the jaws of the seemingly ever eager, adipose finned recipients. Also, I am immodestly glad to announce, of beaching them too – as I had landed an unprecedented (for me) dozen fish in a row without loss. I should have read the omens and seen that the portents were against me, like the distant grey storm clouds blowing up the fjord. Having thirty pounds of salmon already banked by mid morning, (beat switch over being at ten), I felt pretty nonchalant, content and, to be frank, clever. Once again, I should have known better. My guide, the head gillie, had waxed lyrical about the past glories of the pool, but admitted that perhaps the current prospects were rather more rose tinted than real.

I waded out beyond the rock and cast a line across the stream, enjoying the feel and sight of it swinging round below me, the little fly flickering and glistening across in an enticing arc. I looked closely at the rock formation and texture of the cliff in front of me, and at the back eddy as the water hit the wall and bounced round. The snow on the far off fjord was clearly visible in the sunshine, a soft, shining layer of reflection, and to cap it all an imperious red throated diver swam past on the stream. Its sleek grey head and flashing red throat hardly even turned in my direction as it bobbed past, then upended and dived, disappearing into the swirling depths, and then surfacing like a float fifty yards downstream, alert and elegant. I would do a lot to have water control like that!

When the line pulled tight, I was instantly dragged out of such idle reverie, and attached, mentally and physically to the vital force at the other end. Another one I mused, greed and self-congratulation rising prematurely. As I like to play fish fairly hard so as not to draw out either the stress for the fish or the fisher, I jacked up the drag, raised the rod into a springing curve and leant in. The response was truly electric, and knocked me into a completely different frame of mind. A few whirring revolutions of the reel and all that pre-emptive confidence disappeared as fast as did the line. The fish ran upstream, straight onto the backing at an unstoppable, uncontrollable speed that left me beginning to shake, mentally if not quite physically. Then commenced a tug of war, with the obviously hefty specimen nose down to the riverbed and refusing to budge, so much so that even with maximum strain it felt so like a dead weight that I was convinced that I was stuck fast into a rock. That awful sinking feeling began to creep over me, my innards feeling like lead, plunging down to my unsteady feet as I struggled over the gravel to raise both the fish and hope.

Fortunately such doubt was soon and abruptly dispelled as the reel again sprang into action. In fact, afterwards the drag was noticeably weaker and I suspect the poor old ball bearing and disc must have more than met their match! The wild, almost frighteningly powerful force suddenly ripped off downstream, with me stumbling afterwards, the rod arched, the reel emitting an increasingly high pitched metallic scream. There is nothing more tedious than reading exaggerated tales of other's fishy imaginations, but after twenty minutes my first twenty-pounder broke surface. Remember that I had one of fourteen pounds caught just an hour before on the bank behind me, so I could gauge the size honestly. It surfaced in a long, curving, dolphin-like roll, a nerve firing length of shoulder, dorsal and tail, before plunging down and off again. With heartbeat doing overtime by now, and the adrenaline pumping, (doubtless the both of us), I remembered to lower the drag as the great hope swirled in front of me. I kept telling myself not to rush it, that a large fish ninety percent played out on a short line was at its most dangerous, the tension, direction and angle on the hook hold being continually changed and strained. Time and again I could pull the head up and round, but the fish summoned the strength, momentarily pulled off balance, to tip down again and just would not be drawn to the bank where I planned to beach it. The riverbank where I was standing had a perfect, gently sloping incline to the water, but my prize stayed just that few yards further downstream where the shingle dropped almost vertically into feet of water. A certain element of desperation began to creep in as I wished for a helping hand and a netsman. Even more, I begged that this magnificent animal would do the decent thing and admit ultimate defeat, a trophy in the waiting, a glorious photo on the wall, the spring balance scales pulling way, weigh-down. As I backed away up the bank, drawing the surface floundering fish towards me, the rod tip sprang up, the electricity switched off, the world suddenly went slack and I watched that beautiful catch sink, exhausted, slowly, oh so slowly, into the deepening, dark safety of its mysterious world. The line had been cut through, either by rock or, more likely I suspect, by its teeth.

That was how the finest fish I was ever attached do drifted, tail first and in slow motion, out of my reality and into my nightmares. A year later it still haunts me, that vision like a still from a video, deeply engraved on my fishing retina, focussed and clear, refracted through the lens of memory onto the painful images of my mind. But when I trudged, heavy-footed, weary and disconsolate to the pool above, desperate to seek comfort from another soul, to talk out and exorcise some of the pain, I met not the understanding warmth of human sympathy but a frustrated, withering stream of criticism. Didn't I know that Klapperflojt was one of the most famous big fish pools in Iceland; was I blind – had I not looked at those portmanteau pictures on the lodge wall? Just what breaking strain of nylon was I recklessly, idiotically using? I slunk off, feeling even worse, hoping that the fish would at least rub out the rusting hook and survive, not to add a gradual, cruel and wasteful death to an already tragic epic.

But like any Icelandic saga, this has a sequel, of warriors, savagery and titanic struggles. It was a year later, (those fishing tips to my hosts must have paid off as I was invited back!), and the river was transformed into a thin silver ribbon, wending its way gently between the cliffs, placid, rock filled and shallow. It had been an almost snow-less winter and a record, sunny spring, ironic as the rest of continental Europe was awash with storms and filthy, never ending wintry weather. As I looked down at the river almost trickling along, reflecting the cloudless blue sky in a dazzling blue straight out of a Dufy painting, thoughts of large salmon seemed somewhat remote. The air temperature was seventy degrees and the water a lukewarm sixty-one, perilously close to danger levels for salmon. It was time for light leaders, micro-tubes and sunscreen lotion.

However, this is the beauty of Iceland – not just the endless views in the motionless, crystal clear air, but also the remarkable tenacity of the spawning urge. Even in low water, salmon still surge their way through the shallows, their tails and dorsals half out of the water, thrashing spray into the air as they fight their way noisily upriver. Unlike Scotland, where the diminished runs of fish just wait offshore for rain, being swept up by nets, seals and sea lice, in Iceland they seem to run, body clocks regardless of water height, a single minded desire to reach the spawning redds at any and all cost. As you stroll along the grassy banks in the afternoon sun, warm and semi-somnolent after a good lunch, it is a humbling, inspiring sight to see the violent commotion in the pool tails as these marvellous animals struggle up the rapids to spawn and (mostly) die. To be honest, it is almost enough to make you lay aside the rod and merely watch in admiration at the power and beauty of nature.

But not quite! In fact, the weather, apart from being just great to be out in and fabulous for showing off the scenery, was perfect for trying out my new acquisition. I had bought a nine foot, eight weight travel rod, partly for sneaking a day's bonefishing on business trips, and partly to see if my New York friends were not all insane when they went salmon fishing with toothpicks. It proved a real treat, light enough to cast with for twelve hours a day, delicate in presentation and strong enough to play fresh, sea-liced fit fish up to nine pounds. As we drove down to the lower river, I basked in the ruddy glow of an unusual suntan, a fair few fish winkled out of the sparkling waters and a lot of rock hopping fun with my new little rod. I also mused on the fact that the lower river had that old strain of truly big salmon, and that light line and baby rod tackle was tempting but inappropriate. The shadow of Klapperflojt still lingered over me, dark and foreboding.

When we arrived at the lower lodge, Gunni, my guide, grabbed the rods and we set off for the canyon beat, to Langidrattur. (For those that speak Icelandic, the name is very apt. For those that don't, it is too rude to translate!). This is Polaroids and mountain goat territory. From up above, atop the almost vertical slabs of rock, you can peer down into the clear turquoise waters and spot the fish a hundred feet below. It is a fascinating and heart-pumping exercise. As is the descent, slithering, scrambling and clambering down, hoping not to end up on a sheer, impassable ledge thirty feet above the water and remembering always to leave yourself a route up and out! It is a good way to work off the lunch, whilst your guide watches, amused, up above amongst the arctic willows. Before departing, I had discussed what tackle to take. Gunni commented that to take a net was bad luck, and it was so much easier to climb down with the baby rod…

In fact, we had spotted a pair of fish, one three times the size of the other, just beside a rock. Of course, from up above it is easy, as the rocks gleam bright sandstone coloured in the pellucid waters, and you can mentally fix an image of the rock shelves, boulders, stream and lies. At water level, it all flattens out and becomes one stretch of very similar looking boulders. It is depressing to fish away, heart thumping from the sheer physical effort of getting there and the anticipated excitement as you know that your fly is swinging right past a fish, only to feel the blank disillusion of an empty drift uninterrupted by tug or flash of silver. When you ascend the canyon, disappointed, to go and fish the next pool way down below, you cast a glance back. What fisherman can resist seeing if the fish are still there and why they didn't take? Only then do you see that you were in fact fishing in the wrong place, behind the wrong rock, the angle and distances all distorted from water level.

This time we decided to fish the run into the pool first. It always surprises me, (a euphemism for saying that I never learn), how salmon will lie with their tails literally a foot above the sill, where the water quickens into a gliding vee before spilling into the shallow rush of the next pool. Gunni directed operations from above, by sign language, and I swung a couple of fly patterns within inches of their noses. The fish were obviously unimpressed and unmoved. Gunni waved me on down to the main event, and headed off to act as taxi service for other beats. Fortunately my mental map was easily fixed, as there was a man high rock at the head of the pool behind which I hid, just the rod tip peeping out as I flicked a mere few yards of line out and across. I could almost sense the feelers of my Red Francis fly pulse and vibrate just below me as they swung past the rock lie. It was a difficult drift due to the very narrow, fast current, the fish hanging just beyond it, and on the second cast I decided I needed to change angle and move up to reduce the drag. As I wondered just how to improve the drift without scaring the fish, one took: that sudden awareness that there is a weight at the other end of the line. You cannot remember the 'take' – one minute there is a steady, undisturbed drift, the next moment a fish is on. There is nothing better than spotting fish from on high, absailing down a cliff and then casting to a known lie and hooking a salmon. It is pure mathematical poetry. Hope and anticipation transformed into fact, emotion and excitement. A quavering heart beat turned into a thumping one.

As was the rod tip as I waded out and strode down below the fish. There was a perfect little beach, of volcanic black sand, ready made for the conclusion of events. From downstream I could make the fish fight both the current, and me, directing it away from the other fish so that I could later return to lure it too, undisturbed. Unfortunately, such presumption didn't quite take into account the current encounter. My opponent simply swam off downstream, not in a reel spinning run, not even in a dramatic display, merely in an unconcerned show of power. I don't think it really realised that I was attached to it and trying with all my little rod might do to haul it out of its natural element onto dry land. This regal procession continued way beyond my lovely little beach, and I struggled up a rock to try to get above the beast at least to put some upwards lift on its head, and to survey the battlefield. As I did my heart sank. Here I was, alone in the canyon, with no net, no gillie, and, frankly, no chance, attached to, yes, the big one with a light rod and line. The fish just swam around the canyon, in and out of the deep green gullies between the rocks, around and around, whilst I maintained an ineffectual pressure and watched. I had a long leader on, and used the leader to line joint as a depth gauge. When it surfaced into the air, I knew the fish was only a few feet down and a chink of hope glimmered through. Then the line would disappear as the fish sounded for the bottom, its great tail waving almost indolently beneath me. I could see every mark along its broad, glistening flanks as it circled below me. It was a tedious tug of war. No action, no histrionics, just a foot won here and then lost there.

After half an hour I think the fish finally understood what was happening and made one short, but not very exciting run and leapt, or rather sloshed across the surface, sending nerve-jarring waves lapping menacingly to the rock upon which I was perched. I clung on, both to the rock and rod, as the fish went nose down again for another twenty minutes, solid and immovable, just a steady throbbing of its tail transmitting its rock-like presence up the line. With an hour up, the fish was circling in ever smaller circuits, on a sort of predetermined route below me and for an instant, for just a hope thrilling second, it rolled, unbalanced and belly up, a great expanse of white signalling a temporary defeat, flag-like, before it regained control and kicked off again to mid river. I stood, half bored by the stalemate, half excited by the ever so dim prospect of a glorious victory, (how to lug the beast back up the canyon?!), but never really alight as I felt so under-powered, so weak and useless in the face of this magnificent swimming machine. Once on land, the fish would be awkward and useless, a flapping, gasping wreck, but getting it from water to dry land seemed an almost impossible task. As the fish rolled again, I began to hope, and drew on the rod, trying to slide the fish towards me, to a small indentation in the rocks that was going to have to act as a landing place. The great silver head came near, a great wake making wedge, then with a final kick of its tired tail it managed to cartwheel around and swim feebly a few yards out to the safe blue waters. With a net and a gillie it would have been all over. Wearily, on both sides, the tug of war recommenced. There was now just a short line between us, between life and death, dream and nightmare, when, again, yet again, the curse of this tragic saga resurfaced and the rod tip bounced up, tension gone, all gone into the deep green void as the fly flew free.

To me Iceland is all about elemental geology, and the play of light and colour upon it and upon the sentiments. All around you lie the gentle lush green and yellow of buttercup fields in the sun, the fjord ridges illuminated, stark and domineering in the sunshine. The lichen and wild flowers startle with their vivid primary colours, clinging perilously to the black cliffs and sprouting from the seemingly barren grey scree and stones. The rocks present an ever-changing panoply of hues, from ferrous orange through all shades of pink, blue and grey to volcanic black and pumice, lunar grey. The water flows peppermint blue and green as it glides pure and cool between the foreboding, almost frightening walls of the canyon, a throw back to the ice age and ice creamy glaciers above. Eventually, as one day fades into the next, the sky is washed purple and blood orange as the sun sets behind the volcano. It juts up, an Egyptian pyramid of a silhouette against the still blue of a midnight sky, throwing the snow on the fjord into reflected pink streaks. The sharp lines and ridges of the mountains are outlined like a Chinese water colour, all black and white and ethereal.

But the most emotional palette of all comes with the fish - the pristine beauty of a silver flank fresh from the sea, the metallic dark shoulder of a porpoising roll, the white belly of a much hoped for surrender. Finally, sadly, you sink into the deep, utter blackness of crushing despair as the silver, white and blue all merge into oneness and natural unity again. The dream drifts back to reality, the fish back into its element and the fisher to another day, another rose tinted sunrise and another set of dreams and nightmares to be made.

The once famous Church Pool on the Thvera, Iceland.

Langidrattur – the one that got away, if only…

Aegisdufoss, the Lower Falls on the West Ranga. Europe's most active volcano, Hekla, in the background.

Into a fish on a typical Ranga pool.

CHAPTER 22

Sand Castles

'The sound of the little burns in the early morning, overhanging tongues of peat, sailing bubbles and foam flakes...'
Neil Gunn 'The Silver Darlings' 1941

Seaside holidays are always supposed to be fun for kids, though my childhood was spent with the deserted, windswept beaches and frigid waters of the Irish Sea rather than the sardine packed topless beauties, (or not), of the Cote d'Azur. The water off the Isle of Man was described by my grandfather as 'bracing', the sort of comment upon which an Empire was built, and lost. Immersion was only possible for a few minutes, before the physical extremities began to turn blue and a shivering retreat was called for. Instead, I preferred to stalk along the tide edge with a little blue bucket. This was not, like any normal child, to build sandcastles, but to look for a telltale hole and worm cast, and then to play search, dig and tug of war with a foul smelling yellow lugworm. If that failed, it was off to the fishmonger who, in those far off days of plenty, was always happy to give a few old mackerel or herring to a keen youngster to use as bait. There was something fascinating about those iridescent dark blue and black zebra stripes along the back of a mackerel, its torpedo, mini tuna shape suggesting exotic far off oceans, the chunk of bait glistening and flashing below the waves. To this day I still haven't encountered a fish that fights as powerfully.

I used to sleep in what must have been the loft of a converted stable, and I would wake early, look at the light slanting in through the curtains onto the wooden rafters and listen to the weather. If it was pouring with rain, battering incessantly against the windowpanes, a good book inside in the warmth beckoned. Or maybe some cooking, wrapping brandy snaps around wooden spoon handles and filling them with oodles of whipped cream for tea, (no one knew how to spell cholesterol then). If it was windy but dry, fortunes prospered, so that a trip to the pier was possible, rod and float at the ready. But the rarest and most blessed of all was a true summer's day, the sea swelling gently and rhythmically in the sun, ultramarine under a clear blue sky, perfect for boating. Hurriedly I would help cook breakfast and gather the tackle. We had two boats, one a rubber dinghy that I would paddle out into the bay with my grandfather. He was the motor, I was the fisher, as we bobbed along the inlets and gullies, searching the flat sands for a catch, sneaking up on ringed plover as they scurried over the rocks and little pools left by the receding tide, probing for a stranded morsel. Overhead the ever raucous oystercatchers would wheel, in their smart black and white livery with that ridiculously long, fluorescent red beak, for ever open and chattering. I can remember the excitement of my first catch – a plaice, my first flatfish, a strange prehistoric shape with those odd eyes staring upwards at you. It was maybe eight inches long, but had unfortunately engulfed the hook – even at a tender age I had some qualms about killing undersized fish – but this one was going to die anyway, so was triumphantly transported home for tea. It probably filled less of a mouthful than one brandy snap, but was, of course, twice as delicious!

The other boat was a fifteen foot sailing dinghy in which, weather providing, we would venture further afield in search of cod and anything else that came. Mostly it seemed to be the ugliest scavengers of the seas, dogfish, wrasse and eels – the first with a skin so rough that it was used as sandpaper, the second literally exploding from the sudden change in depth, as if blowing bubble gum out of its mouth. Worst of all was the eel, a terrifying beast, writhing, curling and biting, and almost impossible to kill. But occasionally we caught something more civilised and edible, and I would sit eagerly on the bows as we motored home, ready to jump off onto the quayside and drag the boat up onto the trailer, then scampering up the beach to tell my grandmother what wonders we had caught for supper. Poor thing, she was forever gutting fish and making fish pies – probably the best way not to hurt my feelings whilst making the less culinary delicacies of the sea at least moderately palatable!

It was only twenty-five years ago, but seems a time of plenty, even without rose tinted nostalgia. Being September, we picked wild mushrooms in the morning on the coastal fields, and off the pier you could see schools of mackerel and pollack, a lesser member of the cod family, milling around below. The little blue bucket was soon filled and we had to give fish away. The herring boats lined the pier, the fishermen salting the fish and throwing them into casks for immediate shipping to Russia. If you turned up with that same little blue bucket they would happily let you pick up the stray fish that had fallen – it never crossed my mind that one might actually have to pay for a herring, plump, silvery and red eyed in its freshness. By the time I was in my late teens, every herring was picked up off the floor and none were spared, and mackerel were no longer visible in schools below the pier. By my twenties, the pier stood deserted, the fishing boats moored up, European Union catch quotas already filled and fishing stopped for the season. The flags, painters and ropes fluttered and clanked in the sea breeze, a sad reminder of the plentiful days before, a noisy lament for the much abused sea and its fast disappearing stocks. As I write this a decade and a half later, the Environment Agency in the UK has just announced that it is considering a ban on all fishing, rod and line as well as net, for migratory salmonids. It is an appalling thought. Are the fishing hotels, gillies, tackle shops and support industries in England, Scotland and Wales all to stand denuded of guests, empty, bankrupt and silent sentinel to a once thriving nature, to rivers and lakes once full of health and fish, now stark and dead? No longer the creak of oars across a loch, the expectant drift of salmon fly across the stream, the night time vigil of a lonely sea trout fisher in a deserted glen as the stags roar and the sun drops slowly behind the midnight mountains?

Certainly we did little to further or engender this decline of stocks! Standing on the pier with my all purpose sea fishing rod, which was more akin to a snooker cue than a willowy, curvaceous fishing wand, I hurled my bright green and red bubble float overhead into the rolling swell. I watched it bounce cheerily up and down the waves before it would disappear with an audible plop as some greedy pollack swallowed the bait. One cast seemed to have attained Herculean proportions, sailing effortlessly into the sky and defying the laws of gravity. Amazed at my suddenly found casting prowess, (professionals can apparently propel their weighty projectiles well over a hundred yards into the briny), I wondered just how I had achieved this epic state. A loud screech from above answered with a swoop and angry beat of wings. My line was well and truly wrapped around a herring gull, a large and angry creature that was very ill amused at its undignified descent from the clouds and did little to help our efforts to unravel it, (luckily it was not actually hooked). They have sharp beaks and powerful neck muscles, do herring gulls.

At night, I have caught many a bat when sea trout fishing, always wading ashore to try to find a branch to put them on so that they can get over the shock and fly off. (Their wingspan is too great so that if you place them on the ground they cannot take off). One of my most interesting catches was years later in Devon. I was fishing a small, deep run above a weir, a well known lie for salmon that have just ascended from below, but a pool where I have never managed to land a fish – having only, sadly, lost a spring salmon there as described earlier. Each time I go, I hope that this is going to be the day, and each time I come away having fished it diligently and, (I think), quite well, but still with no tale to tell. So when my little mepps spinner was flicked upstream under the branches and just over the deep hole where I had hooked and lost that salmon a few years earlier, I reeled in with some hushed expectation and was thrilled and not too completely surprised when a sudden thump announced success at last.

From my limited experience, sea trout take sometimes with a crash, sometimes with the most delicate suck, more of an impression of subtle interference than of an active pull. But the reaction when the rod is lifted and the hook bites in, is always the same – a reel spinning series of leaps. Salmon on the other hand seem, in the initial stages, more pensive, often just shaking their head in wonder and discomfort rather than high tailing it for the sea. Well, this beastie did neither. It just plunged down and headed downstream, with unstoppable power but none of the usual tail and head thumping. The reel spun, my heart beat, and the rod arched and nodded, but something was awry. I splashed my way out of the river wondering just how big this salmon was, when with a great plop, a large, ugly black head surfaced below me. For a moment I wondered how it had got there without me noticing, until I realised the depressing truth. I was firmly attached to it. If gulls are uncompromising, cormorants are even worse, and tougher, and beaching one is neither an easy or delicate affair.

But nights sometimes come up with better surprises, such as salmon hooked when sea trout fishing, all hell breaking loose on light tackle in the inky darkness. That's real fun! More recently, I was up on the

North Atlantic coastline. It had been one of those days, well couple of days really. Driving up north in July, not a time that I usually fish in the Highlands, was a lovely surprise. The rivers were running full and healthy, the broom was a blaze of yellow colour, the foxgloves were bright in their pink and purple colours, perfect triangles of dripping bells, and the lupins reminded me of Iceland. One of the great delights of fishing at different times in the same places is to be able to see the differences in the seasons, how nature alters costume and colour, how flowers succeed each other, migrants come and go, the light and mood changes. I could spend hours watching the play of light, cloud and shadow on a mountain, the suddenly illuminated, spot lit detail of crevice and cranny and verdant green, then the dark black shadow creeping over as a cloud flicks off the electricity, and the detail disappears into sombre shade, the greens fading to greys and blacks, gentle summery beauty into a more stark, imposing drama.

Rain had for once been bountiful, so the fish were supposedly running up Loch Hope. As we emptied eagerly out of the car, the silver birches glimmered and rustled in the sunny breeze and we dived for head nets and midge spray as the vicious blood suckers made us pay for the balmy welcome. But the wind failed, coming, going and changing direction. Setting the boat drift was difficult as the strength and direction of the breeze was so unpredictable and the water surface was hardly ruffled by a wave or the spreading rings of a leaping fish. We tried and tried, I fished this fly and that, floating line, sunk line, all to no avail. Finally, rowing between drifts, I stripped off the whole line and let it trail, or troll behind us when a big, fresh sea trout took hold. The gillie whooped happily as a wild, large creature ran and hurled itself repeatedly into the air. At such distance, frankly, it is all luck, as I had no control, and obviously my cards were not reading well that day, as with one final assault into the air the line went limp and the fish crashed home to safety. We paddled on in abject silence.

The next morning dawned fair, and the prey turned from migratory to resident trout. It looked good over the bacon and eggs, and I dispatched my parents off onto what I hoped would be an interesting and moving trip through the Clearance villages up InverNaver. A century ago the Scottish landlords had brutally evicted their tenant crofters, burning their houses in favour of sheep. It is perhaps the most savage and guilty period of Scottish history, a time of venal brutality and, in my opinion, as bad if not worse than anything that the English have committed. This was their own people, valued at less than a flock of sheep. As my family set off up the glen, we headed west, across the sun bedecked sea lochs, in hope of a fair day. It had been a record season, three and four pound wild brown trout aplenty, and our last visit had been unlucky, a day of cold wind, endless rain and no fish. Today was to be different, the windscreen wipers redundant, the windows open. The dreaded Loch Caladail was going to be tamed, and the trout lurking arrogantly therein.

Until we arrived that was. From up above on the roadside the water looked calm, a lovely steady ripple and breeze. Perfect we mused. By the time we were shoving off, the rain started. The wind veered to the northeast, strengthened and chilled both the marrow and any hope. Not a fish rose. The odd valiant olive and hardy sedge hatched and floated by, but undamaged, not a neb or fin or rise in sight. It was truly depressing, even more so in a season when the catches were so good when the weather was right. Sometimes luck can play a cruel hand in this noble art! I was so fed up that I actually took time off from fishing, something I rarely do. I just enjoy being out with a rod almost whatever the conditions, and I am also paranoid that the moment I leave, the weather will change, the fish will throw themselves upon any hook in a mass suicidal frenzy and I will regret it for ever after. You know - you flog the water all day, with no reward, then leave for an early dinner only to be told that there was a fantastic evening rise. I headed off to look at some limestone caves where a river, ironically of the most incredible orange-brown peat colour, like a rushing stream of rust, had simply eroded away the soft underbelly of limestone and suddenly plunged through the roof of a cave. It is a spectacular sight, though what a waste of what looks like it could have been a nice salmon river, but even the most bionic salmon cannot jump fifty feet vertically!

That done, my father and I were idly browsing through the tourist office whilst the wind snarled outside and threw the waves in crashing fury upon the seashore, when we decided to go on a puffin hunt. Not in the Icelandic sense, when in August they set out upon the cliffs with the strangest little nets on incredibly long handles and try to catch the little birds as they fly. Of course, rather like Bambi and deer/venison, or little bunnies, we down south tend to wince in outraged horror at the idea of eating a cute little puffin. But when times and climate were harsh, and food scarce, puffins were a vital source of energy and nourishment. As the most common breeding bird in Iceland, (an estimated ten million) they are not in great danger form the paltry human population that is a mere fortieth as numerous. It is also a dangerous 'sport' as the cliffs are perilous, and every year some crazy puffin hunter plunges to his death. The flesh tastes rather liverish and is a blood black red. They are the most comical of birds, waddling about their burrows with those vivid, bright striped triangular beaks full of little fish, though scientists inform us that they are very domesticated – they mate for life and dig separate toilet burrows!

Still, the puffins were as elusive as the trout, and the walk out over the sand dunes and along the cliff tops was invigorating but as fruitless as a drift across the loch behind us. I discovered later that they leave at the end of June. I was really up north for the grilse-sized brown trout, (west coast Scottish grilse seemingly getting smaller and smaller these days, down to two pounds or even less). But the Cape Wrath Hotel also owns the bottom beat of the River Dionard. It was full of water and, unusually, fish. Needless to say I had eschewed this opportunity, having just returned, smug and self satisfied, from Iceland. Jack, the owner, had kindly offered me a rod, and said I could borrow his tackle. I had ungratefully refused – why waste my time chasing small and infrequent Scottish grilse I thought, when I had a freezer full back home. When I returned to the hotel and asked nonchalantly if the river had offered up more, an eight-pounder was produced. But with a difference – it was not, as thought, a medium sized salmon, but a huge sea trout! How hard can you kick yourself?!

Decidedly, it was not my lucky day. Still, that evening, a fine and very fairly priced wine list having rather lifted the gloom, I decided to avoid the World Cup final, all be it France against Brazil, and head loch-wards. Remembering that long distant success on Loch Borralaidh, I hoped that the evening would bring calmer weather and the much hoped for hatch of midge or sedge, when the big fish really do come up from the deeps to feed and the fly fisher has a more than even chance. Does lightning ever strike twice?

The loch surface was indeed calm, not a rise to be seen, but peaceful it most certainly was not. Since my last visit, in early spring, hundreds of kittiwakes, terns and black headed gulls had nested on the island, and the din was unbearable. It was an endless, raucous disharmony, a loud, jarring noise, worse than even the most grating horrors of modern classical music. One thing about fishing at dusk is that everything seems to soften, to dim and slip into darkness, it is a soothing, gentle time to be out. I quickly left my favourite piece of bank and headed for the far side, away from the island and its ghastly cacophony.

Still nothing rose, but as the distant hills lost their form and merged into simple monochromatic grey presences, I waded in, trying to remember that wonderful first fish that had taken just along this very bank. This time I had both rod and reel intact. Hoping for a repeat performance, I saw a rise, whipped the line back and forth until I judged, in the gloaming, that I was far enough out and cast a hopeful line into the fading twilight. The reward was a sharp tug – a fish, not big, not quite what I was hoping for, but ever so welcome. Usually the brown trout up here run and jump in a silvery imitation of their migratory brothers, but this fought strangely, and as I drew it towards the shingle, the pale reflection was not of a brownie. It was longer, slimmer, with a rather outsized, deeply forked, swallow-like tail. The flanks were of pale white silver, with peachy spots all over, and fins of ripest apricot. It was a pretty, lovely fish lured up from the depths, seldom caught on the fly. A fish that remains in just a few deep lakes and lochs where it was stranded by the last ice age, an ancient hangover from the days, millennia ago, when the giants carved out the rocks, ridges and glaciers as if with an enormous ice cream scoop. It was an arctic char.

CHAPTER 23

Innocence & Guilt

'I fish because I love to; because I love the environs where trout are found...because I suspect that men are going along this way for the last time, and I for one don't want to waste the trip...and, finally, not because I regard fishing as being so terribly important but because I suspect that so many of the other concerns of men are equally unimportant - and not nearly so much fun.'
Jon Voelker 'Testament of a Fisherman'

One trouble with living in Paris without a car and working for a multinational that involves much jet lagged globe trotting is that I ignore the wonders that are almost on my doorstep. When I was invited by friends up to their cottage in Normandy, I was literally transported to a different world that I thought only existed in picture postcards, and yet it was only an hour and a half away from downtown Paris. It is a vast area of flat fields where you begin to understand the ever present might of the French farmers' lobby – everywhere was sown with crops, munched by cows or churned by combine harvesters. The houses were all steep, pointy roofed and often thatched, window boxes built into the thatch and dripping red with geraniums, the facades all white plaster and wood beams – rather Tudor in style, utterly quaint and picturesque. It was nice to see hedgerows left scruffy with wild flowers, a hare bound across a field and a lovely sunset wash pink across the fields, a layer of thick blue misty haze lifting rather eerily from the ground as the land cooled down. Everywhere, we were surrounded by familiar names – known mostly from the cheese shop, land of Pont L'Eveque and cider. But best of all is the wonderful local custom of the 'trou Normande' (literally 'Norman hole'), where a palate-cleansing glass of neat calvados is inserted mid meal to liven the spirits and whet the appetite for further over indulgence.

I suspected that there was partly an ulterior motive to the timing of my visit, and was impressed when Max, my hosts's six year old, dutifully showed me to my room and bathroom. He then grabbed me by the hand and dragged me off to the garage to show me his latest toy – a metal stick. Chattering away with great enthusiasm whilst I looked somewhat lost, he removed the end cap and out popped a nine foot French pole, which was proudly handed to me. I have never fished with a pole, and was relieved when Max ruefully announced that he thought that the float and 'other bits' were back in Paris. In fact, this was not so, and Kathy, his Mum, produced a small winder with float, lead shot and hook, kindly telling Max that I was there on holiday and not to be bothered by little boys wanting to go fishing. Of course, the truth was that I was probably as keen as the six year old!

One of the delights of fishing is its ability to absorb totally all the senses and the mind, to the exclusion of anything other than the rippling flow of water and ringing splash of a rise. It is a sort of immersion in nature and the gentle obsession of deceiving its finned, swimming inhabitants. It carries with it an almost childlike innocence, and rarely do I see aged adults behave with such youthful eagerness – it is quite charming. It also, in my case, has an almost Proustian ability to transport me back to long summer days of childhood. So what better than to be able to pass on this most treasured gift and at the same time participate in the true innocence of a youngster's first casts, and just for a moment borrow back some of that lost, enchanted world of one's past? I hurriedly knotted the nylon to the one end ring on the rod, (there is no reel), threaded on a float, a couple of weights and the hook. I then stood on the lawn and showed Max how to swing the line out – just as my great uncle had to me almost exactly twenty-four years previously on a lawn in Devon.

Of course the ensuing bird's nest, a phenomenal tangle for just a few feet of stiff nylon, was a test of such rose-tinted patience as well as my eyesight! As lunch was digested, (poached Icelandic salmon, appropriately), we headed off to the fishing 'lakes' under a searing sun. When we arrived, I saw a delightful looking little chalkstream, very fast flowing and full of healthy weedbeds and watercress, and, yes, that wonderful quickener of the heart beat, a few waving tails. Who needs caffeine? I then noticed that my 'chalkstream' was in fact off limits for fishing and was actually merely a man made conduit between metal fish rearing tanks and a number of rather green, stagnant looking ponds. There was also, (for me), a most unusual sign which I had to read twice to ensure that the lunchtime wine had not got the better of me, as it stated that any artificial bait was banned but any real one was okay. As a size sixteen Blue Winged Olive is not much use on a float and pole, this was probably just as well. What was not was the actual bait on offer – happily sold along with the cokes, candies and chocolate bars. 'Vers de farine' – if ever you see this, turn about fast and run. They are truly disgusting, a sort of vast grub, yellow-white, wriggling, odious smelling and about ten times the size of a maggot. Armed with this ghastly packet, we headed for the beginner's pond.

Max, showing remarkable delicacy for his years, was most unkeen to handle the squirming bait, so I was reminded of far off days with maggots, camp stools and little rods aside the Thames and had to do the necessary. My poor mother, I once put a maggot bait box in the fridge and I can still mentally hear the screams – of course the box was empty, (and in fact I had even cleaned it), just the idle whim of a malicious sense of humour. As you can imagine, after that anything even remotely resembling fishing boxes was banned to the garage! Anyway, the shoe was firmly on t'other foot now, and vengeance wrought as I had to deal with the disgusting bait, spewing out white goo as I hooked the poor thing. Still, the excitement was palpable – the pond was only a few yards in diameter, had a narrow band of weed around the edge and then a circle of open water in the middle in which a number of very visible trout milled around aimlessly, (presumably put in there that morning). Max could see them and was vociferous in his excited demands and urge to extricate one. I tried to explain that they could see us as well. Still, with these fish this was probably not a problem, no need for camouflage and crawling on one's stomach, the very audible 'plop' as weights and float landed indelicately into the water surface was actually quite useful as it grabbed the fish's attention and, ultimately, their mouth.

I have to say that even though I have caught a fair few rather more wised up fish than these poor, naive, tail-less farmed fish, the nervous tension was quite contagious. We swung the line out and when a fish turned, locked on and gave a kick of the tail in our direction, I don't know who was the more excited, Max because he could see the fish, or me because I knew what could or could not happen. I desperately wanted him to catch his first fish in the half-hour we had before my train left. Well, he is obviously destined, or should the word be fated, to be a fisherman, as the first fish kicked, splashed and ended up flapping on the grass ready for the barbecue, and a second followed suit. It was interesting to see the amazement and horror when I had to kill the fish – he wanted desperately to show off his prize to his father, but winced visibly when I applied the fatal blow. As did I, but then I was hoping that the animal that was really hooked was also for life, but at the other end of the line, and for many, many pleasurable years too.

But I cannot help feel a twinge of sadness at the same time. My first trout was a wild sea trout than ran and leapt and left me all a-tremble in the dusky shadows of a Devon summer's night. It was taken twenty years ago in a river then full of clear, peaty tinged water and fish. I can only look back and wish I knew then what I do now, and could have fully benefited from the relative bounty, rather than splashing around as an eager, hopeful but desperately inexperienced tyro. In contrast, Max's first trout was of similar size but genetically worthless, a misshapen impostor, a poor apology for a rainbow, stocked into a tiny pond and ready only for slaughter. I cannot help wondering if there is more significance than mere co-incidence to all this? What future is there for the budding keen youngster today?

This July I managed only a hurried weekend trip down to Devon. After the record cool, wet spring and early 'summer', the river was flowing two or three inches above the usual dead summer level, and looked good. The cattle had gone, as had the barbed wire fences, (rubber waders relax!), and the banks were a lovely colourful mess of towering cow parsley and pinkie-purple balsam waving in the breeze, (just waiting to snag a slightly over generous cast at night, and cow parsley is very, very strong). That night I waded out into my favourite pool, Station Meadow, where that first fish, and my first salmon came, and my feet slithered and slipped over the pebbles in ankle deep water. The riverbed was covered in green algae. With this year's unusually high and cool water levels this was not a critical problem, but with the normal summer lows and what pathetic dribble of water is left warming up to sixty degrees, oxygen levels deplete. At night the algae breaks up into thick foamy soap suds, sucking even more life giving oxygen out of the water. Many sea trout are left floating belly up, ventral fins flapping in the air in a sort of tragic wave goodbye to health and life.

Worse still is the smell as you wade along, and the slushy brown cloud that rises from your waders. Pure treated sewage, which comes down from the new holiday camp behind on the hill, a distinct shitty smell that wafts up the nose. Just what you expect when fishing one of the finest sea trout pools in Dartmoor. If all the holiday makers have to chuck their faeces and detritus into the river, (which I would contest), they should have put the pipe a mere four hundred yards downstream, below the weir, where a good, reliable flow of turbulent water is guaranteed to disperse the foul muck. Of course, extending that pipe for the few extra few yards was no doubt costly, so they dumped it into the nearest access point where the river fans out and trickles, ankle deep over the stones, leaving the sewage to settle between floods into a thick, noxious brown carpet.

About four miles below this, the Teign's main tributary, the Bovey, runs into the Junction Pool. As all meeting pools are, it is a fine holding stretch for fish which stop there, deciding whether to nose their way up the Teign or the Bovey. The water has eroded away the high, reddish-brown clay bank, and from up top on a late summer's day you can, even now, see shoals of schoolies – small, silvery sea trout. They shoot, missile-like, out of the water, or, more subtly, just roll their burnished flanks, a rippling flash of underwater silver. It is an engaging sight, and one that breeds great confidence for the ensuing night's sport. But not for much longer it seems. Indeed, when/if I visit the river next year, the Junction Pool may not be there. Yes, I choose my words with care – it may not be there.

Why? Simple – because the actual riverbed holds fine deposits of valuable ball clay. So what you might well ask. So the local clayworks has decided to enrich their private shareholders and divert the two rivers. Damn them off, send them down a new course, and then dig up all that lovely clay. What of the badgers, otters, (rare as they be) and nesting sand martins that all use the current riverbank? Or, need I add, the fish in the Junction? All sacrificed to increase earnings per share? At the same time, the Environment Agency, due to the drastic decline in fish stocks, wishes to close down the neighbouring River Dart to all fishing, (rod or net) and restrict the Teign to mandatory catch and release on single barbless hooks until at least July. As said earlier, they may also impose a complete ban on all fishing for migratory salmonids throughout the U.K. As said, I fear for young

Max and his hoped for future as a would-be fly fisherman.

Unfortunately the decline is still debated, (like Nero whilst Rome burnt), and scientists, politicians, greedy short-term landlords and commercial interests all discuss, argue and pontificate. The issue is left to learned journals and debating halls, whilst the fish continue to be hoovered up at sea, eaten alive by fish farm sea lice, polluted and netted to extinction. One man – Mr Orri Vigfusson – and one charity – The North Atlantic Salmon Fund (NASF) – struggles and continues to do good, negotiating with governments and commercial interests to buy off all interceptory netting and trying to find sustainable alternative employment for the netsman. Their success has been encouraging, due to straight, almost zealous hard work and determination, leaving more salmon to return to the spawning beds, if the UK river owners and UK Government would only give them a chance. As Orri has stated, with the Northumberland drift nets still slaughtering tens of thousands of (mainly Scottish east coast) salmon, the UK is not capable, or worthy of managing this valuable natural resource. I have tried what little I can to help raise money for NASF, a percentage of all proceeds from this book going there, and have argued with commercial interests, but it is a tough cause. I suggested to major retailers of factory farmed salmon, that they should put something back by supporting the NASF, if only to be more environmentally conscious when the horrors of fish farming finally do hit the headlines. I suggested to magazine editors that a charitable donation to the NASF could only help, but they sadly replied that commercial interests mitigate against it.

Is Max going to be able to fly fish for wild Atlantic salmon when he is my age, or will he be reduced to 'landlocked' stew pond fish stocked unnaturally in concrete reservoirs? The answer, and the responsibility, lies entirely in our hands.

CHAPTER 24

Ireland's Crown Jewel

'The feeding is superb...Small wonder that Corrib trout are fat and have flesh as red as a carrot'
T.C. Kingsmill Moore 'A Man May Fish' 1960

Six piece travel rods are the sanity restorer of the modern 'business executive'. They should be available on the National Health. What is it about air travel that transforms a normally reasonable human being into a mindless idiot? Why the mad panic the second the plane touches down to leap up and grab all the incredible mountains of 'hand luggage' that have been squeezed and rammed into the overhead lockers, just to stand, squashed and uncomfortable, for five minutes until the steps actually arrive? Why the rush to be the first to switch on the mobile phone?

However, though flying seems to bring out the most irrational, short tempered intolerance in most, there is one time when I really relish it, like a schoolboy playing truant, or sneaking off behind the bike sheds for an illegal smoke. When? When I have a tiny travel rod secreted in my hand luggage. What a lovely feeling to know that along with the portable phone, computer and filofax there is secreted a rod, reel and box of flies. It boasts the prospect of a few hours away from a world of stress, the chance to sneak off to some calm, sylvan spot to cast a fly on new waters, full of unknown promise and hope. Somehow it gives a much rounder shape to business meetings, and all those identical hotel rooms. They look much more like home with a rod propped up against the trouser press and an anti midge spray next to the neat little bottles of shampoo, conditioner and bath foam!

Even better when the venue happens to be Ireland, where anything is possible and pleasant surprises guaranteed. The first was when the owner of the Glenlo Abbey Hotel in Galway called me to arrange some fishing over the weekend. It was one of those delicious moments, the meeting of two different worlds, the sudden coming together of two orbits. With typical, soft Irish charm, so different from the hard reality of email and fax, he chattered away as if we were old friends. Even more of a coincidence, we realised that we had a mutual friend in common, John, a Dublin insurance broker that I had worked with over a decade previously. Years ago he had said that he had contacts with the Western Regions Fishery Board and would one day get me on to fish the famous Galway Weir Fishery. Alas, our paths parted and he never could, but every time I saw pictures and articles about that most unique and prolific of salmon beats I wished that I had managed to take him up on his kind offer. Now, out of the blue, I had a hotel owner asking me if I would like to fish there. Ten or twelve years of interest and desire suddenly culminated in a simple fax – 'bring double handed rod, chestwaders and small flies, size ten'. It is amazing how much pleasure and anticipation a mere ten words can conjure up!

So, after a short flight from Dublin, I found myself on a sultry Friday night in July sipping a glass of France's finest, (okay, so business does have its upside...). We were seated in the converted Pullman carriage of an old Orient Express train, luxuriating in the silky smoothness of the finest cabernet and the amazing intricacy and opulence of the compartment's inlaid woodwork. Outside the wonderful tangerine hues of a panoramic sunset sank across the unruffled waters and islands of Lough Corrib. Not quite how I had expected to dine in Galway. And from the sublime to the ridiculous, the next morning I gathered salmon rod and gear and ordered a taxi to the city centre to go fishing. As I said, surprise seems to be endemic here.

The Galway Weir Fishery scarcely fits the stereotype image of a salmon pool. It doesn't snake its way between rocks, tree lined banks and distant mountains. It is hardly the picture of an idyllic wilderness. As you fish down it you walk along a neat tarmac path alongside the cathedral, trying not to catch the marigolds in the flowerbed behind you or make a fool of yourself in front of the half hourly tourist buses that grind past on the bridge and the Saturday afternoon shoppers who hang over it to watch you. It is a very public place to catch a mistimed cast in your ear, lose a fish, or, worse, (in all senses), misjudge the seemingly innocuous, gliding flow below the weir and take a step too far. Unfortunately that last prospect was, the day I arrived, not on the cards, unless I was quite suicidal. Salmon fishing with the fly is best when just two of the sluice gates are open and gushing water over the weir. With four open it becomes difficult, and with the full six the standing wave at the top is four feet high and the whole beat, (less than a hundred yards long), is white water down to the bridge. Needless to say in this wettest of El Niño summers, I faced the Full Monty, a frothing, rushing series of waves and white caps hurtling the fly line round in one impossible rush. That old dream was looking a little tarnished. The frustration mounted every time a grilse hurled itself into the air, well out across the stream and inaccessible with a fly, the splash disappearing in the watery maelstrom the moment it landed. It was but a momentary vision of heart pulsing excitement disappearing as quickly as did the false hope that it aroused. Meanwhile, the traffic would drift by in an endless procession, the shoppers would watch, lose interest and wander off, all unaware of the little drama being enacted below.

However, if the fishing was literally a wash out, the day was still a pleasure. To have finally fished the famous pool was a treat, the list of past fishers a positive roll call of celebrities from all worlds, political, sporting and entertainment. I spent the day enjoying the banter, chat and 'blether', and the remarkable warmth of the local fishers' welcome. I gathered a huge memory bank of stories, (all true!), lots of useful information and dreams for the future. Had I brought a spinning rod and a few Irish rubber tails I might still have struck solid silver, though I was really a month late for the peak grilse run when the record catch was eleven in a day to the fly and seventeen to a shrimp! The fishing should only have cost me the princely sum of twenty punts for the whole day, but with the river so high and being a foreign visitor there just for the day and with only a fly rod, the manager waived the charge – what Scottish river would do such? The locals insisted that I share their lunch, good humour and expertise. After I had netted a fresh little grilse for one of them, he refused to fish on and thrust his spinning rod into my hand urging me to use it as my fly rod was useless in that heavy water and he wanted me to catch a fish. I was frustrated and fishless, but charmed.

As I strolled across the walkway above the weir, I found myself glancing back up Lough Corrib. The weir starts the short river that drains all seventy square miles of the mighty lake. I couldn't help musing that I really was in the wrong place at the wrong time, as the weather up there looked just grand for trout fishing. Of course, it had indeed been one of those fabulous, all too rare days up on the lough, when flies hatched and fish rose in continual abandon, as I discovered when drowning my muted sorrows in the bar. I bumped into my guide and boatman for the morrow, Jim, and was immediately dragged upstairs to admire the catch; beautiful plump wild brown trout, olive-brown backs and high shoulders, gleaming thick black-spotted silvery flanks, buttercup bellies and shovel-wedge tails. I gulped, (air and drink), and began to mutter to myself about what could have been. As I had to leave at midday, we fixed a rendez-vous at an unholy six thirty on the Sunday to squeeze in as much fishing as possible, hoping against hope that a repeat set of conditions would reward us for such an early start.

After much hard experience, I believe that wild trout on limestone lakes are often not too prone to rise to an artificial fly, preferring the juicy nymphs, shrimp and fish fry down below. Cold easterlies or northerlies blow hope away. You cower in multi-layered woollies under a leaden sky, cursing the elements, the boat pitching relentlessly, rainwater sloshing around your feet, soaking everything in sight however much you try to keep it high and dry. Everything goes limp and damp, bottoms, sandwiches and enthusiasm. At the other extreme, tourist postcard days are equally useless, though far nicer. The water stretches out in an endless mirror of clearest blue, the sun shimmering, the boat motionless, every movement sending a wake of ripples out to shatter the calm. No, let's be honest, to catch good bags of wild trout on the fly you need good luck and an eclipse of the three precious moons. A steady, mild wind and decent rolling wave; a sustained hatch of flies and a dimpling rise of fish and you are in business. But we all know how often full eclipses occur...

Could I seriously hope for this twice in two days? That might be stretching even Irish hospitality to the limit. We drove up to Oughterard, the fishing centre of Corrib where every bed and breakfast sports a leaping trout on its advertising board. It was a lovely soft morning, perhaps a little too gentle on the wind and wave for a perfect day, but promising. We drifted by the hundreds of islands, and the boat was quickly adorned with the brilliant green delicacy of mayfly and the bustling, dark bulk of sedge and murrough. It is said that you take far more, and bigger fish on Corrib on the troll than on fly, and that fly-fishing in the early morning is only for masochists or fools.

Jim confirmed that the first statement was true, but so what – who wants to subdue such beautiful, wild spirits on a trolled lump of metal and a telegraph pole of a rod? Meanwhile, as the varied cocktail of fluttering wings, wriggling legs and proud antenna floated by, the odd one disappeared in an audible slurp. There was no doubt about it – both flies and fish were out to play. We watched sheet-like grey rain tumble down on distant Ashford Castle, across the lough in front of us, whilst we basked in the sun. Behind us the islands and trees were spotlit in verdant green. We motored past Inchagoill to Jim's favourite spot and I wafted out a team of three Irish flies – a Golden Olive Bumble to carve an enticing mayfly wake; an Irish Dabbler in the middle, and a dark claret Murrough for the big sedge. It positively bristled with alluring antenna and subdued hope.

It was a nerve-racking moment. Jim was a real expert, having fished for the national team, and a more passionate and enthusiastic trout man I have never met. It was contagious, but I was still aware that I was expected – by both of us – to perform and not louse it up, an apt phrase as we chatted and agreed about the tragic collapse of Irish sea trout stocks and the ugly proliferation of nets and cages offshore. Meanwhile the fish boiled and splashed at the flies. I covered a rise here and there, and just to keep me hoping, the odd fish would torpedo vertically into the air, nose first, tail flapping, making my heart thump. But nothing would take hold properly, or at least I couldn't hook one. The minutes flew by as relentlessly as the waves and wind, pushing us ever onwards towards departure time and the barren concrete greyness of the airport runway. Jim urged me on, desperate that I should take my first Corrib fish on the fly. I struggled to concentrate, to stroke the bushy bob fly through the waves, willing a fish to rise and swallow.

One took just as I was lifting off to cast again, a horrible moment with the rod held way up in the air and the fish cavorting and splashing on a loose line as I struggled to regain contact. A few seconds later it all went slack. Another pulled hard and I struck back, to feel nothing but the empty weigh of water. I was amazed that such a mouth-tugging heave can result in nothing. We turned, went back to the top of the drift and tried again, changing the flies, determined that one would finally take hold for good. Suddenly there was another knock, this time met by an instinctive and savage lifting of the rod. There ensued three sea trout-like leaps, a run under the boat and contact was finally made. Without doubt, a fly rod and not a stiff trolling rod is the right tool, as it bucks and bends to every lunge, leap and dive of the fish. The reel sang that ever-sweet song and the line ran out almost to the backing. Jim was probably more worried than me, giving a stream of helpful advice and encouragement, evidently enjoying the moment as much as I was.

Until that devilish Irish surprise sprang out of the bag again. Suddenly the fish, and line, just started to run out remorselessly, quite unstoppable. The backing knot bumped its way up through the rod rings and then jammed stuck. For a hideous moment I thought the four-pound breaking strain leader would part. However, the top two sections of the rod gave way first and plopped gently into the water. I suppose this was the lesser of two evils, though it didn't seem so at the time. I wondered what on earth was going on when Jim realised the awful truth. Whilst the fish was firmly hooked on the top fly, the bottom fly was equally well stuck into a rock underwater, one of the risks of fishing with three flies at once. Meanwhile we were drifting forty yards away with half the rod floating overboard. Jim calmly suggested that I keep the line tight, reach overboard and rescrew the rod together, whilst he whipped the bows round, started the engine, and motored above the fish. As we floated over the rock where the line and fish were snagged, he grabbed the net, somehow released the fly and then netted the trout. After that we laughed, shook hands and sunk to our knees in united relief, grateful humour and utter delight. A beautiful, fat Corrib trout lay in the boat, conjured aboard by one of the most deft and amusing pieces of boatman's wizardry I have ever seen. As Jim said, Lough Corrib really is the jewel in the emerald island's crown.

CHAPTER 25

Redemption in the East

'Fishing restores perspective. When we escape to the solitude of quiet waters, the day's fleeting troubles seem to evaporate into the mist; in the presence of Nature, spiritual order is restored.'
Criswell Freeman 'The Fisherman's Guide to Life' 1996

'Dear Adrian. The fishing is good, the West has taken over 500 and the East over 1,000 including a 27 pound fish, the largest in Iceland this year. Regards, Throstur'.

Now, after just five weeks of the season, including the early, lower catching ones, this is not exactly a poor record. Given that I was booked on the Icelandair flight the next week, you would have expected salmon catching prospects to be pretty rosy. My confidence should have been 'Hekla high' – up in the clouds just as the Fuji-like peak of that magnificent volcanic backdrop that overlooks the River Ranga. But I have one of those sotto voce confessions to make. I can almost visualise the Bateman-like cartoon image of shocked old fishermen falling off the dark leather armchairs in Reykjavik's Hotel Borg, spluttering into their cognacs. Here was a man who had failed to catch a salmon on the East Ranga, one of Iceland's most prolific and accessible salmon rivers, flowing just and hour and a half's drive south east of the capital.

Well, there you have it, the cat is out of the bag and the salmon very definitely not out of the water. In three years, I am ashamed to admit that I had never even hooked a fish on the East Ranga, let alone landed one. A little explanation may help here. No, not excuses, just background to help you understand this remarkable feat of non-salmon catching. In the early days when Throstur Ellidason first started his smolt rearing, it was principally on the West Ranga, the river that springs from beneath Hekla. I have already written about its broad, gliding stream of steady but unostentatious power, offering uniquely stable water height, colour and temperature due to its volcanic spring origins. It looks calm and genteel, but much less so when you wade in it and feel the full push of that seemingly innocuous stream. In contrast, the East is deep, cold and fast, the sort of river where you wade as deep as you dare and then 'heel in', digging your boots into the shifting pebbly sands and leaning back into the current. Not a place to slip. It also, unfortunately, comes from the glacier, and can colour into a milky-grey and chocolate soup after heavy rain up in the mountains. When the smolts were mainly released into the West Ranga, the East was the 'also ran', generally fished first slot on arrival day when still trying to acclimatise to the fact that you were not behind a faceless computer screen, but in mid salmon river. After that first afternoon we always moved on to the prime West beats. Only on the last morning of the week did we return to the East. It was a truncated session finishing early, the mind already on the suitcase to be packed, that latent sadness welling up as the minutes ticked away and another week's fishing flowed inexorably downstream and away for one more year.

Thus the East never really received the full throttled attention it deserved, well not from me at least, my mind always being airborne thirty thousand feet somewhere above the Atlantic, not the best place to lure a salmon. The more I fished those first and last sessions without even a heart contracting tug, the more I slipped into an easy acquiescence of the fact that this was just practice time, not serious fishing. Until 1997 that was, when a huge smolt release plan started on the East. Suddenly a day on an East beat became the peak chance, and we drove over in tense anticipation to see how clear the river was. If we were greeted by a cocoa-like flow, how bitter the disappointment, knowing just how many argent flanks were concealed, safely, therein.

Standing beneath the long black cliff on East Beat 7 on an early August afternoon in 1998, I had something to prove. As a supposedly proficient rod and, worse, one who had twice spouted in print on the river and was thus given presumed 'expert' status, it was my moment of truth. The chips were down. The water was milky enough to hide my feet when knee deep and the wind, ever welcoming, was straight upriver and into my face. Meanwhile the current fairly raced by, carving its way in broad swathes through the pitch-black volcanic rock, making wading a hazardous affair. A first chuck saw the line sail valiantly into the buffeting gale and the fly land in a wind-swept heap a few feet behind it, like a novice's first, hopeless cast. Prospects were not looking too good, and I am a bit old for beginner's luck!

But there is one element in this tale as yet unmentioned – Peter. He is the rock upon which my Ranga success is so often founded, a guide of amazing charm and enthusiasm, and one who shares the same views on salmon fishing as I do. He dislikes crowds and loves to seek out fish in places that are seldom fished, not staying all day flogging the best known but heavily fished lies. It is easy to be seduced by the repeated belly flops of bored resident fish, but I doubt that they are frequent takers. Their surface activity is probably caused by the sheer tedium of seeing yet another shrimp fly, but is enough to convince some rods that they are the only fish in the whole beat. Hence they stand and cast for a few more hopeless hours, ignoring the unfished but less reputed pools just down river. Peter and I head off for the distant, rarely visited pools and, surprise, surprise, often find a fair few fish there too, and ones that having never seen a fly are more likely to oblige.

The only snag is getting there. Icelandic guides look slim and weightless, but are obviously some strange genetic intermix of mountain goat and fish. Struggling along behind, splashing, spluttering and trying not to float off, I have a distinct lack of gravitas. So when Peter muttered that as the water was high and fast, and the wind unfriendly, we, (note the 'we'), could get a much better drift from the other side beneath the towering black cliff. I grabbed the wading stick, which for once I had remembered to bring, and followed as best I could. The water was about forty-two degrees cold and swift, so it was a chilling experience. I had to lift my arms and rod above my head to keep them dry, the swirling would-be bath doing its best to drag me down in its icy embrace. Once safely across, it was a choice of absailing down the near vertical larval cliff or a quick slide down a steep bank of shifting grey sands; a sort of ski in neoprene chestwaders and then a hefty plop as I landed in the river, fortunately still upright and thankfully into only a foot of water. Peter waved and headed back across the river as if it were an afternoon paddle. I shook myself alert and sent a line out across the churning stream.

He was right of course. With the wind partly sheltered by the cliff and from a less confrontational direction, it was an easy cast to cover the nearside salmon lies which I had so struggled to reach from the other bank. Child's play. A couple of yards of line pulled in, lift, swing, a punch of the shoulders and out it catapulted, landing with a brass tube fly plop, then cutting into and swinging across the milky stream. Flies in such conditions of wind, wave, water temperature and colour are neither subtle nor pretty. In 1997, a new creation had swept all before it, both in terms of vast salmon catches and the even louder ringing of the fly shop cash tills – the Snaelda. This lumbering beast is quite simply a brass tube tied carrot shape with black wool and a silver rib, and a small black hackle at the neck. I suspect the hackle was put in to add respectability to this ugly fly as it is, I am sure, totally superfluous. I never bother to tie it in and have not noticed any drop in catches. However, the critical bit is the thick, long tail of black hairwing with silver crystalflash strands glistening and intermingling. The toilet brush from Hell you would muse. Still, it works, it really does, and how!

However, over those long winter nights with only the Seine to remind me of clear flowing water, requiring some feat of the imagination, I had softened the pattern and added some colour to the Snaelda. I replaced the black tail by a mixture of bright red and yellow bucktail. This homemade fly also had the added advantage of costing about a quarter of the Reykjavik shop bought version. I really didn't expect to catch much, but I tied it on. Peter looked at it, half swallowed an Icelandic expletive and christened it 'The Ugly'. I preferred the more technical name, The Garry Dog Snaelda, a lovely fusion of Tayside and Ranga, Scotland's greatest salmon river and Iceland's most prolific. Somehow it seemed appropriate, a blending of disparate rivers and pleasures. I lobbed it into the wind. Brass tubes may be miserable to cast, but if projected with some force they really do fly into the teeth of most gales. It quartered round, the lurid toothpaste colour intermediate fly line shining through the cloudy water until stretching and straightening out below me. I took a step down the bank and relaunched the projectile, again watching that fluorescent arc settling nicely into the current, trying to dispel all memories of work and to sink into a more rapt reverie of Icelandic salmon fishing; to deepen the concentration and heighten the senses, to imagine that ugly fly as it swung its gaudy, bewitching path across the current, hopefully right in front of a fish's nose, startling and enraging it to take. I have to admit that I was still suffering from my East Ranga inferiority complex, and it was me that was startled into action when the line pulled tight. Stupidly only half believing, I tentatively raised the rod, to be rewarded by a kick and a throbbing intensity. Could this, at last, be it?

Ironically I had been forced to fish the wrong rod, as my fifteen foot ten weight, best suited to dealing with heavy tubes and buffeting winds, had been converted by Icelandair from a three to a four piece. Despite being inside a very solid rod case the middle section was smashed in two. Even more inexplicably the solid metal wading stick with it was seriously bent – was there some poltergeist up in the cargo hold? I used the replacement rod, a twelve foot eight weight that is perfect in gentler weather. As it bucked and kicked I stumbled along the gnarled bank in an effort to get alongside the fish and force it to play me as well as the current, rather than vice-versa. Then the hook came away. The line flopped to the surface and drifted aimlessly around. The fly hanked up on some weed and everything went awfully limp. I cursed myself for having obviously done something wrong. Why is it that after a fish is lost I always think I made some grave mistake and spend hours pondering it, when it was probably just bad luck and a poor hook hold? The curse of the East had enjoyed another guffaw at my expense.

Determined to have the last laugh, I checked the fly, waded back to the top and threw it out again, this time with a touch of venom, an extra punch into the wind and the miserable Fates that had sent it. Five minutes later the rod kicked again, and this time I reacted with a swiftening heart beat and urgent purpose. Being on your own in a fast stream under a cliff with no net and no suitable beaching place, and an angry, recalcitrant salmon stampeding round the pool, is a recipe for a lot of nervous exhaustion. But eventually the poor fish succumbed and was unceremoniously hauled ashore, a spray of silver scales glimmering against the incongruous pock marked black rock. At last, at last, at last – number one and counting!

Two more were successfully beached, one other hooked and lost, and I was left reeling with unexpected success. Even better, the next morning dawned, far too early, bright and balmy. The white, plastic wrapped hay bales looking like huge golf balls, neatly ranged across the almost artificially green grass fields; a weird, unworldly foreground to the immovable blackness of the triple triangled mountain, the massive icing spread of the glacier and Hekla mingling with the clouds, head in candy floss. The air was so clear the scenery looked sharp and stark, razor edged in its brilliance, etched, not shaded, in bright light. And we were back on the East, a further chance for redemption. By now over confident and eager, I cast with ease down the main run, what joy to fish in shirtsleeves and watch the leader curl, unblown, across the water, cobra-like and landing far away with a controlled, delicate splash. It was as nearly effortless as I can achieve, not exactly poetry in motion, but at least fairly limpid prose. A salmon rose, as did my spirits, exactly where it should do, having obviously read the same textbook, just off the main stream. I angled my cast with consummate ease and thought, calculating the perfect drift and waiting for the line to pull hard and prove me right.

Of course it didn't. Damn it, why not? I fished with extreme care all the way down, and not a tickle, not even the sight of a fin. I waded out, back up and fished down again, with glowing self satisfaction and growing ill ease – conditions were perfect, a pseudonym for dead easy, and even I could manipulate a line with some skill. The fish were there but just not playing ball. At the end of my second immaculate run, Peter strolled up. I grumbled ungratefully that I thought I had covered the pool pretty well, and he said that he had seen a fish head and tail, like a large trout, just behind me. Grudgingly I took the Ugly for a swim again, and Peter whooped with delight as the fish took, bang on, right where he said it would. But it didn't fight like a salmon. It bored rather than ran, a dogged persistence rather than a lightning display of athleticism. As the water had cleared overnight, we caught a glimpse of a broad shoulder, not of silver, but of darkest greyish-green, and as the fish rolled belly up, tired and defeated, the river flashed orange. A sea-run arctic char, a chunky five pounds of it, a colourful and very tasty throwback to the Ice Age. I was delighted. As the other rods gathered round and camped on the most obvious and reputed holding pool, Peter and I did our usual trick, waded across the river twice and fished the whole beat in a series of rushed casts. Two more silvered specimens plumped out the net by lunchtime, and I began to wonder at my luck – it had been well worth the wait!

The afternoon was a salutary reminder that Icelandic weather is 'changeable', as I believe the meteorological phrase goes. The wind stiffened and rain began to tumble down. Most rods headed for the car, or the warmth of the lodge, (or was it the whisky I wonder?), but we decided to fish on, trying to beat the river as that dreaded milk began to churn again. One fish of extraordinary strength responded. It kept fighting literally beneath my feet as I walked along an undercut grass bank, worried that it would collapse and dump me into the deepening stream. I struggled to keep the rod out across the river to persuade the fish to move out from under its cosy overhang. Peter had retreated to the car a hundred yards away, but was watching with binoculars – what a guide! On seeing that distant, watery vision between the windscreen wipers stop casting, he rightly presumed what was up and came scampering down with the net. Time and again I tried to force the fish up and out, and every time it surged beneath the bank, boring down with astonishing power and persistence. It was becoming embarrassing, as I just could not tire this devilish beast. Yet we could see it was not a big salmon. Eventually we realised that this was not a salmon at all, the small head and deep, powerful shoulder finally giving it away. A six-pound sea trout, heavily spotted and lilac flanked, as lovely a fish as you could wish to catch. It crowned a wonderful triple-specied day, and a glorious consolation after all those fruitless casts on the East. Mecca found in the East at last.

Postscript (2001)

As said, 2001 saw what is probably my last visit to the Ranga. Our first session on the East was, yet again, washed out in a chocolate flood of disappointment. But we finished our week, fittingly, on East Beat 7, on Scollatangi, where the Ugly was christened. The water was clearing, a faint milky cloudiness tinging the icy blue. Perfect. An indecent ten grilse were hauled ashore the black sand beach. A wonderful, if poignant, end to my Ranga saga. Mecca indeed.

CHAPTER 26

Last Cast on the Don

'Out of the running
blackness of a river pool
a white salmon unplugged
itself and fell back
in a smash of light'
Norman MacCaig 'Go-between' 1966

You should never go back to scenes of former, more youthful triumph. It is always disappointing, as the stark blackness of cold reality cuts through that lovely roseate glow of misty reminiscence, and nostalgia turns rusty. Things never seem quite the same, wishful memory having blurred the unacceptable edges of the passage of time. These days, especially in migratory fish terms, you are likely to find that a river that was once full of childhood epics and salmon, is now running empty of fish, just old fading photos and the odd lingering memory left to recall former glories.

Still, to coin a very apt cliché this El Niño summer, every cloud has a silver lining, and there was no shortage of those this year, (clouds I mean), heavy, black and full of life giving rain. Whilst it may have been the worst season this century for sunbathers, cricketers and worshippers of the celestial golden orb, for gardeners and fishers it has been one long series of refreshing precipitation. Chalkstream riverbeds that have run dry every recent summer were suddenly transformed back to bright crystalline watercourses full of fluttering flies, grateful flowers and even happier trout. Growth was abundant, hard work for the river keepers and bank mowers, but like a shot of much needed blood for Nature.

All this rain meant that rivers were, for once, well stocked with water, grilse and school sea trout. I am not a great fan of spinning, mainly because I am not very good at it, and am never quite sure how to tackle the problems of weight, speed and angle of spinner retrieve. But I do enjoy idling up small streams on sunny days with a tiny rod and a small upstream mepps spinner. You sneak along the bank, trying to lurk unobtrusively behind the overgrowing bankside foliage, and flick the tiniest of spinners upstream, past the ever-visible phalanxes of schoolies and into the slack deeps under the far bank where the salmon hold up. It is not easy – a hesitant cast, wary at the thought of spooking the shoal, lands the spinner short, with a loud splash, right in the middle of it. In the blink of an eye a once peaceful pool full of gently wavering tails is transformed into a nightmarish scene of startled sea trout swimming round in circles. Fishing is over. Equally, an over-exertion lands the cast straight into the overhanging trees, and playing a branch as it rustles, swings and seems to pull back elastically has the same end effect. A little silver spinner is left dangling as a new tree ornament and a critical reminder of your incompetence. Meanwhile the fish have disappeared. They just vanish.

Sometimes, just now and then, the spinner arcs delicately over their heads, lands on the far side like a ballerina and twirls back in a voyage of rising blood pressure as a sea trout sticks its nose literally an inch behind it and glides across the stream. It is awful – as you simply run out of room, and the fish looks up, surprised to see this alluring bait disappear into thin air, and very unimpressed to see the large human figure behind it. It is almost funny – the fish seem to make one last dart after the spinner, and then finally twigs the full implications of the tall green clad, rod holding figure. They stop immediately and turn, drifting back to safety whilst your heart beats wildly and you desperately but vainly will the fish to take! A breathless second cast will, for some reason that is beyond me, usually disturb the whole shoal. They either just move, in a sort of co-ordinated side step, further over and under the trees, or start swimming in circles, milling around. Either way, the fun is over.

The last time I tried this, I was so frustrated that I decided to take a fly rod down as well, for the hell of it. I have often read tales in magazines of catching sea trout on dry flies in broad daylight. I was highly sceptical, but willing to give anything a shot. As I strolled down to the river, far from the roads and crowds of sunbathing families, I decided to give the deep head of the pool a quick cast with a spinner first. I placed my fly rod in the bushes and rounded the corner to try my luck. A few minutes later, I returned, as expected without success and keen to float a dry fly. I put down the spinning rod and went to collect the other one. But it wasn't there. The rod was of little commercial value, but it was my first real fly rod, and had taken my first sea trout, brown and salmon. It was a cheap length of fibreglass, but it linked back to my childhood and to so many nostalgic memories. With increasing desperation, disbelief and mounting anger, I hacked through the the bushes with my landing net, cursing the thoughtless, thieving swine who has stolen the last, most treasured relic of my fishy beginnings.

A fortnight later, in September, I was due to be in Aberdeen on business on a Friday, (mere coincidence!), and had planned to spend the Saturday with friends on the Dee, in a last backend fling after salmon. I have still not landed a fish on the Dee, nor, in fact, a salmon in Scotland for two years. It was high time to put this to rights. Until, that was, my friend and host decided to be invited to the Spey that very day – not an offer to be turned down, even for me. I cursed my ill fortune, as Friday meetings held next to fine rivers are a rarity! Still, chances to muse on what might have been are rare, as I found myself in my office discussing half billion dollar investments in drilling rig construction in the Caspian Sea, and what political risks this might represent. To be honest I was struggling to comprehend the tortuous legal structure when a friendly face popped by my office and asked if I had a minute.

Wearily, grumpily and rather churlishly I replied yes, if it was just one minute. He was an American-Egyptian who had worked for a short while down the corridor and had been moved to Aberdeen. As he was a keen fisher he had asked me for some advice which I had readily given. Anyway, he announced that he now lived in Monymusk. Hmm, I mused, that is on the River Don, scene of that much-regaled epic encounter with a seventeen and a half-pound spring salmon. I looked up from the forest graveyard of paper in front of me. Monymusk, uh huh? He had free access to fishing for salmon and trout on the Don. Caspian go hang, he could have five minutes! Anytime I happened to be up, if I just gave him a day's notice, we could fish – and, oh yes, the river was full of water and salmon just at present. Now at this stage, the meeting rather degenerated. My colleague across the table was, ironically, recently transferred in from Caracas and the man with whom I had been bonefishing. He too put down his pen. When was I next up north? Well, as a matter of fact, the following day, and with a 'free' Saturday that should have been on the Dee as well.

Thirty hours later, I found myself standing in chestwaders beside the Boat Cottage, wondering at my good luck – and bad. To be back on the Don – so unexpectedly – was a sheer impromptu delight. It was ten years since I had been up there, and much Scottish and Icelandic water has flowed under my personal fishing bridge in the meantime. Yet that one fish still remains the finest I have ever managed to land. Looking now, the river seemed so small. I can remember struggling to wade and cover the water a decade ago with new chestwaders and a single-handed rod. Now, the waders were, remarkably, the same, all be they patched up, but the rod had long gone, as had, I hope, some of the inexperienced and rusty casting. The Don seemed so intimate and friendly, easy to wade and no problem to cover – indeed, the only fly I lost was from an over eager cast into the far bank. It was gratifying to find that the intervening ten years had seen my limited skills improve apace, but that my desire and pleasure remained the same. I was horribly impatient to get in there and have a crack!

Ah, but I mentioned bad luck as well as good. We get back to that rain again - just a bit too much of a good thing. The river was high and black, pushing down with some urgency, a mass of ale coloured froth, creaming along like the head on a half-finished pint of stout. Wading in it was eerie, my legs disappearing into the impenetrable black water, invisible below the knee. Behind, two rumbling eye-like lights glowed in the distance as a combine harvester worked into the night. Pheasants skittered along the fields and a fantastic flotilla of upwinged flies sailed down the river, completely ignored by the famed Don trout. It was so frustrating! I knew that just a couple of feet below that foam speckled black surface lay dozens of salmon, almost motionless in that acidic, peaty stream, just a sinuous curve of the tail holding them on station, completely unlikely to budge one inch for a fly. I was so close and yet so far – again.

So I was left to daydream, and to ponder the quality of life. Kal, my generous host, paid less to rent his delightful, large old crofter's cottage than I did for my small flat in Paris. Here, his neighbours were the kingfisher and dipper, and the pair of osprey that still nested on the beat above. His kitchen window and conservatory overlooked the heather clad moors up to the mountain, the bedroom view sloped down over the garden to the river. As he said, the nearest human, (there was only one), was a couple of hundred yards away in a little 'castle house' (an architect's whimsical folly), and he could literally watch the trout rise from his bed. There was even a gardener thrown in! His morning commute was half an hour or less to the office where I had just been working. On a nice day in the summer he could fish before breakfast, or just sip coffee on the porch and watch the sun, and trout, rise – and be home in the evening in time for a pint, dinner and the evening hatch.

But not on the next morning, he couldn't. It was early, cold and very bleary, (maybe the local hotel bar accounted for that) and the river had dropped a mere couple of inches and ran black as the just vanishing night. It was still hopeless. We fished through the motions, then retreated for a huge consoling and warming breakfast. It would clear by lunchtime the locals predicted. I pottered around to kill time, (I hate being in the middle of nowhere beside a salmon river which is effectively unfishable, there is no way of concentrating my mind on something else or of finding alternative ways to divert my attentions). I ended up driving upriver in search of nostalgia and sunshine – all I received was a torrential downpour and the depressing sight of the hills upriver at Strathdon receding into the mist and rain. It was like a Turner painting, the rain slicing across the sky in a slanting grey sheet. I could almost feel it permeating through the heather and peat and filtering yet more acidic pitch black sediment into the river.

By early afternoon I could resist no longer, and as I had to leave for the airport at teatime, a few last salmon casts for the year seemed appropriate, regardless of the conditions. I met one of the local experts, a man who took, himself, about a third of all the fish off the stretch. He kindly informed me that I was, unwittingly, poaching his beat as I was on the wrong side of the river! Being a free guest is bad enough, but then stealing someone else's water... In fact, the other bank was far better, so he selflessly offered to be my gillie for the afternoon, and we waded across. As we did, the sun nipped out from behind the frowning dark clouds and the sky warmed from grey to azure. It was as if a huge light bulb had been switched on overhead.

We both noticed them at the same time. Our feet that is. To understand the excitement that this engendered, you have to be on a salmon river full of fish with just two hours before your flight out, and to see that the water is just clearing into perfection. As every treatise states, the bonanza time to fish is on a falling, clearing river. Suddenly I glimpsed a chance, a small window of opportunity between the next deluge of peat surely heading down from the hills above and my plane taking off a few miles below. Just a chink in the armour, but maybe enough to give that last salmon of the year, the first in Scotland for two years and a tangible throwback to that beautiful spring fish just a beat and a decade behind. It was tantalising.

My would be gillie suggested a small, drab fly. Looking at the still dark brown water I thought something large and colourful would be needed to show up. I compromised, putting my bigger fly on the end and a small Munro Killer on a dropper – something I never do, as fishing with two flies seems a double incitement to disaster. The foam had gone, the water turning from dark ale to amber whisky, and still the flies floated down unimpeded – not a brown neb to be seen. But then the surface was thrown into spray as a salmon finally showed. We were in business. They really were there, and the water really was just clearing enough for success. A sudden pull off the reel sent my heartbeat into overdrive, but nothing else – a yard of line span off the reel but the fish came away, unhooked. Somewhere out there a very lucky, surprised salmon was returning to his lie, free. I lifted, paused and rolled the wrists again, trying to propel the fly right under the far bank, an easy cast, and let it swing right through the main salmon lies, a small run of water between two just visible streams. Suddenly, another tug completed the circle, accompanied by a cartwheel in the air, sending golden spray flying across the river.

He weighed about five pounds, a small cock salmon to gladden the heart, a little gem of pleasure snatched from the river, the runway, and the coming closed season. Caught – as you will have surmised – on the wee dropper. Oh yes, and when I returned south a letter was waiting for me. An over zealous, but well-intentioned fisher had picked up my rod, thinking it had been lost or forgotten. Sometimes it does pay to go back after all.

Mark Bowler lands a good sea trout for Hazel on Loch Dionard.

Dawn mist – breakfast view from 5 Rivers Lodge, Montana.

Tough training ground: big fish country on the Beaverhead.

Scenic drifts down the Big Hole.

CHAPTER 27

Montana – Big Fish under a Big Sky

'You think of your own insignificance, and the ridiculous side of so much of daily life. You need to contemplate more, to look around you. Whatever the generally held view, the world has a beauty that surpasses understanding'.
David Hockney Interview with Connnaissance des Arts 1994

Houston is one hell of a long way from Montana, but it was there that both this book and my dream trip to the Far West began. The sprawling highways, endless traffic and ostentatious oil wealth of Texas might seem a strange place to link to Montana, but Houston does offer some great fishing stores. Browsing through them, I discovered what I term the transatlantic form of 'angling literature'. This was a far cry from the rather dull, instructive but humourless how to do it works that we so often find on the bookshelves back home. Instead, I found writing that was much more discursive, chatty, and amusing. It was reflective, sometimes even slipping into the philosophical and largely autobiographical. I bought up suitcase loads and read them eagerly, wondering why we no longer produced the Greys, Farsons and Plunket Greene's over here. Whilst pouring over such tomes, two desires welled up in me, just like an infant stream wending its way to Montana. I wanted to fish in the West, and to write my own, more European version of tales by the log cabin. To ease the temptation, the tackle shop opposite my hotel just happened to advertise a lodge in, guess where, Montana.

Hence, in late September 1998 I found myself wending my way up through the meandering forest hill roads out of Butte, deep into the night and bitterly cold, watching cautiously for the deer that lined the verges and peered into the headlights with their bright red eyes. When I awoke later that morning for a daylight view of Montana, I was – for the first time of many that week – awe struck by the massive arena of the Rockies. A thick film of blue grey smoky mist curled up from the valley floor, accompanied by the incessant honking of a thousand cranes waking up from their nocturnal roost. The rising sun flung a pink grapefruit hue across the mountains as I breakfasted, out from behind the frowning dark clouds and the sky began to glow like one of those vast Hockney landscapes.

About one hundred and ninety years ago, after the Louisiana Purchase, Thomas Jefferson sent Lewis and Clark off to explore, to seek out the fabled Northwest Passage to the Pacific. The Continental Divide lies just a few miles down the road, and it puts it all into scale when you consider the limpid, infant waters flowing rapidly beneath your feet in Montana are destined to join together to form the Jefferson, then the Missouri, then the Mississippi and finally, almost a whole massive continent away, to spill out into the steamboat, jazz, and crawfish boils of ever so distant New Orleans. Everything here is sculpted on a vast scale.

Lewis had more than his fair share of travails back in 1805. Having found the River Big Hole and named it Wisdom, he was chased by a bear, charged by three buffalo bulls and awoke to find a large rattle snake hanging in the tree beneath which he had slept. Add dysentery to this and you wonder how he ever made it! Now the great adventure is remembered everywhere, but the buffalo are long gone and exterminated by the whites, the Red Indians pinned back into nearby reservations and ghastly alcoholism. General Custer met his match not far away across the Plains and as current day sages sadly comment, the whites brought the indigenous Indians one of their greatest gifts – the horse – but with it one of their greatest evils – alcohol – which the Indian metabolism simply cannot digest and cope with.

For once, man has actually improved the natural habitat from a trout's point of view by impounding the snow melt waters of a mountainous winter behind the Clark Canyon Reservoir dam. This creates one of the most fabled tail waters in the West – the Beaverhead. Because the water flows from the bottom of the reservoir, not the top, the temperature is pretty steady, giving an unusually long and stable growing season for the trout below. Though the banks are littered with the remarkable constructions of the ever-industrious beaver, the river actually owes its name to a rock, just opposite the lodge, which supposedly looks just like the snub nosed head of a beaver. Despite looking at it from all sides in all lights, I couldn't help wondering if the dreaded alcohol hadn't in fact arrived rather earlier than history recounts...

What really was lifelike was the pair of twin buffalo rocks as we sped up towards the dam. The road carved a wide swathe through the gorge and between two hump-backed ridges that really did bear an uncanny resemblance to that once abundant animal, an ever present and sad reminder of the indiscriminate slaughter of forty million buffalo just a century ago. It must have been a spiritual place. Nowadays reverence is saved for the river that flows below. As we pulled the car into the dam 'recreation area' to launch the boat down the almost vertical slipway, there was an almost mythical feeling. The air was thick with the heady, overpowering scent of wild sage, and antelope were grazing on the arid hillsides. The river curved and cut a rapid flowing vein of clear green water between the banks crowded with willow bushes. Lime coloured weed beds waved indolently in the stream - it was like a magnified, outsized chalkstream. The kingfishers were of huge proportions, osprey and golden eagle soared overhead, and we knew there lurked the most amazing trout just below.

But this was not a myth, it was Montana, and the fisheries board regularly monitors and electro-fishes the river to check its health. There has been no stocking for quarter of a century, and the river now supports a head of about two thousand wild trout per mile, with a four-pound fish every forty yards. Let me just repeat that. There is a four-pound wild trout just waiting for you in the current every forty yards – these days the mere length of an average tournament cast! Like a carefully weighted nymph, let me leave that statistic to sink in and entice...

It was therefore with a sense of scale and fervid anticipation that we stepped into the boat and launched off into the foaming spume below the dam outflow. It was also here that the fun and learning process really started. Having fly-fished for over twenty years, and pontificated in print and over many a fireside whisky, it is rare that I find myself a complete beginner when trout are concerned. I am always, I hope, willing to listen, question and improve, but I expect to be a fair way up the learning curve. Montana was a delightful return to the baseline. It was a breath of fresh air from this Wild West frontier land that swept away much of the dogma, snobbery, and received wisdom that we all carry around with us. Any such surplus baggage had to be flung aside in the swift flowing purity of the Beaverhead's crystalline waters. My mind kept returning to one image - a picture of those wonderful trout – big, fat and plentiful, and unutterably wild.

But as I said, I had a long way to go before I was actually able to catch one! Coming from the south of England, I generally think of dry flies as being delicate, tiny representations of specific insects, or at least general imitations of fly life, which are flicked gently upstream. The Big Hole is a fast flowing freestone river that riffles, glides and charges between steep canyon walls, offering a lively habitat for rainbows, browns and the indigenous whitefish (a grayling look-alike without the sail dorsal fin). Just to throw me in at the deep end, we started by fishing two dries, one attached to the bend of the other by a yard of nylon. What surprised me was not the technique, but the flies themselves. You have to see a 'Parachute Madam X' to understand this. It is huge. Back home, we consider a crane fly/daddy-long-legs to be a large mouthful, but you should see the (grass)hopper flies out west. They are great big juicy representations of the natural, large and brawny, their legs almost kicking in the stream. In the smaller version I think they will also make brilliant crane flies (now there's an idea for next year...).

Even more shocking, in name as well as pattern was the huge rubber legged, foam bodied 'Chernobyl Ant'. I am no purist but this stretched even my stiff upper lip! But let's be honest - such aesthetic qualms do tend to melt rapidly in the heart thumping excitement of a swirling rise. The flies are ugly in all senses, but if beauty is in the eye of a trouty beholder, then they could pass as fine art for me. True, if I saw one crawling on my bathroom floor I would run for cover, but these monstrous bugs offer three great advantages. They never sink, they are always visible and being such a succulent morsel they are swallowed with abandon by larger fish. In my book that's not too bad a CV for a dry fly is it? Besides, some of the closer Hopper imitations really are works of the highest fly tying skill.

The trouble was that however appetising and attractive such dainty morsels were, my reactions were still back in the Ice Age. In the first, humbling few days I missed fish after fish. Learning to control the line, both to avoid drag and expedite the chances of a hook set whilst drifting downstream was a whole new ball game, and the fish hits were lightning fast. Time and time again my ever patient guide, Matt, would exhort me 'hit, HIT, HIITT!!' as I reacted woefully late yet once more, and another silver flash and splash signalled the spitting rejection of a substantial trout. On one calm stretch before a rapid, we saw four dimpling rises. I was fishing two dries, but however we changed the menu, the fish would only rise to the Royal Wulff. As Matt backrowed to slow the boat, I curled out four careful, hopeful casts, had four long, rolling, slow motion head and shoulder rises and hooked precisely none. Then the placid waters, with an almost heavy surface film, ran flat and peaceful, not a dimple again as we anchored and waited for a re-rise. Opportunity had knocked and had been wasted.

But the dry fly part was in fact the easiest. The major learning curve came later on the Beaverhead, when trying to control a fast flowing deep nymph between the weeds and right under the banks. I began to realise that the tighter I cast into the bank, the more fatties came out for lunch. The rig was a shock – a bright red yarn strike indicator, split shot and two nymphs, barbless size twenties, on 5x fine nylon. Once again, there was strict logic behind all this. To get unweighted mini flies down to the fish in such narrow, confined runs and so rapid a stream, and to have any hope of a hook up, requires pretty desperate measures. The addition or subtraction of one shot could, and did, make the difference between backing ripping runs and blank indifference. In fact I have to admit to an almost mesmeric fascination with the indicator, which was simply a bunch of yarn strips tied together and combed out into a sort of blushing red lily shape. It was very pretty, like watching a flower bob, swirl and float down the stream, twisting, slowing and reacting to every invisible mini current, to every breath of a stream within the stream. It was an object lesson in water currents and line control, and, once again, in rapid reactions.

You have to remember that knowing that you are drifting over a three or four-pound wild rainbow every couple of minutes does terrible things to the blood pressure, and missing hit after hit does even worse. All those magnificent trout wasted as you drift downstream, leaving all that hope and golden chance behind you – and there's no heaving the boat back upriver to try again. On my first day on this most exacting Mecca, we drifted off the main river, anchored the boat and set out to wade-fish a side channel. Here I was on terra firm and had a chance. In Montana most of the land we drifted through was privately owned, but the riverbed up to the average high water mark is public, so that as long as you put the boat in and out on a public piece of land, you can drift, wade and fish in freedom.

We jumped overboard and surveyed the pool. The river hit the wall of a steep canyon and angled to the right, leaving a mini channel of calm, deep water on the far bank beyond a weed bed, and otherwise scurrying over the shallows before spilling out into a deepening round hole. It was perfect. Just thirty feet above us a golden eagle circled effortlessly. Looking at the rugged, arid hills, I half expected John Wayne to appear at any moment, and had to pinch myself back to remember that this was not a movie, nor a fishing dream, but reality. Matt showed me the tension cast, whereby you lob the rig out, mend upstream, let it drift, mend back up and over the indicator, then feed line and mend downstream as the rig drifts away below you, still 'hunting'. When drag becomes inevitable you just point the rod straight at the fly, lift and swing the whole lot upstream. After a while it is easy, no need for willow-grabbing backcasts or tangling false casts, just an easy lob back into the pay zone.

Down the flower would drift, twisting in the swirls, hesitating as the current slowed, sliding to the left in a mini side stream, semaphoring an endless message up the line. Decoding it was the key. At first I was far too slow. The merest hesitation, hint of a deflection, and Matt told me to set the hook. If it was merely weed or current, no matter, it was just a lift off and recast. I tried to understand, and eventually the dawn broke, and rosy fingered light filtered into my addled mind. The yarn landed with a spilt shot plop, righted and floated, curled a bit and then curtsied – did not disappear in a heart and arm wrenching vortex, but merely dipped a fraction. Instead of my usual, hesitant half lift 'was that a fish', I heaved upwards. The yarn did not fly skyward, but rather stabbed down, and a vital, thumping kick at the other end meant I was attached to a two pound brown. I was there, at last.

But the biggest revelation was left to the last afternoon. The weather had been most unseasonable for fall – bright sun and midday temperatures well into the seventies, time for shirtsleeves and sunsets. It was great for a fisherman's soul, and suntan, but sweaty in neoprene's and not exactly ideal for fishing. On the last day, the weather gods showed us what it could have been all week, and at one stage we had to pull ashore and hunker down in the boat in what can only be described as Hurricane Beaverhead. Trying to cast was simply impossible, the line being hurled out of control straight downwind, the rain thumping horizontally into suddenly inadequate waterproofs, lightning streaking down to the riverside and clearing the river of rods in an instant! Just like everything else in Montana this squall was on a vast scale. The tricos had been hatching in abundance, and the side eddies and under bank whirls were just littered with their swarming masses. Even more to the point, the rainbows were just beginning to turn on to the only fly that they seemed to be willing to take, a minute Sparkle RS2, specifically tied by Matt and lethal. The sudden temperature drop killed the rise stone dead, and I ruefully pondered on the two monsters that had, as often, left us way behind.

Playing these rainbows on such fine line and small barbless hooks was a lottery. Why use barbless you might ask? The obvious reason is to support the catch and release ethic, but if you probe deeper I suspect that the C&R is as much for the guide and rods as the fish! Trying to clear weed from the flies in a mad, finger fumbling haste to get them back out into the purple patch, I twice stuck the fly beyond what would have been the barb, and less caring rods have been known to hook their guides often. But when you do hook them, (fish, not guides), what a spectacle lies in store! Jay, owner of the luxurious Five Rivers Lodge where we were staying, had commented that he had hooked seventeen big ones this year on the Upper Beaverhead, and had lost the lot – and he has fished here for over a decade and surely knows how to handle a fish. I hooked ten and landed five, and broke on none – which apparently was either lucky or a good effort. They fight as I imagine a steelhead must. Think back to that flowering nod again, then lift and hit, the blood pressure soaring. There is a leap and splash, then a long, long run into the backing. You follow frantically in the boat, there is an acrobatic cartwheel in a shower of dazzling spray and then it all goes slack... Once again that word, it was 'awesome' and humbling, and far too often it was a straightened, or weeded little nymph that trailed disconsolately back.

One fish that we reckoned at about three pounds or twenty inches, took whilst I was wading. It was another lesson learned, as the fish will happily take a mere couple of rod lengths away – no need for long distance casts that only reduce the chances of a successful hook up. Matt asked if I wanted to land it. What an odd question I thought, until I saw the backing disappear and realised that to land it we would have to leap into the boat and follow, oars flailing madly, thus leaving the blessed honey hole. We did, (I am glad to say), and we had to chase that beast down under the bridge, and around the corner before finally netting him an honest hundred yards below where he was hooked, no exaggeration. It felt epic, but somehow not unusual.

But as I said, the grand finale came on that last afternoon when the storm subsided and things returned to a cool, cloudy norm. Note the last phrase – cloudy. It took Matt about a second before he handed me the streamer rod, which he had been itching to use all week. I looked with horror at the two inch fluorescent yellow 'fly' before me, sprouting hideous yellow rubber legs and an even worse name, the Yellow Yummy. Ah well, when in Montana... In fact, even here, selective feeding (or attack) was prevalent as we attached a smaller black crystal Woolly Bugger to act as an extra choice and maybe a Yellow Yummy-chasing, trout-seducing fly. Thereafter all the fish took the black one.

Streamer fishing is a technique, I dare not use the term art form, all of its own. It is not at all like my idea of lure fishing, aimlessly casting for the horizon and stripping back in. It is a rapid search and attack, a sort of blitzkrieg sweep. As the boat drifts down, you prospect under the banks, casting into every back eddy and whirlpool, more of a lob than a cast, plopping the beast as close to the bank as possible and then twitching it out with jerks of the rod top. It is exhausting, repetitive, very visual and, when the fish are on, unbelievably 'hot'.

Let's float back to the Beaverhead. It is narrow, deepish and fast, rushing through banks lined with overhanging bushes and the tree felling edifices of the all-gnawing beaver. Overhead a rather wild, bright white light streaks out between the looming, fluffy grey cumulus. It is cool, but tense as you stand in the bow. You support your thighs in the leg rest to stop you lurching overboard as the boat spins in the rapids, or thumps a rock in the riffles. The rod is held in your right hand, your forearm now weary and aching, two huge, garish flies hanging down limply at the ready. Your mind is focussed on just one thing – getting that fly right under that grassy bank.

You concentrate on the mechanics, trying to peer beneath the surface and willing another large brown to crash out of his hole and engulf your fly in a rage. You are drifting towards a large, overhanging willow. Behind it swirls a back eddy the size of a coffee table in a small indentation in the bank. Matt warns you to get ready and cast right in the moment you drift below the tree. You remember to check behind you – there is nothing worse than missing the hot spot by hooking and losing the fly in the bank behind you. The cast has to be accurate – a yard too far and good bye fly and hello willow; a yard too short and no dice. But it lands bang in the hole, twitch, twitch, the gaudy flies darting and glistening out from the hole.

Suddenly all hell breaks loose. There's a golden flash underwater as a fish sees the intruder and turns. A log-like brown speckled back follows the fly, and then, literally, the rod top thumps down as the fish lunges viciously at the fly, kicking water into the air with its shovel of a tail. It is so aggressive, so fast and furious that it is almost frightening. Matt whoops with excitement as you see that broad, burnished flank launch airborne in an arc of golden colour, then plunge down for the bottom, whilst he heaves on the oars to get over to the side and drop anchor. Let the big one out of the hole and into the fast current downstream, and the curtain on this drama will fall in mid scene. You check for obstacles, for tree trunks in the back eddy as the fish throbs and tugs for freedom, your heart beating apace. It really is wonderful action – from tiny little undercuts below the bank we had three pound brownies launch themselves at and savage the fly, and one positive submarine that followed out to look. Matt yelled to recast, but as the boat drifted on I really only had one chance at an accurate lob and he wouldn't come out again. It is maybe not a method of delicacy or finesse, but for sheer excitement and large fish, streamer fishing surely takes some beating.

For me to appreciate this sunny trout fisher's heaven was hardly surprising, but I went with my close friend and impromptu (i.e. press-ganged) sub-editor, who had never fished before, and I was amazed and delighted to see her reaction. At first there was just a passing interest in what was at the other end of her line, and a relaxed enjoyment of the blissful weather and glorious canyon surroundings.

Barren, dusty hillsides and rocks towered up above us, the banks lined with cottonwood trees already decked in leafy yellow-orange and autumnal gold. The sparkling waters glinted in the sun, each sinuous bend of the river giving on to more wonderful vistas and distant mountains. After having been bent double in many a leaking, back aching Scottish rowing boat, a state of the art floating machine is sheer, unadulterated self-indulgence. You can luxuriate in a swivel seat, proper backrest, and leg supports. It has everything you could ask for when either fishing or just lounging in the afternoon warmth reading about the epic adventures of Lewis and Clark nearly two centuries ago in the very same waters that you now float. But by day three she was leaping out of the boat at the take out and wading off to continue fishing, whilst the so-called pros gave in and packed up. She caught a whitey on the nymph and a smallish brown, and hooked into two Beaverhead monsters before, as sadly predicted, hanging on too tight. We watched the rod point pull down towards the fish before smartly springing back, slack and empty – the first of many, no doubt.

Whilst her determination increased, she admitted that fishing was a fine excuse to be totally immersed in nature. It gave a chance to watch, enjoy and appreciate all those wonders that we are usually too busy to notice, or too far away, suffocating in some concrete grey city of exhaust fumes and over stressed individuals. But it was also a fantastic tonic, an all-embracing escape from work, a pursuit that heightens the senses and concentrates them all – to the complete exclusion of work pressure and similar extraneous thoughts. Another convert I am pleased to say, and I couldn't put it better than that. Perhaps she will now think me slightly less eccentric than previously!

It is difficult to convey the potent cocktail stirred by the majesty of the scenery, the sheer scale of it all and the almost unrealistic expectation engendered by the fishing. From the moment you blearily open the shutters at the lodge to that last reluctant cast of the day is an unending dream of hedonistic, sensual pleasure, basking in the mellow fruitfulness of nature and the tense anticipation of fishy delight. But if I had to try to define, or encapsulate my vision of southwest Montana, it would be the endless vista of mountains stretching out in all directions under the ever-changing light of that Big Sky. You really feel as if you are on top of the world, the air caught, motionless in the brilliant illumination of the afternoon sun. The views are spaceless, timeless and humbling, reducing petty human priorities to their just irrelevance in front of the massive stature and epic proportions of nature.

The ridges hump, jut and tower around this vast arena like an imposing boundary wall, a speechless, immovable audience watching the human antics on the Great Plains below. Apart from the sheer vastness of it all, it is the complete spectrum of light that nature's palette throws upon this wonderful backdrop that continually challenges, fascinates and inspires. From that icy, pastel dawn through the shimmering afternoon, the rivers glistening a reflecting blue, the wave crests sparkling as if with a myriad rhinestones in the unexpected sunshine, to the sinking blood orange of a fiery sunset. As we drifted home one evening, the clouds massing vermilion and purple, a bald eagle perched on a dead tree just by the riverside, a stark, majestic silhouette against the glowing embers of the day. Underneath, rustling amidst the willows, a startled white tail deer looked up and scurried off, its fleecy white rump bouncing along. It jumped into and swam across the river before gracefully leaping up onto the far bank and bounding off across the meadows. The mountains began to lose form and blur into a heavy grey-blue mass, outlined, etched in a white yellow light rising up through layers of ever deeper blue to the ceiling of stars above.

It was like an endless movie, apt in this land of the Wild West, played out on the panoramic wide screen of the surrounding Rockies. Just to cap it all, as we reluctantly departed, the peaks were coated with a fresh dusting of icing sugar snow, harbinger of winter to come and the end of another fishing season. As we hit the highroad we couldn't resist glancing back, and saw the rings of one last trout rise spreading gently across the placid waters. It imprinted a freeze frame picture on the memory to enrich, warm and gladden the cold, dark months of a fishless winter, a final farewell and invitation to return from the glorious rivers, mountains and wild trout of Montana.

Fishing Locations & Contact Details

The following is a list of contact, travel and fishing details for the locations mentioned in the text, which I have tried to ensure is accurate at the time of going to press, though keeping up to date with current email and internet addresses is a thankless task. All, except perhaps the River Kjarra/Thvera in Iceland, are readily accessible to the public, though obviously early booking for the more popular sites is advisable. The costs quoted are only rough guidelines from 2000/2001. I hope that you get to fish one or many of them; be it the most exclusively expensive or humbly simple, they all offer one priceless pleasure – the chance to enjoy wild fish in wild places.

ENGLAND

River Teign, Dartmoor, Devon

Salmon, Sea trout and Brown trout.
Salmon – 1st February to 30th September
Sea Trout – 15th March to 12th or 30th September
Brown Trout – 15th March to 30th September

Fishing :
The Teign is a small, wooded, peat-tinged stream that runs off Dartmoor, and is one of the best sea trout rivers in England. It used to have an early run of big spring salmon, but as everywhere this is now just a memory. Salmon appear, these days, in May/June as do the bigger (2-5lb) spring sea trout, though a few can be taken in April. Grilse and smaller sea trout (1-2lb) run in July, and August sees the school peal arrive (small sea trout 0.5-1lb). A run of salmon also comes in September, but sea trout by then can be red. Given rain, grilse runs can still be good and I had 3 in 3 mornings in late August 1997. Salmon fishing does depend on water and many pools require a spinner, being deep, slow flowing and overhung with branches. The usual hot spots are the deep holding pools above and below the weirs/bridges (Sowton/Ashford/Bridford/Newbridge) and the junction with the Bovey, but there are many little pots in between that are seldom fished. A car is essential, as you need to try a spot and then move on. Sea trout fishing is best at night with small (6-10) flies, unless after rain when daytime spinning can be effective in coloured water. The most used spinners are Rapalas and Flying C's, though I prefer to spin upstream with small gold or copper Mepps in sizes 1-3. Sea trout flies are standard, Alexandra, Peter Ross, Squirrel and Silver, Black and Gold etc. As many pools can be slack, a fly with some wing movement can be effective, as are wake lures late at night (Muddler Minnow or any foam bodied fry fly will often bring up fish when all else fails). A single-handed rod is all that is required, or a nine foot light spinning rod. Thigh waders can be useful,

though you rarely need to cast more than a dozen yards.

The Upper Teign is known for its wild brown trout, which are small but prolific and rise well to a dry fly in the spring. Small olives, black gnats and terrestrials do well. They also have salmon and sea trout given adequate water, and in wet years the upper river can fish better than the lower as the fish run straight through. Fishing tactics are the same as for the Lower Teign. The river runs through Dartmoor and is very pretty.

Contact: Lower Teign Fishing Association – day tickets are available at Tackle Trader, Wharf Road, Newton Abbot, S. Devon (01626 331613)

Cost: £15-£25 sunrise to sunrise depending on which beat.

Upper Teign Fishing Association – day tickets for brown trout available at The Anglers Rest, Fingle Bridge, Drewsteignton (Tel: 01647 281287); James Bowden & Son (Ironmongers), The Square, Chagford (Tel: 01647 433271) and Exeter Angling Centre, Smythen Street, Exeter, (Tel: 01392 436404). Bowdens also sells evening tickets for sea trout, and the Anglers Rest sells 7 salmon tickets a day. Drewsteignton Post Office and the Clifford Bridge Caravan Park also have some tickets.

Cost: £5 a day for brown trout (£15 a week), sea trout £7, salmon £15.

NB Since 2000, there have been Environment Agency restrictions on spring salmon catches (any salmon caught before 16th June has to be returned, but any method and barbed hooks are allowed – a pretty useless fudge).

Chalkstreams – Hampshire/Wiltshire

Brown trout, grayling (both wild) plus stocked browns and rainbows.
(Also salmon/sea trout on bottom beats of the River Test).
Trout – April 15 or 1st May to 30th September or 15th October
Grayling – 16th June to 14th March (seldom fished after January)

Fishing:

Dry fly and (sometimes) upstream nymph. The fish (browns and grayling) on the upper reaches and tributaries of the rivers are mostly wild. On the Itchen they are often stock browns, and on the Test browns and rainbows. Best time is May/June, and some rivers (Avon, Itchen, Test) have the big drake mayfly hatches. The Bourne is better later in the summer, July/August and is my favourite. Salmon/sea trout fishing is available on the Test, with heavily weighted 'lifted nymphs' as well as more traditional night fly fishing for sea trout. The salmon are rather a nostalgic memory, but the sea trout can be worthwhile. Flies are legion, but as general imitations I would hate to be without an Adams (dry) and Goldhead Pheasant Tail (nymph). Beyond that there are literally hundreds... This is where the cult of the dry fly began.

Contact:
Wiltshire Avon at UpAvon:
Peter Prince, 33 The Old Tractor Yard, Rushall, Pewsey, Wilts SN9 6EN.
Tel: 01980 630008 Cost : £40 a day (small, slightly canal-like beat, no need for guide, smallish fish, great for beginners/youngsters).

Famous Fishing (on 19 chalkstreams) :
William Daniel - William Daniel <FamousFishing@compuserve.com>
Tel: 01722 716210 Fax: 01722 716050
Email: enquiries@famousfishing.co.uk
Web: http://www.famousfishing.co.uk

Cost: From £50 to £160 per rod and £140 for a qualified guide (+VAT).
Tackle provided. Good guides and super rivers to fit most needs (from beginner to expert and, dare I say it, corporate fat cats too).

Travel: less than 2 hours drive from London via M3 or M4.

NB Rod Fishing licences are required in England, available at post offices, tackle shops etc. Cost depends on duration and type of fish sought.

BERMUDA

Personally I am not a fan of deep sea trolling, and have only done it once so I cannot recommend any specific boats or skippers. There are many available locally and on the internet. One lucky friend, Magne Seljeflot, who catches human-sized tuna, recommends:

Captain Allen DeSilva, Mako Charters, 11 Abri Lane, Spanish Point, Pembroke HM 02, Bermuda
Tel: Boat 234-8626 Office: (441) 295-0835 Fax: (441) 295-3620
Email: mako@ibl.bm Web: www.fishbermuda.com

Cost: US$1,200 a day (6 person)

I am told that there are bonefish too, though I have not fished for them.
http://www.bermudabonefish.com, Tel: (441)292-2190, jhpfish@ibl.bm.

ICELAND

River Kjarra/Thvera in Borgarfirdi, West Iceland
Salmon, Arctic Char and Sea Trout.
June-August (12 weeks, 14 rods)

Fishing:
The Kjarra is the upper river, and involves a lot of walking and hill climbing. Fishing is now by fly only (and the Thvera is heading that way too – happily so). Flies used are small (12,14, microtubes in low flows), on floating lines, with standard local patterns (Red & Black Francis) and especially small black bodied flies (Stoat Tail, Blue Charm, Munro Killer, Black Sheep, Hairy Mary). The lower river, The Thvera, is more open and a double handed rod can be useful, (The Kjarra and the top canyon section of the Thvera can easily be fished with a single hander), and the same flies but maybe in size 8/10, down to 12 in low water. This is an early river, the fish in June are the biggest, up to and over 20lbs, and July sees the main grilse runs averaging about 6lbs. On the Thvera especially there is always the chance of a big fish, and a second run comes in later in August – always use strong nylon! The fishing is expensive and very booked up, but the scenery, lodges and salmon runs are excellent, dream fishing – one of the top ten rivers in Iceland.

Contact: Jon Olafsson, Spordur
Tel: 354 587 0860 Fax: 354 568 0645
Cost: Top 'wild' river in Iceland in 1999. Details upon application – obviously it is expensive and booked up well in advance.

Travel :
Two hours drive north of Reykjavik. There are daily Icelandair flights to Keflavik (Reykjavik) from Heathrow/Glasgow and European capitals. Transport to the lodges is provided from Reykjavik or Keflavik.

River West and East Ranga – South Iceland
Breiddalsa – East Iceland
Minnivallalækur & Upper West Ranga (Trout) – South Iceland

Salmon, Sea trout, Arctic Char, Brown trout.
Salmon – Ranga – 20 June to 10 October (best July-August)
Breiddalsá – 1st July to 30 September (best Aug/Sept)
Sea Trout – best in September
Brown Trout – Minnivallalækur – 1st May to 15 September

Fishing:
The West Ranga is a spring fed river that offers almost guaranteed water height, clarity and temperature (8-12 degrees C). The wind can be strong, so a double handed rod is useful except in sunny calm weather when a single hander can be used. I use a twelve foot eight weight which is perfect. Lines are usually sink tip, intermediate or a full floater with sinking leader, though sometimes a straight floater will work. The most popular fly is the Snaelda, a one inch brass tube, but standard patterns in size 6/8 are also effective (Francis, Shrimp, Collie Dog) as are the Sunray Shadow and tube flies. The East Ranga is faster and colder, and can run cloudy with snowmelt and unfishably dirty with rain. Brass tubes (Snaelda, Francis) are used with slow sinking line types. The season opens in July with bigger fish, up into the twenties, the main grilse runs (4-8lbs) coming in towards August. September sees sea trout into double figures. The 2000 Ranga catch (West and East) was over 3,700 salmon and 400,000 smolts were released in the spring.

Brown Trout – the Upper West Ranga also offers exceptional fly fishing for wild brown trout, especially in June, though I have seen fish of 8lbs and 12lbs taken in August 1998 and 1999! Throstur can also arrange brown trout fishing on another top river, Minnivallalækur, where in May/June 1999 the trout averaged over 5lbs and six were caught 10-12lbs, mainly on streamers and nymphs. It is as perfect a trout river as I have ever fished. May 2001 saw a fish estimated at 20lbs taken (yes, a wild brown trout).

In 1997 a smolt release programme was instituted on a river in the East of Iceland at Breiddalsvík – the River Breiddalsá and tributary Tinnudalsa which give fantastic views, lodging and classic single handed fly fishing in waterfall/canyon scenery. At present, as salmon returns (many of them big 2 sea-winter fish) are just being established, access is both cheaper and easier than the Ranga. The river takes 6-8 rods and is a late one – August and September being best. There is also excellent arctic char fishing, (and nice browns). The rivers do depend on water. Smaller flies (8-12) and standard patterns with floating lines and maybe sinking leaders are all that is required, especially shrimp patterns (Red and Black Francis). The head guide, Sudi, prefers silver, or even gold hooks. The lodge is one of the most comfortable I have seen and the scenery unequalled.

Contact: Throstur Ellidason, Angling Service Strengir, Smárarima 30, PO Box 12024, 132 Reykjavik, Iceland. Phone/Fax: 354 567 5204
Mobile Phone: +354 893 5590
Email: "Angling Service Stengir" <ellidason@strengir.is>
Web: http://www.strengir.is

(NB at time of printing, it is not certain that Throstur will still be leasing the Ranga in 2001. As he is the man who had the vision, patience and sheer guts to create this fishery, and the landowner's wealth, this is a great shame and injustice).

Cost :
Ranga (Salmon) – US$800-US$1,000 per day (US$500 September)
Browns – US$200-300 per day, Sea Trout - US$500 per day in September
Breiddalsá – (Salmon/sea trout/char) – usually in combination trip with Ranga, but will stand on its own merits very soon as catches progress.

Non fishing guests pay $170 per day
Rod sharing is allowed and significantly reduces costs, and as Icelandic salmon fishing days involve a full 12 hours of fishing, is very practical.

There is also excellent arctic char fishing on the Hvolsa River in a self-catering lodge at US$390 per day July-September.

Travel:
The Ranga is at Hella, 1.5 hours drive southeast from Reykjavik and Throstur will pick you up. There are daily Icelandair flights to Keflavik (Reykjavik) from Heathrow/ Glasgow, plus several European capitals and New York. Breiddalsvík has a very small airstrip for charter flights, or the scheduled airport is an hour away at Egilsstadir and the gillies act as taxi service.

Federation of Icelandic River Owners :
Web: http://www.arctic.is/angling/rivers.html
Info on Rivers Grímsá, Midjardará, Rangá, Breiddalsá, Laxá í Dölum, Vídidalsá, Laxá Kjós, Lake Thórisvatn, Laxá in Thingeyjarsysla, Vatnsdalsá trout section, Langá, Hítará river + trout and char fishing.

IRELAND

Lough Corrib, Galway, Ireland

Brown trout, Salmon.
February 15th to 30th September

Fishing:
Flyfishing (and trolling bait!) for magnificent limestone wild brown trout, (and some salmon in the summer), that run well into double figures on the troll and up to 5lbs+ on fly. The record trout is 22lbs! The duck fly (midge pupae) come early, in March/April, then olives and Mayfly, then usual summer sedge etc. Traditional flies (Green Peter, Duckfly, Murrough, Dabblers) and more specific dry/nymph imitations are used according to the season and hatch. The lough is huge (44,000 acres) and a good boatman/guide essential both for safety and local knowledge. Best time April/May and September, high summer can be difficult, (though trolling produces monster fish).

Contact: Currarevagh House, Oughterard, Connemara, Co. Galway, Ireland.
Tel : 091 552312/552313 Fax : 091 552731 (Built in 1842)
Email: currarevagh@ireland.com
Cost: B&B €75, Dinner €32, Fishing guide €85 per day.
Irish Blue Book Web (country manors, hotels etc, some with fishing):
http://www.irelands-blue-book.ie

Glenlo Abbey Hotel (5 star)
Tel: 091 526 666 Fax: 091 527 800
Email: glenlo@iol.ie Web: http://www.glenlo.com/subpage.htm

Cost: IR£100-200 a night, dinner IR£38, breakfast IR£12

Guide: Jim Riddell Email: riddellj@tinet.ie Tel: 087 2578485 £110 a day 153 Lurgan Park, Murrough, Renmore, Co. Galway (a great experience)

There are many fishing bed and breakfasts and small, inexpensive fishing hotels on Corrib, centred around Oughterard. A brochure – 'The Great Fishing Houses of Ireland' is available from Bord Failte, Irish Tourist Board, 150 New Bond Street, London W1, Tel: 0171 5180800, Fax 0171 493 9065
Email: info@irishtouristboard.co.uk, Web: http://www.ireland.travel.ie

Oughterard Tourist Office – Tel: 091 552808 Fax: 091 552811

Galway Weir Fishery, Galway, Ireland
Salmon: 1st February – 30th Sept., Sea Trout 1st June – 30th Sept.

Fishing:
A short beat in the middle of Galway City, right by the Cathedral, but renowned for prolific runs of salmon, now declining, though the average is still over 900 a year. Best time is June for the main grilse run. Fishing is by fly or spinner, Glenlo Abbey or the WFB (see below) can arrange fishing by the day or half day, though prime time is popular and booked up. Try small Irish Shrimp patterns (or spinners). Apart from the River Moy, this must be one of the most productive stretches of salmon fishing in Ireland (or Europe). A new beat has just been added further down, at lesser price.

Western Fisheries Board, Weir Lodge, Earl's Island, Galway,
Tel: 091 563118 Fax: 091 566335 Email: info@wrfb.ie
Web: http://www.wrfb.ie/
The angling report is updated each week.

Fishery Manager, Galway Fishery, Nun's Island, Galway City
Tel 091 562388 Fax 091 562930 E-mail: shartgalfish@eircom.net

Cost: May 21st to July 15th, there are 2 sessions per day, 06.00-13.00 & 13.30-20.30 at £45.00 (Euro €57.14) per session, New Beat £10.

Travel:
There are domestic flights from Dublin to Galway, or to Shannon which is a couple of hour's drive away. Dublin itself is 3.5 hours by road.

The Great Fishing Houses of Ireland, P.O. Box 6375, Dublin 4, Ireland.
Phone: +353-1-668-8278, Fax: +353-1-660-5566
http://www.irelandflyfishing.com/index.html

NORWAY
Ostermarka Trout Lakes, Oslo
Brown trout

Fishing :
There are 400 lakes, 90% with trout, in the forests above Oslo. The closest to the City (by the garbage dump, or at the foot of the ski jump) are the most heavily fished, further up into Normarka/Ostermarka they are more remote (45 minutes by car, plus

a half-hour walk). Bank fly-fishing in hill forest, peaty trout lakes with traditional wet flies and dries (midge, ant, emerger, caddis, dragon/damselfly). As the water is dark, I find gold, orange and black loch style flies work well, as does the trusty KeHe. The fish are not large, mainly under a pound. You can also spin, which in some parts, with steep pine forested banks, can help casting considerably. Wading is inadvisable, but wellies are a must. There are also sea trout in saltwater within 10 minutes of downtown Oslo, and the River Drammenselva has salmon fishing just 40 kilometers away.

Contact:
General fishing tax licences are available at post offices. For specific details on fishing, local licences (salmon/sea trout/brown) and exact locations, try any of the fishing shops in Oslo such as Nordisk Fiskeutstyr, Villmarkshuset, Christian Kroghs Gate 16a, 0186 Oslo, Tel: 47 22050542.

Travel:
Flight access to Oslo, then by hire car or bicycle (it is easy to hire both).

Cost:
Minimal, day or week permits and tax licences cost usually under £10.

SCOTLAND

For general information on accessibility to fishing in Scotland, the best reference is 'Trout & Salmon Rivers & Lochs of Scotland' by Bruce Sandison, published by Merlin Unwin in 1997, updated 2001.

Limestone Lochs & River Dionard, Durness, Sutherland

Brown trout, Salmon, Sea trout
Brown Trout – best May/June & September
Salmon – grilse runs depend on water July – September

Fishing:
Limestone Lochs Caladail, Borralaidh, Lanlish, Croisspol, by boat and from the bank (Lanlish is bank only). Fly only, especially during summer evenings and nightfall. Traditional wet flies, plus dry olives, sedge, buzzers and (in autumn) daddy long legs, plus fry imitations. Difficult fishing for big fish, average weights seem to be growing in the last 3 years – Croisspol 1lb, Borralaidh 1.5-2.5lb, Caladail 2-4lb, Lanlish 4lb+. Caladail produced many 3-4lb fish on small (18-22) dry flies last year. Splendid silver flanked browns that look, fight and taste like sea trout. Best catch in 1999 was 8 trout totalling 32lbs!

Also salmon and sea trout fishing, fly only, on the bottom beats of the River Dionard, best season is July to September depending on rainfall and consequent runs of fish. Fish can be red later in the season. Single-handed rod and usual smallish salmon flies (size 6, 8). A typical Highland spate stream – lovely fishing after rain amidst splendid scenery. Also some nice sea trout – in 1998 an 8lb fish was caught in July.

Contact: Jack Watson, Cape Wrath Hotel, Keodale, Durness, by Lairg, Sutherland, Scotland, IV27 4SW.
Tel: 01971 511212 Email: jack@capewrath.co.uk
Fax: 01971 511313 Web: www.capewrathhotel.co.uk

Cost: Boat £15, bank £10, hotel B&B £35 a night, River Dionard £25.

River and Loch Dionard, Sutherland
Salmon and Sea trout as above.

Fishing:
For the bottom beats of the river see above. For the rest of the river (6 beats) and the excellent sea trout loch at the top of the system it is possible to book the whole river for a week. A lodge (for 8) and flat (for 2) are available for accomodation. Strath Dionard is an SSSI (Site of Special Scientific Interest), with breeding greenshank, merlin and eagles, set in wonderful scenery, but does need rain. If the river is out of water or fish, the limestone lochs are nearby, and there are plenty of less challenging trout lochs in front of the lodge. The main loch is remote, pitch black and right under the sheer cliff of Foinaven where the golden eagles nest. It also has lots of fish in it! A beautiful place to fish, and lovely fly water, given rain.

Contact: David Allingham, White Hall, Syderstone, King's Lynn, Norfolk, PE31 8SB, England. Tel : 01328 823233

River Kirkaig/Upper Inver/Upper Oykel, Sutherland
Salmon, sea trout (and brown trout on numerous lochs).
Salmon – 11th Feb to 30th Sept (Oykel) or 15th Oct (Inver/Kirkaig)
Trout – 1st April (lochs) 1st May (rivers) to 4th October/26th June
Sea Trout – 1st July to 15th October
(prior 1st July all fish must be released)

Fishing:
The top and middle beats of the Kirkaig require some mountaineering and lots of walking amidst spectacular scenery and great fly water. The lower beat is right by the road and much easier on the legs. The Inver is an easier, bigger river, but these days lacks fish. Double handed rods are needed on both in high water, otherwise single handers in summer with standard flies, (large sizes in fast water, even weighted tubes, especially Collie Dog and Willie Gun on the Kirkaig). The Upper Oykel is a typical heathland stream, and the loch good too. The hotel is very comfortable, food excellent and it commands magical views. Absolutely classic fly fishing for the relatively energetic, but heavily dependent on water for the summer grilse runs. Back end fish can be red (or black) especially on the upper rivers. The Kirkaig still has a few big fish in June, up into the 'teens of pounds – exciting sport. This is my idea of quintessential Highland salmon fishing in marvellous scenery, fly water and comfort (midges apart!). Also hundreds of trout lochs available.

Contact: Nicholas Gorton, Inver Lodge Hotel, LochInver, by Lairg, Sutherland, IV27 4LU
Tel: 01571 844496 Fax : 01571 844395
Email: stay@inverlodge.com Web: www.inverlodge.com

Cost: Trout £5 bank, £10 boat, £25 river (pre July 1st). Estuary sea-trout £15 a day, salmon £90. Price for full board would be £100 a day (less for longer stay packages).

Loch Hope & Altnaharra Trout Lochs Sutherland
Salmon, Sea trout, Brown trout.
Salmon 1 March – 30 September
Brown Trout 15th March-6th October

Fishing:

Loch Hope now offers about the best boat fly fishing for sea trout in Scotland, (about 500 a year, plus 10 salmon in 2000), the fish beginning to run in June. Traditional loch style wet flies and dapping, a Blue Zulu is a great starter as a bob fly. Majestic scenery too. I favour the South End beats, though Middle Bay can be exciting. Personally I hate trolling for salmon on Loch Naver, though later in the season the top end is fly fished and does hold good trout, but I prefer the brown trout fishing on Lochs Loyal and Craggie, and especially Slaim which also holds salmon up from the Borgie – a lovely river to fish given water, and one that still maintains spring runs. There is trout fishing at all levels from quite difficult (Loyal) to reliably generous (Slaim) to downright easy small fish for beginners (Meadie). The gillies can advise. There are 13 hill lochs to fish, and in 2000 the best trout scaled 6lbs! The hotel is comfortable with good food and wine. There are also spate salmon rivers (Mudale, Strathmore), plus occasional access to better known rivers such as the Borgie and public waters on the exclusive Naver and Helmsdale.

Contact: Anne Nielsen, Altnaharra Hotel, by Lairg, Sutherland, IV27 4UE, Scotland.

Tel/fax: 01549 411 222 Email: enquiries@altnaharra.com

Web: http://www.altnaharra.com

Cost: full board is around £79 and fishing Loch Hope £40 a day, plus £38 for a boatman/gillie. The trout lochs are £25 per boat and salmon rivers from £25-50 a rod day. Professional fishing/casting instruction also available at £100/£60 a day/half day.

If travelling north to Sutherland by car, you will probably pass via Lairg/Bonar Bridge, in which case it is well worth visiting the Falls of Shin, especially during the summer when salmon and sea trout are running and jumping. There is a good Visitor Centre for food and shopping:

Tel: 01549 402231, email: info@fallsofshin.co.uk

Web: www.highlandescape.com/fallsofshin

Trout Lochs, Caithness

Brown trout

Fishing:

Traditional loch style fishing, boat and wading, for brown trout on Lochs such as Watten, Toftingall, St Johns. Watten fish are as silvery as sea trout, and St Johns has a good mayfly hatch. Best season May/June and September. The little Wick River also produces, surprisingly, about 300 salmon a year given enough rain.

Contact. Hugo Ross, Fishing Tackle Shop, 56 High Street, Wick, Caithness, KW1 4BP, Scotland.

Tel: 01955 604200 Email: hugo@hugo-ross.co.uk

Cost: £20-30 a day for trout.

Sutherland & Caithness Trout Angling. Web: http://www.fishing-highland.co.uk

River Tay, Perthshire

Excellent Spey casting tuition and fishing on Murthly Castle and Glendelvine Beats of the River Tay in April/May, (plus fishing in Iceland, Russia and elsewhere):-

Contact: Michael Evans, Little Saxbys Farm, Cowden, Kent, TN8 7DX.

Tel: 01342 850765 Fax: 01342 850926

Cost: 3 day Tay course £340-£390 + VAT (excludes accommodation)

River Dee, Aberdeenshire
Salmon, Sea trout
Salmon : March-September

Fishing:
The greatest spring salmon river. Small flies on floating lines in gin clear waters. Also a goodish (and often ignored) run of sea trout starting in June. Nowadays salmon have to be returned on many beats. These beats on the Lower Dee are good, and easily accessible to everyone. Take a wading stick as the river is broad and the bottom can be slippery in the surprisingly pushy current.

Contact:
Durris Beats – James & Meg Anderson,
West Mains of Keithock, by Brechin, Angus, DD9 7QD
Tel : 01356 626037 Fax : 01356 626041

River Don, Aberdeenshire
Salmon, Sea trout and Brown trout
Salmon - 11th February to 30th October
Brown Trout – 5th April to 6th October (may differ slightly on some beats)

Fishing:
Classic salmon fishing by fly or spinner, throughout the season. The Don still retains a spring run, a big fish autumn run and is also the best brown trout river in Scotland and maybe the whole UK, and mainly on dry fly. The March Brown and Olive hatches bring up wild browns of three and four pounds, (best fish recently topped six – to a dry fly!).

Contact: Forbes Estate Office, Castle Forbes, Alford, Aberdeenshire AB33 8BL, Scotland.
Tel: 019755 62524 Fax: 019755 62898
Email: Castle@castle-forbes.com

Cost: Castle Forbes Trout £20 per day, £75 per week.
Castle Forbes Salmon £25-45 per day, £110-190 per week.
Accommodation at special all-inclusive rates available at
Castle Forbes to Forbes Estate fishing tenants.

Colin Hart, Grant Arms Hotel, Monymusk, Inverurie, Aberdeenshire, Scotland, AB51 7HJ.
Tel: 01467 651226 Fax: 01467 651494
(The Paradise Wood beats are aptly named.)

Cost: Double room £65, trout £15, salmon £35 per day, £175 week.
An 18th century coaching inn, with 13 fishing beats over 10 miles.

South Uist Estate, Western Isles
Brown trout, Salmon, Sea trout
Salmon/Sea Trout – Feb/March to 15th/30st October but best in summer
Brown Trout – 15th March to 30th September

Fishing:
For wild machair brown trout (May/June, September), and salmon and sea trout (July-September). By boat or wading, (the lochs are shallow and generally easy to

wade in chestwaders). Fly only, using traditional loch flies (don't fish for the browns without a KeHe or local fly Charlie Maclean as bob fly and Silver Invicta/Kingfisher Butcher as point). Machair trout are often up to 2lbs and over, amongst the best lochs are Bornish, Grogarry, Stilligarry, West Ollay, East Bee. In 1998 over 1,000 wild trout were taken, best 3lbs14oz, with 242 over 2lbs and an average of a pound. 150 sea trout below 1.5lbs were returned and 182 kept, up to 8.5lbs, plus 92 salmon up to 12lbs.

Contact: Lochboisdale Hotel, Lochboisdale, South Uist, Outer Hebrides, HS8 5TH
Tel: 01878 700332 Fax 01878 700367

Cost: Trout £22 per boat, Salmon £28-£55 depending on season, gillie £35.
Weekly rates for dinner, bed & breakfast around £55 per person day

South Uist Tourist Office Tel: 01876 700286

North Uist, Western Isles
Salmon, Sea trout and Brown trout, (best seasons as above).
Season as above.

Fishing:
Traditional loch style boat fishing in peaty waters. Uist is mainly water, there are lochs, and fish, everywhere you look, in all directions! The sea trout can be of a nice size (5lbs).

Contact: Lochmaddy Hotel, Lochmaddy, North Uist, Western Isles, HS6 5AA, Scotland.
Tel: 01876 500331 / 2 Fax: 01876 500210
Email: info@lochmaddyhotel.co.uk Web: www.lochmaddyhotel.co.uk

Cost: B&B £80 double room, dinner £18, trout fishing free but £15 a boat.
Salmon/sea trout £20-45 per rod per beat per day.

North Uist Tourist Office Tel : 01876 500321

Travel:
Either by car ferry from the mainland to either Lochboisdale or Lochmaddy, or via British Airways to Benbecula from Glasgow, where you can hire a car and drive across to the Uists. Ferries are operated by Caledonian MacBrayne.

Web: http://www.calmac.co.uk (with full timetables),
Email: reservations@calmac.co.uk
Tel: +44 (0)8705 650000 Fax: +44 (0)1475 635235

Scottish Tourist Board : http://www.visitscotland.com/

VENEZUELA

Los Roques, Venezuela
Bonefish, (+ Barracuda, Spanish Mackerel, Jack, Tarpon,)
Season : year round, but best January-October

Fishing:
Sight fishing with fly or spinner for bonefish on the Carribbean flats, and in the mangroves. Fishing can be by boat over deep shoals of fish, or the more exciting, but challenging wading the shallows for feeding and tailing fish. A bonefish swims at over twice the speed of a salmon! Specific tackle is required for each species (especially tarpon rods which are very strong, and reels with huge amounts of backing and

serious disc drags). The bonefish average 3-5lbs but can go 7-10lbs. Los Roques is an archipelago of 48 islands set amidst the azure Caribbean Sea in a Venezuelan Nature Reserve. Flies used, size 4/6: Gotchas, Crazy Charlies, Clouser Minnows etc or spinners: Diamond Jigs (brown, white, & yellow) and Wiggle Jigs (brown, white, & yellow).

Contact:
I stayed at Pez Raton Lodge, which can now be booked through Frontiers
18 Albemarle Street, London W1X 3HA
Tel: 0207 493 0798, Fax: 0207 629 5569
Email: london@frontierstrvl.com, http://www.frontierstrvl.com/ or for the USA
Tel: 724-935-1577, Fax: 724-935-5388, Email: info@frontierstrvl.com).

Cost for 7 nights/6 days fishing double occupancy/boat US$ 2,995.
Otherwise Linea Turistica Aereotuy can arrange flights/lodging on Gran Roque or a yacht and fishing:-

Caracas: Boulevard de Sabana Grande, Edificio Gran Sabana, N-174, Piso 5
Phone: (582) 7616231; (582)7616247; (582)7618043; (582)718483
Fax: (582)7625254
Email : Tuysales@etheron.net

Cost: US$1,500-US$1,800 for 5 day all inclusive package

There are also several private tour operators that offer package trips at upmarket sites such as Macabi Lodge, full advertising on the internet, eg:
http://www.chapisportfishing.com/

Travel:
Most major European airlines fly daily to Caracas, and there are several domestic flights a day to Gran Roque, which takes under an hour.

UNITED STATES

Rivers Beaverhead, BigHole, Jefferson, Ruby, Poindexter Slough, McCoy (Spring Creek) – Montana

Brown and Rainbow trout (plus Whitefish, Cut-throat, Brook trout).
Season: All year, but realistically the fishing is spring to autumn.

Fishing:
Flyfishing, drifting and wading, with dry, nymph and streamer for big fish. Tactics vary throughout the season, depending on weather, water flow and hatching insect life, which can be anything from tiny baetis, midge, BWO, and caddis (sedge) through to huge terrestrials (grasshoppers/craneflies in the fall) or the famed salmon fly hatch (June) on the Big Hole. Heavy Woolly Bugger streamers also work well, especially in late season when it is overcast. Five weight rods (maybe 6 for streamers) and lots of backing required. It is easy to buy the fly of the moment locally, or the guides will tie them. The big rainbows and browns, especially in the top section of the Beaverhead below the dam where they average over 3lbs, are awe inspiring in their acrobatic power and the Rockies are magnificent. There are also various spring creeks for 'chalkstream' type fishing which put the Itchen and Test to shame. The lodge, hospitality and food are top grade, and the guides patient and knowledgeable. Bring lots of layered clothing, as the weather can be extreme and very changeable. Wild trout in the 3-5lb range are, literally, common…

Contact: Jay Burgin, Five Rivers Lodge, 13100 Highway 41 North, Dillon, Montana 59725-9533, USA.
Tel: 1 800 378 5006 or 406 683 5000 Fax: 1 406 683 6470
Email: fiverivers@mcn.net

Cost: US$400 per rod per day based on 2 people sharing a room/boat and guide. Spring creeks are about $80 a day extra (remarkably good value).

Travel:
Once in the USA, Delta flies from Salt Lake City to Butte, Montana where Jay will pick you up. There are many internal domestic flights to Salt Lake.

This, and other trips, can also be booked through Westbank Anglers (I booked through the Houston shop opposite the Galleria, on Westheimer. They know the fishing well, and, of course, all the tackle etc needed):
http://www.westbank.com/westbank/default.asp

Fish & Environmental Conservation Contacts

North Atlantic Salmon Fund

The indefatigable Icelander, Orri Vigfusson, has done more to buy off netsmen (intelligently, in a sustainable fashion) than anyone else, and left many more salmon to spawn in the world's rivers as a result. By buying this book you have already contributed to the fund, and I hope you will continue. Otherwise we will leave a sad, salmon-less world after us.

North Atlantic Salmon Fund.
Skipholti 35, 105 Reykjavik, Iceland.
Tel: +354 568 6277. Fax: +354 588 4758.
Email: NASF@gamefishing.co.uk. Web: http://www.gamefishing.co.uk/NASF/

The Wild Trout Trust (Britain & Ireland)

Created in 1997 in order to conserve the wild trout of Britain and Ireland through the protection and restoration of their habitats.

The Wild Trout Society, 92-104 Carnwath Road, London SW6 3HW.
Web: http://www.wildtrout.org Subscriptions: join@wildtrout.org

Trout Unlimited (USA)

Founded in 1958 to conserve, protect and restore North America's coldwater fisheries and their watersheds.

1500 Wilson Boulevard; Suite 310, Arlington, VA 22209-2404, USA.
Phone: (703) 522-0200 Fax: (703) 284-9400
Web: http://www.tu.org/

The Salmon & Trout Association

Formed in 1903 by the Worshipful Company of Fishmongers in the City of London, the S&TA represents the views of game anglers, with 115,000 individual and club members throughout the UK. S&TA promotes a conservation-based agenda together with the Anglers Conservation Association (ACA), fighting abstraction and pollution and influencing the management of our Water Industry. There are 3 focus areas :- education, conservation of the aquatic environment and political lobbying.

Fishmongers' Hall, London Bridge, London EC4R 9EL.
Tel: 020 7283 5838 Fax: 020 7626 5137
Web: www.salmon-trout.org

The Atlantic Salmon Trust

Set up in 1967 when stocks were beginning to start their steady decline and many salmon fishers felt the need for practical research. The Trust is still involved in the encouragement and direct sponsorship of research projects, but has widened its activities to act as a centre for information on wild salmon matters. It tries to make sure that decisions on salmon management are taken on an informed basis.

Moulin, Pitlochry, Perthshire, PH16 5JQ, Scotland.
Tel: 01796 473439 Fax: 01796 473554
Email: Salmontrust@cs.com Web: http://www.atlanticsalmontrust.org